# The Assault on Authority

# The ASSAULT on AUTHORITY

### Dialogue or Dilemma?

**William W. Meissner**

ORBIS BOOKS
MARYKNOLL, NEW YORK

## *Table of Contents*

# Introduction

Ours is a time of crisis—crisis on many fronts. It is uniquely a time of crisis of authority. The traditional notions and institutions of authority are being challenged on all levels and in many contexts. The authority of civil government is being challenged in the streets, the authority of ecclesiastical government is being challenged in a variety of ways, the authority of traditional offices and ways of exercising power are being challenged in almost every facet of contemporary life.

There was once a more or less general presumption in favor of authority structures. That presumption no longer seems to be operative. The attitude toward authority has become more ambivalent. Men distrust it, fear its power and are threatened by its potential abuse. The paradox, of course, is that as the structure of society becomes more complex, men come to depend increasingly on the functions of authority. The growing complexity of culture and social action and the increasing interdependence among the individuals who compose society bring with them a demand for an increase of the resources of society to preserve order and organize the cooperation of individual effort. Modern man has become more dependent on authority and in consequence has also become more susceptible to and sensitive to its deficiencies. This is the core of the "crisis of authority."

The response to this crisis of authority has been a gradual democratization of the structure of authority. There is an increasing emphasis on individual freedom and responsibility. The watchword is decentralization. In politics there is increasing concern for the prerogatives of local government. In education there is an increasing demand for student participation in academic government and decision-making processes by which educational institutions are run. In the Church, there is an emerging emphasis on collegiality and the meaningful participation of the laity.

All authority derives ultimately from God. But it exists only in intellectual beings. It involves man on the level of his distinctively human capacities—his freedom and intellect. Authority must respect man's free choice and judgment. It must be distinguished from absolute independence on the one hand and from the subjection of coercion on the other. In the first instance, the exercise of freedom is carried out without any advertence to the consent of the other; in the second, the will of the other is forced or imposed on the individual without his willing acceptance. Rightfully understood, authority involves the imposition of one person's judgment on others in a different way. It is operative only where it is given free acceptance and recognition. It becomes something else when it becomes an exercise of power in violation of personal freedom. Authority in its authentic sense is not the exercise of power.

The association of authority with power in the more traditional formulations has led to a more or less univocal concept of authority within the Church. The unfortunate fact that this more or less static and uniovcal concept no longer answers to the concerns and preoccupations of the contemporary mind has begun to operate to the detriment of the Church in its attempts to meet the modern world halfway. The lapse is not simply a conceptual one. Father John McKenzie[1] has pointed to a number of concerns over the exercise of ecclesiastical authority which seem to have had the effect of tarnishing the image of authority and diminishing its prestige.

The first issue is that of segregation. The role of ecclesiastical authorities was unfortunate in that in such a large social issue, involving as it does so many profound moral issues, the hierarchy was slow to assert its leadership. The situation was—and is—undoubtedly very complex and in any case difficult for Church authority. Any position was bound to be controversial and to leave one or other faction unhappy. What seems to have evolved, however, is a situation in which many honest Church members find themselves forced to oppose their ecclesiastical leaders on grounds which seem to them primarily moral. By and large, the American hierarchy vacated their rightful moral leadership and allowed it to pass into other hands.

A second difficult issue is that of birth control. The problem was difficult enough before the publication of *Humanae Vitae.* Before that event, it was largely an issue of morality; since that event, it has also become an issue of authority in the Church in the most profound sense. The general sympathy with the authoritative position on birth control has been seriously eroded. The apparent lack of sympathy in the opposite direction and the seeming unreachability of ecclesiastical authorities on this issue have not increased the willingness of an already burdened laity to accept authoritative directives. The remarkable willingness of priests and even bishops to speak out against the papal encyclical was evidence enough of the crisis in papal authority that the encyclical has intensified. The crisis clearly has been present for some time.

McKenzie also points to a growing awareness of and sensitivity to the abuses of ecclesiastical power. There is nothing new in the abuse of such power, but the climate in which it takes place is changing and subjects are becoming less tolerant of it. The exercise of power often seems arbitrary and authoritarian. It often gives the impression of injustice and vindictiveness, however one might argue the merits of a given case. The newspapers are constantly supplied with stories having to do with condemnations of books, suspensions of priests, dismissal of teachers—in many instances without publicly justifiable reasons. There is also the apparent affiliation and identification of ecclesiastical authorities with the vested interests, the socially and economically privileged classes of society.

It is difficult to argue that those who hold authority in the Church are at fault. Whatever one's moral judgment in these matters, it is apparent that the hierarchy has gotten itself a bad press. And the upshot of it all is that well-disposed and sincere Christians find themselves in good conscience opposing the authorities of the Church on what they feel conscientiously to be moral grounds. There is somehow a failure of leadership at the least. In any case, the willingness of the community at large to accept the legitimate directives of ecclesiastical authority is strikingly diminished.

In the face of such crisis and the accompanying erosion of prestige, it seems futile and destructive to try to return to the traditional formulations and structures of authority and refurbish and reinforce them. That would seem only to intensify the very problem it seeks to cure. What is needed is at one level an evolution of new structures of authority which permit its exercise in such a way as to respond to the contemporary demand for freedom and responsibility. Along with this evolution of structure, there has to be an evolution of formulation so that the exercise of authority is paralleled by an emergent concept of authority which underlines its implicit congruence with individual freedom and maturity.

The notion of authority in the Church must be broadened and deepened. The traditional notion dealt with a capacity vested in an individual by reason of holding an office. The primary authority of this kind in the Church is the authority of the bishops. It is an authority based primarily on power. Catholics have become accustomed to this form of power and its abuse. Its style is bureaucratic, autocratic, paternalistic and even arrogant. It is a style of pomp and power that somehow obfuscates and obliterates the Christian ideal of authority as service. It is more a distortion of real authority than an authentic form of authority.

In addition to the long-predominant authority of office, there is an authority of the community. This is the authority that belongs to all members of the Church by reason of their membership in the community of the Church. It is the right of every individual, singly or in concert, to be taken seriously, to be listened to, to take action and to accept the consequences and responsibilities of action. It may be carried out by submission or by protest. The danger is that submission may be identified as obedience and responsible protest with self-advantage. The authority of the community may sometimes follow, but it may sometimes lead; it may cooperate with commissioned authority, or it may oppose it. It has no other legitimacy than that of Christian responsibility.

What is lacking in the Church and what is desperately needed is effective communication between the hierarchy and the rest of the Church. Communication has been undermined by the authoritarian and bureaucratic modality of expression. Communication is a two-way street. There can be no real communication in a vertical direction. Communication is a horizontal phenomenon. Communication is impossible in any meaningful sense unless authority speaks to authority, unless the authority of the community brings to the dialogue an equivalence of dignity and legitimacy which enables it to speak face to face with the authority or office.

A similar crisis exists on many levels of the social structure. There is a crisis in secular authority no less than in religious authority. One can look at almost any segment of the social organism and find there the symptoms of unrest and distrust that mark the conflict. The two areas that press upon public awareness in contemporary society are the crises on the campus and the Negro movement. One can look at both these efforts with a jaundiced eye and see them as misguided efforts by powerless and underprivileged groups to gain power and influence. To do so, I believe, is to exercise a prejudice and to miss the deeper significance of these developments for the evolution of social structure.

Dynamic forces at work within our society are moving toward a recasting of social values and a reorganization of social structures. The parameters of social organization are being transformed in a direction which places an emphasis on individual freedom, individual expression, and individual responsibility. More to the point, there is a pressure toward acknowledgement of the principle of distribution of authority. The principle would hold that if a man is expected to submit himself to a social order and to abide by the prescriptions of that order, he should also expect to have a reasonable voice in the determination of those prescriptions. The ancient model of the university, in which learned men determine the content, mode, and context of what is to be communicated to learning men, is no longer satisfactory. Whatever one may think of the demagogic absurdities of student extremist groups à la SDS, it seems to me that there is an underlying dynamism which has a valid impact on social processes. The problem is, of course, that the instability of adolescence is prone to act in the face of frustration; and extremist groups, by and large, do not allow themselves sufficient perspective to envision constructive alternatives.

The so-called student revolt, as I see it, has a basically constructive drive behind it. It is an attempt to reform the structure of authority in the university. It is an attempt to break through the authoritarian and more or less bureaucratic structure of the university so that the student can begin to exercise himself as a determining force in the university community. His demand is that, if he is to surrender himself to the university for a period of years, and if he has to put himself or his family in financial bondage for what the university gives him, he has a right to have a say in what the university is, does, and teaches. One can argue inexhaustibly whether or to what extent such a claim is valid, possible or advisable. My only point is that it is there. What is needed is the effective building of student community as a means of redressing the balance of power and to establish a meaningful dialogue between the bases of authority in the university. Students can achieve a real part in the dialogue only insofar as they can achieve a real sense of community which will provide the structures of authority with which the dialogue can be joined. Without community, there can be no dialogue, only obstructionism.

The Negro problem is much more complex and difficult. It is compounded by problems of education, employment, housing, cultural deprivation, poverty, and prejudice. But it shares the aspect of revolt against white authority structures. The black man feels victimized, trapped, helpless in the face of the society in which he lives. The spectre of white paternalism which lives on in the welfare system is demeaning and devaluing. The black man has little recourse but to feel the pangs of impotent rage and frustration, and to strike out in the blind hope that by destroying what afflicts him something better will take its place. That destructive power has been unleashed in unfortunate race riots and other gestures of protest and sabotage of white authority.

The destructive potentialities of this situation have been neutralized in some degree by the more effective black leaders. The NAACP, under the leadership of Roy Wilkins, and the Southern Christian Leadership Conference, under Martin Luther King and now his followers, have been reasonably effective forces working toward the acknowledgement, not just of Negro rights, but of human rights. The degree to which this has been achieved is due to the effectiveness of these leaders and others in building a sense of community—and a correlative sense of identity—among black people. The Black Power movement—vague and unstructured though it may be—is a potentially healthy step in this direction. The problem has been that black leadership has been splintered by a competition for power and influence and even control of government funds. Black frustrations are only too easily subverted to factious and destructive ends by inflammatory leaders who find greater satisfaction in obstructive and destructive protests than in constructive efforts to build the black community.

The point is not that the black movement in this country has many problems, but that it contains an essential dynamism which must have its ramifications for the evolution of social structures and civil authority. The black people are protesting an injustice which has come upon them in virtue of historical circumstance, socio-economic process, and prejudice. They are seeking to alter this situation. They are seeking, not just change, but social change in the structure of authority. They are asking, "How does a minority group, so deprived and so subject to prejudice, find within the structure of society a way to have its basic rights preserved when the structure of society does not see fit to acknowledge or act to preserve those rights?" We must not deceive ourselves that passage of civil rights legislation by the Congress automatically effects the preservation of basic rights. One cannot legislate prejudice out of existence. That basic question is directed substantially at the organization and function of authority structures at all levels of society. It is a variant of the basic question that is being posed at many levels and in many areas of contemporary life. How must the traditional structures of authority be modified—in the Church, in the university, in society, in business, etc.—so that social structures and order can be maintained, and so that the contemporary demand for individual rights, individual freedom, and individual responsibility can be achieved.

The world of business, as well, is being invaded by young, active, dynamic graduates of the university system. Their arrival, in ever increasing numbers, presents a challenge to corporate structures. They do not accept the traditional business incentives and corporate objectives. They are much more highly trained than their predecessors of a generation ago and they have been making it quite clear that the traditional routes of access to positions of responsibility are not adequate. They are not inclined to work their way up in the company hierarchy. They do not want a company schooling in stifling routines. They want responsibility and the opportunity to express themselves in a manner commensurate with their training and backgrounds.

For large corporations to accept and integrate this influx of young talent, the corporation must endure changes in its authority structure. The reluctance of such structures to change has created a shift of many bright young executives to smaller businesses where responsibility and the opportunity to shape business policies according to their convictions and values is more readily available. These demands are being met both because of a shortage of qualified personnel and because the rapid advance of technology puts a premium on recent training—both factors which put young executives in a strong bargaining position.

Thus, powerful forces are at work in the business community, as in other segments of society, creating pressures toward decentralization, wider distribution of authority, increased emphasis of individual responsibility and initiative. The more or less authoritarian, hierarchical structure of the corporation is becoming an archaism. The business community is being forced to re-evaluate itself and reorganize itself as a matter of economic necessity. Unless the business community as a whole can make itself an attractive and compelling context in which talented young people can find what they are looking for, there will be a brain drain away from the business sector, and the best minds will find what they want elsewhere.

The problems of authority which are displayed at large in society and the Church are mirrored in more human terms on the level of the religious community. There the structure of authority is brought into direct confrontation with the reality of individual lives. The crisis of authority has asserted itself there as well. At that level the authority of commission is confronted by the authority of the community also, but it is confronted in addition by another form of authority which is much less explicit at the level of larger social structures. I refer to the authority of maturity which belongs to each individual, not by reason of commission to an office, not by reason of his membership in the community, but by reason of his maturity and adult humanity. This latter form of authority comes more to the fore where the dialogue of authority is at the interface of the individual and the immediate community.

The evolution of authority must take the direction of the amplification and integration of all these forms of authority. The notion of authority must become diversified. The shift must take place from the univocity of an authority of power to an analogous notion of authority which embraces the diversity of its manifestations. In the pages that follow, we are proposing a notion of authority conceived in terms of relation. The notion of authority as relation has the flexibility necessary to permit the broadening of the basis of authority to include more than a mere basis in power. The analysis that emerges has application analogously at all levels of the implementation of authority. At whatever level, the authority relation calls for the inner response of human beings in freedom and responsibility.

The analysis intends to say little more about the contemporary issues of authority or its philosophical nature. Rather it is directed at the understanding of the inner face of authority. It takes its stand at the complex interface of individual and social structure and seeks to understand the complexities of the authority relation in that context. The concern is originally with the inner psychic mechanisms and the patterns by which they interact with and respond to the social systems at work in the community.

The analysis is directed in the first instance to the religious community as such, but the principles and mechanisms of the authority relation have analogous application to all levels of social structure. Further, the psychological literature on authority is sparse. Psychoanalytic concerns with authority have not gone much beyond the rudimentary framework of displaced attitudes in relation to the father figure. What passes here is rooted in analytic theory and may hopefully provide some further development of the understanding of authority.

The concrete structures of authority are in fact evolving. The process of decentralization is at work in the Church. Collegiality has emerged as an increasingly operative principle of Church organization and administration. The priests' senate has become a feature of diocesan politics—a creature of very recent vintage—but its impact is being heard and felt in significant terms. Within religious groups, a variety of experiments are under way to give the reality of the authority of the community some institutionalized means of expression and influence. These trends will continue. They are far from passing experiments that will not outlive the enthusiasm of the moment. They are emerging and will become more or less permanent structures in the Church's social organization.

The direction of such changes is to bring into real structure the diversity of bases of authority in the Church. The imbalance in favor of the authority of commission is in process of correction. Structures are evolving to give a place to the authority of the community and the authority of maturity. The triad of bases of authority must come into mutually regulating balance with each other. The structure of the Church may then rest upon three legs rather than upon only one or two. The fruitful tension and dialogue between the three bases of authority can bring new life to the Christian community. It is only when the balance is achieved that real communication can take place in the interest of building the community. Only in this way will authoritative presence to the community become meaningful and the mature bases of the authority relation be realized.

A primary locus for the evolution of such balance and meaningful interaction within the relation of authority is the religious community. There, more than any other place, the conditions for the evolution of attitude and structures of authority are optimized. It is there that the reality and presence of the community enters into the closest and most intimate dialogue with the inner life of Christians. There, better than elsewhere, the inner mutuality of the authority relation can be realized. There the mechanisms of identification and sharing of values have their most intense and least diluted influence. The religious community, therefore, is a unique matrix within which the evolution of the structures and concepts of authority can take place. The Church, facing as it does the crisis of authority, needs to have such structures evolve so as to witness the mutual engagement and regulation of the bases of authority. That solution is what it desperately needs and increasingly seeks. To that purpose, the following considerations will focus on the religious community with the anticipation that formulations discovered there might have their analogous application elsewhere.

# Part I

# Conceptual Aspects

The Concept of Authority

Leadership and Authority

*Chapter 1*

# The Concept of Authority

Undertaking a discussion of this nature, since it deals with a concept which has been so thoroughly considered on the theological and philosophical levels, may require some justification. I suppose my concern with the concept of authority stems from the overriding impression that many of the problems which confront the contemporary Church and religious organizations in particular are rooted, conceptually and emotionally, in difficulties related to the concept of authority. Not only the Church, but society in general, is agitated by what might be called a crisis of authority. What I propose to undertake, then, is an examination of the multiple aspects of the understanding and exercise of authority. In so doing, I am not at all concerned with the philosophical or theological implications of the concept of authority. I am concerned with the psychological and sociological implications. That is not to say that the theological and philosophical considerations of authority are not in themselves significant, or that they are not in many ways related to the primary focus of our present concern. They simply represent different approaches. It has been my impression that in many ways the "crisis of authority" is not really a crisis of authority at all, but rather a crisis in the usage of authority. While the concept of authority itself has been well worked out, little attention has been paid to its less conceptual aspects. Therefore, we can concern ourselves in this chapter with some of the less traditional significances of the concept of authority.

## The Traditional Notion of Authority

The more traditional notion of authority had focused primarily on the definitional aspect of authority and on the moral or ethical justification for the use of authority either in the political organization, the state, or in the ecclesiastical organization, the Church. Vatican II, for example, speaks of the Pope's authority in the following words: "Hence by divine institution he enjoys supreme, full, immediate and universal authority over the care of souls. Since he is pastor of all the faithful, his mission is to provide for the common good of the universal Church and for the good of the individual churches. He holds, therefore, a primacy of ordinary power over all the Churches."[1] The fundamental notion here is of a divinely instituted power, vested in the pope by reason of his office, which gives him authority to rule, guide, and teach the universal Church. A similar notion of authority, applied to the political realm, can be found in the constitution on the Church in the Modern World. Speaking of the goals of the political community, the decree reads:

> Individuals, families, and various groups which compose the civic community are aware of their own insufficiency in the matter of establishing a fully human condition of life. They see the need for that wider community in which each would daily contribute his energies toward the ever better attainment of the common good. It is for this reason that they set up the political community in its manifold expression. . . .
>
> Many different people go to make up the political community, and these can lawfully incline toward diverse ways of doing things. Now, if the political community is not to be torn to pieces as each man follows his own viewpoint, authority is needed. This authority must dispose the energies of the whole citizenry toward the common good, not mechanically or despotically, but primarily as a moral force which depends on freedom and the conscientious discharge of the burdens of any office which has been undertaken.[2]

The concept of authority employed here regards it specifically as a property of the group. Moreover authority in this context has a specifically paternal function. As Simon[3] indicates in his perceptive analysis of political authority, the paternal function of authority is only one function among what must be regarded as a diversity of functions of authority. Thus authority is regarded as aiming at the proper good of the governed. It is needed for the survival and development of immature and inadequate persons. Consequently authority is made necessary, in this sense, by the deficiency of the governed. It presumes the inability or the incapacity of the governed to organize and direct their own activities toward their own proper good. The proper good here, of course, is not always the individual good, as distinct from the common good. The common good toward which authority directs the common efforts of the governed may indeed be equivalent to the proper good of the individual members of the community. It is plain, however, that paternal authority has an essentially pedagogical aim. It seeks the attainment or maturation of the capacities of the governed to enable them to govern themselves effectively. Properly considered, then, paternal authority should really be aiming at its own disappearance and therefore, commits a fundamental abuse whenever it outlives its necessity.

Authority, however, also has the function of bringing unity into the action of the community. But unity of action requires unity of judgment. When the action or the means of action are unique and determined, authority is required only insofar as the members of the community can be considered inadequate, either because of the weakness or perversity of their wills or the ignorance or incapacity of their intellects, to perceive and agree upon the unique means. When the means are multiple, and this is the usual case, unity of action requires a determination among the multiple means in order that the community can direct its efforts to a common action. This requires authority which is empowered to decide upon one out of a multitude of courses of action. For example, it is completely arbitrary whether cars drive on the left or the right side of the street, but it is essential to the community welfare that cars drive on the same side of the street. Thus, as Simon is quick to point out, while the paternal function of authority diminishes as the deficiencies of the governed are made up, the unifying function of authority becomes more significant as these deficiencies are overcome. The more capable and understanding the members of the community, the more diverse and variable will be the courses of possible proposed action. Consequently, the unifying function of authority does not originate in the deficiencies of the members, but really in the nature of society as such, and must therefore be regarded as an essential function of societal organization.

Simon also points to a third function of authority, namely achieving the volition of the common good in the community. Authority is necessary, first of all, for the direction of private individual members of the community toward the common good of the community. Secondly, authority is required for the direction of the variety of functional processes, each of which regards some particular aspect of the common good, toward the whole of the common good. Thus, the exercise of political authority has a variety of functions: it has paternal, unifying, volitional aspects. Moreover, it would seem traditionally that among these various functions of authority, the paternal function has been more or less emphasized in the functioning of religious groups. This is valid, not only in terms of the organization of the Church itself, but by way of analogy to the Church as a divinely instituted organization, has application also to lesser religious groupings.

## Social Aspects of Authority

In the context of social actions and interaction, the concept of authority is very closely related to that of power. Power is essentially the capacity to influence the behavior of other members of the group, but authority is not just any kind of power, since it depends upon the recognition by the subordinate members of the group that the one possessing authority may legitimately prescribe patterns of behavior for the group to follow. Social power, in general, rests on more than one basis.[4] In fact, several bases can be distinguished: (1) *reward power* is based on the member's perception that others in the group have the ability to reward his behavior; (2) *coercive power* is based on the perception that others can punish his behavior; (3) *legitimate power* is based on the perception that others have a legitimate right to direct his behavior; (4) *referent power* is based on the member's identification with others; and (5) *expert power* is based on the recognition of a special knowledge or expertness in the other. Authority, thus, as a form of social power is directly related to the exercise of legitimate power, but it is important to appreciate that the authority relationship can be contaminated by other forms of power.

French and Raven[5] have proposed several hypotheses about the bases of social power. For all types of social power, the stronger the power basis, the greater the power will be. The basis of power rests on the perception of the group or of any of the members of the group that the one in authority has this or that quality. It is not enough, for example, that an individual possess expert knowledge in order that he exercise power; it is also necessary that the group recognize him as possessing that knowledge and therefore accept him in the role of expert. It is important to appreciate that the range of activities within which any particular type of power can be exercised will vary considerably. Referent power, generally, will have the broadest range; that is, the range of activities that can be affected or changed by reason of the individual member's identification with the superior or with the group itself is broader than that of any other basis of power. This basis of social motivation is probably most often applicable in religious groups, but as we shall see, it forms a foundation for the authority relation wherever it exists.

Any attempt to utilize social power beyond its range will tend to reduce the effectiveness of that power. Thus, when the superior exerts power on the group beyond the range of that power, he is reducing by an equivalent amount the basis of his capacity to influence the group. Expert power, of course, is an obvious case of this: if the expert tries to use his special power to influence the group in an area where he exceeds his competence, he induces an attitude in the group which tends to disregard his special competence even in the area proper to it. Even in the exercise of legitimate power, the superior can exceed the range of his legitimate authority. The range of authority is established by the formal structure of the group, but it is important to remember that informal group norms of legitimacy are also effective. In general, in addition to the formal, established norms of the distribution of authority, the group itself evolves its own operating standard of what the superior can or cannot legitimately demand. When the superior exceeds the limit established by the group's informal consensus, he exceeds the range of his effective legitimate power and thereby reduces the power itself. It is important to realize in understanding the exercise of legitimate authority that the informal group consensus has nothing to do with the formal organization of authority in the group and takes place independently of it.

With regard to the exercise of reward or coercive power, any new state of the group's system produced by their influence will be highly dependent on the agent exercising the power. Moreover, the more observable the conformity of the members, the more dependent the new alignment will be. If a superior tries to reinforce external conformity by a system of rewards and/or punishments, external conformity will depend on his continued exercise of this type of power. Influence of the superior in virtue of his legitimate power would not be subject to this limitation. Thus, when a system of rewards and punishments, which can often be very subtle, has been introduced to reinforce external conformity, conformity may be achieved; but it is achieved at the sacrifice of more stable and internalized bases of group cooperation. The exercise of coercion results in diminished attraction of the member to the superior and in a high degree of resistance to the superior. Reward, however, results in increased attraction and low resistance. Interestingly enough, the more legitimate the coercion, the less it will produce resistance and decreased attraction. Thus, when legitimate power is joined to coercive power, it mitigates the effect of the latter.

The classic treatment of legitimate authority was that of Max Weber.[6] Weber defined 'imperative coordination" as the probability that certain specific commands from a given source would be obeyed by a given groups of persons. Obedience to commands can rest on a variety of considerations from simple habituation to a purely rational calculation of advantage. But there is always a minimum of voluntary submission based on an interest in obedience. Obedience to the superior can be based on custom, affectual ties, or on a purely material complex of interest, or by what Weber called ideal (wertrational) motives. These purely material interests result in a relatively unstable situation, and must therefore be supplemented by other elements, both affectual and ideal. But even this complex of motives does not form a sufficiently reliable basis for a system of imperative cooperation, so that there must be added another important element, the belief in legitimacy.

Weber distinguished three types of legitimate authority.[7] 1. Rational-pragmatic authority bases its claims to legitimacy on a belief in "legality of patterns of normative rules and the right of those elevated to authority under such rules to issue commands (legal authority)." In such authority, obedience is owed to a legally established impersonal order. The persons who exercise authority of office within this order are shown obedience only by virtue of the formal legality of their commands and only within the scope of authority of their office. 2. Mimetic-traditional authority bases its claims to legitimacy on "an established belief in the sanctity of immemorial traditions and the legitimacy of the status of those exercising authority under them (traditional authority)." Obedience in this case is owed to the person of the superior who occupies the traditionally sanctioned position of authority and is therefore bound by the terms of that tradition. The obligation of obedience is not a matter of acceptance of the legality of an impersonal order but rather as a matter of personal loyalty. 3. Charismatic authority bases its claims to legitimacy on "devotion to the specific and exceptional sanctity, heroism, or exemplary character of an individual person, and of the normative patterns or order revealed or ordained by him (charismatic authority)." The charismatic leader is obeyed by virtue of personal trust in him and in his revelation, or in his exemplary qualities as influenced by the individual's beliefs in the charisma.

It is immediately apparent, of course, that the Weberian categories of authority have a limited usefulness. They are, as he himself insisted, "pure" types of legitimate authority. They are most useful in the analysis of more bureaucratic types of social organization, and probably would find their primary application to such organizations as the army, business organizations or bureaucracies organized along totalitarian lines. It is also evident that religious groups do not fall neatly into any one of these categories but in some sense participate in all of them. The religious subject accords obedience to the religious superior on rational grounds insofar as he recognizes the superior as the representative of a properly constituted legal authority; on traditional grounds, insofar as he recognizes the traditional status of the superior; and on charismatic grounds insofar as the charisma of the superior can be interpreted in terms of the grace of office or the guidance of the Holy Spirit. While this is not a personal charisma of the superior, it is also clear that on informal terms the superior may well exercise a personal charisma in relation to his subjects by reason of his own personal gifts and the measure of respect and trust which he can engender in them.

Weber's categories have also been criticized from the point of view of their cultural embeddedness and their applicability to more authoritarian types of organization. Thus Harrison[8] has pointed out that the organization of voluntary groups, particularly in the United States, tends to be structured along quite different lines. The ideology of such groups tends to be highly antiauthoritarian. They distrust centralization and resist further structuring of the organization in terms of authority relations. On the other hand, some degree of bureaucratic organization is necessary for the attainment of group goals. The inherent conflict heightens social tensions and makes problems in authority and power quite acute. Thus, Harrison concludes, the modes for legitimation of authority are significantly different in this kind of organization than those suggested by Weber's analysis of authoritarian systems.

This raises the interesting question, of course, as to the influence of the democratic emphasis in our own culture in considering problems of authority and the exercise of power. It is important to realize that the exercise of authority, whatever its legitimacy and whatever its formal characteristics within the structure of the organization, is not exercised in a cultural vacuum. Culturally generated and derived attitudes toward the exercise of authority have important implications for the implementation and uses of authority within any formally organized structure. Thus, whatever the conception of authority one attributes to the religious organization, i.e., whatever the degree of one's commitment to the authoritarian ideal of religious authority and obedience, it must still be recognized that religious subjects who are born and raised in a democratic society and whose value orientation incorporates democratic ideals carry within them conscious and unconscious attitudes which must inevitably influence the way in which authority is exercised and responded to within the religious group.

### Authority as Power

Power is an essentially social phenomenon insofar as it refers to the influence of one individual over another or over a group. It is a kind of latent force. Authority, then, is really a form of institutionalized power. Social power, as constituted within the formally organized group, is expressed in and through authority.[9]

The concept of social power often carries within it an implicit treatment as being attributed to a person or a group. The most usual formulation of authority in religious groups, for example, suggests that the superior has the power to command, i.e., that the power of commanding obedience is somehow attributed to him by reason of his office. There is a tendency among social scientists, however, to view power as a particular type of social relationship in which one person adjusts his behavior to conform with a pattern of behavior communicated to him by another person.[10] This is an interesting formulation of the power concept, since it implies the concept of power as a property of social relations which involves ties of mutual dependence among the members of the group. The power or the exercise of power resides implicitly in the dependency of other members of the group. As Emerson[11] points out, the dependency relation of A on B is, first of all, directly proportional to A's motivational investment in goals which are mediated by B; and, secondly, dependence is inversely proportional to the availability of these same goals to A exclusive of any relationship to B. The power relation is really the converse of this, so that the power which B exercises over A can be measured by the amount of resistance of A which can be potentially overcome by B. In these terms, the reciprocal interaction of power and dependence within the group produces tensions which throw into operation balancing procedures which are calculated to reduce the tension. One characteristic balancing operation, delineated by Emerson is motivational withdrawal, by which the dependent person equivalently decreases his motivational investment in the goals mediated by the other person and thereby diminishes the other's power. The group tension can also be decreased by increasing the extension of the power network or by the equivalent diffusion of dependency within the group. This would tend to dilute the power-dependency polarity and thus reduce tension. Another means of tension reduction is the formation of coalitions of two or more of the weaker dependent members of the group against the stronger power-wielding members of the group. In a sense, coalition can be regarded as a characteristic of all organized group functioning. Thus, one can conceive of authority as a power of the group itself exercised through an authorized person whose position is a function of group coalition.

Thus, the legitimate power of authority is equivalently a directed power which can be employed only in those channels which have been defined by the norms set up by the group. The last, and very interesting, means of tension reduction in the group is the emergence of status. By reason of status with its correlative ego-enhancing implications, the motivational investment in the group situation in the more powerful member is increased. Thus, the more powerful person's motivational investment in goals mediated by the rest of the group is increased and, therefore, his dependence on the group is increased. By reason of the reciprocal relationship of power-dependency, this increases the capacity or power of the weaker member to control the more powerful members.

The emphasis on relational aspects of power, while it may not serve the purposes of philosophical definition of authority, does serve the objectives of bringing into clearer relief the multiple aspects which must be brought into focus if we are to achieve any substantial understanding of the practicalities of the exercise of authority. It also emphasizes the fact that authority, narrowly defined in terms of legitimate social power, is made more complex in reality by the interaction of other forms of power which in fact have a wider distribution within the structure of the group. There is an interesting parallel here in the study of leadership. For a long time, thinking about leadership was dominated by the so-called trait approach which tried to delineate those characteristics which both identified leaders and made them capable of functioning as leaders. It was soon found, however, that the bases of leadership were multiple, and that in varying situations different members of the groups showed leadership potentialities. Consequently, students of leadership began to focus their attention, not on the traits of the individuals involved, but rather on the interaction between group members and on the kinds of situations in which different kinds of interaction gave rise to different forms of leadership. It is quite obvious, parenthetically, that the concept of the "superior" in a religious setting is still operating in terms of a fundamentally trait approach.

## Authority as Communication

Another significant approach to the problem of authority puts it in terms of communication. Thus Barnard[12] defines authority as "the character of a communication (order) in formal organization by virtue of which it is accepted by a contributor to or member of the organization as governing the action he contributes." The definition involves a subjective aspect, that is, the accepting of the communication as authoritative, and an objective aspect, the character in the communication by virtue of which it is accepted. Barnard goes on to say that if a directive communication is accepted by a member of the group, its authority is thus confirmed by him. Acceptance admits the communication as the basis of action, while disobedience is equivalently a denial of its authority. Thus, the decision as to whether an order has authority or not lies with the inferior rather than with the superior. This conception of authority is a decided turnabout from more traditional notions. But it emphasizes the notion that even in the most absolute form of social organization, authority rests in some sense upon the acceptance of the consent of the individuals.

The essential point in this formulation is that the necessity of assent is required in order to establish authority for the individual. Acceptance of the communication as authoritative depends upon four conditions. 1. The individual can and does understand the communication. A communication that cannot be understood can have no authority. Given a willingness to comply, the individual who receives a meaningless communication must either disregard the communication or follow his own course of action. 2. At the time of his decision, he believes that the substance of the communication is not inconsistent with the purpose of the group. Equivalently, then, the group ideals and purposes serve to limit the range of authority. Communication of an order at cross purposes to the group purposes would necessarily create a situation of conflict. The intelligent person can be expected to resolve the conflict by denying the authority of the order which contradicts the purpose of the group effort as he understands it. 3. At the time of his decision, he believes it to be compatible with his personal interest as a whole. Thus, the acceptance of the communication is involved in the complicated relationships between personal goals and personal interest and group goals and group interest. In general, the congruence of personal and group goals increases the motivation of the individual member to participate in and contribute to the group effort. Communication of an order which is against personal interest will necessarily reduce the net inducement of the individual to contribute to the group. This approach to authority would regard the existence of net inducement as the substantial reason for accepting any order as having authority. 4. The subject is mentally and physically capable of complying with the order. Any order to do that which is impossible, even though it be only a little impossible, is regarded as exceeding the range of its proper authority.

Despite the emphasis on the acceptance of the individual in the exercise of authority, the proper functioning of authority is insured by the normal compliance of orders given in any effective organization with these conditions, and by what Barnard calls a "zone of indifference" in individuals by which orders are regarded as acceptable without conscious questioning of their authority. The presumption of legitimacy operates in favor of the authority structure. The zone of indifference is characteristically wider or narrower for different individuals and would seem to be related to their personal tendencies toward conformity or deviance within the group. Moreover, group involvement and group participation generally create an active personal interest in the maintenance of authority within the group. A more or less implicit attitude is generated by the informal organization of the group which makes individuals loath to question authority as it functions within or near the zone of indifference. Barnard suggests that the formal statement that authority comes down from above, from the general to the particular, as it were, confirms the presumption among individuals in favor of the acceptability or orders and enables them to avoid challenging such orders without at the same time incurring a sense of personal subserviency or a loss of personal status.

The more objective aspect of the communication has to do with the reasons or characteristics of the communication which induce its acceptance. In the structure of formal organizations, the authority has to do fundamentally with the potentiality for assent among those to whom the communications are sent. The authority imputed to communications from a superior may be based on position (authority of position) independently of his personal qualifications and abilities, or it may be based on superior ability and competence (authority of leadership). When the authority of leadership is combined with the authority of position, the degree of acceptance of the communication is greatly increased. The maintenance of objective authority requires commensurate capacities in those who hold high positions of authority. High positions, not supported by the abilities of those who hold them, have weak authority; as do highly competent men in minor positions. Authority thus depends on a cooperative personal attitude of individual members on the one hand, and on a system of communication in the organization on the other. Communication, therefore, must be effective and relatively efficient, not only for the effectiveness of group adaptation and the normal functioning of the group process, but also for the maintenance and effective exercise of authority within the group.[13]

## Authority as Relation

We have already noted the traditional emphasis in the concept of authority on the power dimension. The relationship between authority and power has been a dominant motif in almost all approaches to the concept of authority whether philosophical, theological, or social. A gradual shift has been taking place from the notion of authority as power to that of authority as a relationship. Authority would thus consist in the relationship between two or more persons by which one party lays claim to the cooperation or subservience of the other party, and the other party accepts this claim. Obviously, the relationship involves power, but the shift in emphasis also involves a shift in the concept of power from that of being a capacity resident in the power-bearing person to the concept of power as a relational phenomenon. Both the bearer of authority and the recipient of authority emerge as important contributors to the functioning of authority. There is a mutuality and reciprocal responsiveness which is inherent in the authority relationship. The relationship is dynamic and reciprocal, so that one cannot presume compliance with authority on the grounds that the bearer of authority possesses a certain amount of power or that he holds a particular office. Authority must, therefore, be regarded as a function of a particular concrete human situation. It should be pointed out that the communication view of authority as proposed by Barnard, is not really essentially different from the relational view. The former emphasizes the mechanism by which the relationship is implemented; the latter brings into focus the implicit relational aspects of communication as such.

It is my impression, however, that the relational point of view must be credited with adopting a broader and more flexible approach to the problems of authority. The approach in terms of power and power relationships has a tendency to emphasize the role of the superior in the power relation. This lends itself to an overemphasis on the exercise of authority in terms of the formal, hierarchical structure of the group as well as in isolation from the dynamic processes going on concurrently within the group, which must inevitably modify and channel the influence of authority within the group. The communications view and other such radically situational approaches to the problem of authority form a sort of polar position in which the more formal and structural aspects of authority tend to be dissolved. Conceived on the communication model, authority tends to be thought of as derived from or constituted by the acceptance of the individual member. It seems more accurate to say that the effectiveness of the exercise of authority depends upon individual acceptance rather than that authority is derived from such acceptance.

The relational view, then, enables us to bring both of these polarities into a more balanced perspective. It enables us to respect the demands of a formal, hierarchically structured organization, as well as to bring into clear focus the dynamic processes, at both the conscious and unconscious levels, which are at work in determining the response of individual members to the authoritative directives of the power structure. Authority, then, can be defined as a dynamic and reciprocal relationship between two or more persons in which one claims to be a bearer of authority, and at least one accepts the claim of the bearer to be authoritative in some area of his own existence.

The emphasis on relation makes it possible to consider authority as involving more than a relationship of power. From the point of view of the subject, the acceptance of authority rests on more than the inherent dependency of the power relationship. The subject may accept or reject the authority of the superior even in the face of the threat of coercion. The acceptance of authority must be based on a broader and more comprehensive view of the subject's motivation to obey. To return for a moment to Simon's consideration of the diversity of function of authority, the conception of authority as based only on power is adequate really only for considering the paternal or unifying functions of authority. There is also a volitional or motivational aspect of the function of authority which is not adequately explained on the basis of power. Moreover, if authority does stem from the nature of society, as we often claim; and if society is an outgrowth of the fundamental nature of man, it would seem reasonable to conceive of authority as being based, not only on the human capacities for obedience (generous though they may be), but also on other basic human needs and capacities. In other words, the acceptance of authority cannot be ascribed merely to the power-dependence dimension. There must also be another dimension or dimensions which we can denominate diversely as gratification, or self-fulfillment, or self-enhancement. I am not so much concerned with the terms here as I am with the concept that the participation of the member of the group in the activities which are structured in terms of authority must ultimately be understood and must ultimately depend on a spectrum of motivations which make it psychologically rewarding, and in some sense fulfilling, for him to participate in the group action. The exercise of authority and the reciprocal response to authority are determined and conditioned by complex human motivations. I would suggest that it is these fundamental, often unconscious motivations which are at work in disturbing and disrupting the function of authority, and that we cannot adequately understand the operations that relate to the authority relation unless we bring these fundamental forces into view.

If we bunch these basic motivations under the rubric of personal interest, we can suggest that as a general rule personal interest is an essential component of the normal development to maturity of the individual. The successful execution of authority, therefore, must respect the demands of personal interest. It should be clear from the start that personal interest is not equivalent to personal wishes, for personal interest may not have anything to do with personal wishes. Putting it another way, the exercise of authority must always respect individual freedom, but individual freedom does not imply license and must be understood in reference to personal responsibility as well as cooperative obligation. Moreover, the successful exercise of authority must not only respect personal interest but must fulfill the demands and obligations of the exercise of power. Plainly, the balance is a delicate and complex one; but the overemphasis or the underemphasis of either dimension, that of power or of personal interest, will result in a distortion of the authority relationship. An overemphasis on the power dimension without concern for the personal interest and needs of the individual member may well result in rebellion. An overemphasis on personal interest to the sacrifice of the directive exigencies of power will result in the frustration of group goals and objectives.

We have tried to thread our way in this discussion through a multiplicity of approaches, all dealing with a very complex concept. Our objective has been not so much to define as to bring into better focus for purposes of further discussion the multiple aspects, dimensions, and implications of the concept of authority. We have tried to show that the trait-oriented, power-based concept of authority which has dominated so much of our traditional thinking on the subject, while secure in its own right, has nonetheless deprived us of the opportunity of exploring the more human and more motivationally oriented aspects of the problem. The shift in emphasis really represents a shift from a question of what is authority to the question of how or why does authority work, or not work, as the case may be. Neither, of course, is an easy question. But I suspect that the problems that are involved in the "crisis of authority" are not really problems in definition so much as they are reflections of an operative model of the operation of authority which may have evolved in relative isolation from the understanding of the factors and conditions of that operation. We can humbly hope that the present discussion and the further extensions of it may help to correct that deficiency.

*Chapter 2*

# Leadership and Authority

In the sociological literature, there is a great deal of overlap between the respective usages of the concepts of authority and leadership. This undoubtedly reflects the rather complex relationship and interaction between them. My position here is that they are substantially different but closely related notions. Authority, while it embraces a mutual relation between superior and subject, is nonetheless embedded in the formal organization of the group. It is an expression of legitimate power in terms of which the superior has a legal right to command, and the subject has a legal obligation to obey. The concept of leadership, however, is not directly involved in such legalistic overtones. Leadership is a form of the exercise of social power, but it is essentially power that is neither legitimate nor compelling. It is a quality or form of action by which the leader elicits the cooperation of individuals in a common objective and successfully coordinates their activities in achieving the objective.

## Bases of Leadership

The respective roles of the superior, who is vested with authority, and the leader vis-à-vis the group are distinct and find their respective bases in different forms of social power. The leader, as such, can influence the direction of group activity, but he cannot thereby assume authority. The superior, however, may assume the functions of a leader and in many concrete situations is often expected to do so. The basis of authority is *legitimate power,* which is grounded in the perception by the subordinate that the superior has a legitimate right to direct his behavior. Let us recall, however, that the basis of leadership may be any of the other forms of social power. *Reward power* is based on the subordinate's perception that the leader has the ability to reward his behavior. *Coercive power* is based on the perception that the leader can punish his behavior. *Expert power* is based on the recognition of special knowledge or competence in the leader. And, finally, *referent power* is based on the subordinate's identification with the leader. While reward, coercive, and expert power enjoy a more or less limited field of application, referent power is by far the broadest basis for the exercise of leadership.[1] The identification of the subordinate with the leader or of the member with the group is responsible for most of the cooperative group behavior in human affairs. We will have much more to say about the function of identification in relation to leadership later on.

## Approaches

The literature of sociology and social psychology has proliferated studies of leadership with great abandon. The high-powered stimulus of World War II with the demand for officer selection and training put a very high premium on the ability to recognize and develop leadership potential. Economic and industrial developments after the war picked up where the wartime efforts left off, and the interest in organizational and managerial aspects of leadership provided a focus of continuing research. Unfortunately, the effort expended has not been commensurate with the yield in terms of understanding leadership.

As we have seen, approaches to the study of leadership tend to cluster into two varieties. Earlier studies tended to favor a trait approach in terms of which the "leader" was regarded as a type of personality that tends to assume a position of dominance within a group in a wide variety of social situations. It became quickly apparent, however, that the same individual was not dominant in different kinds of social interaction. This shifted the emphasis to attempts to discover the personality characteristics of the leader in each of different kinds of situations in which leadership behavior was manifested. The limitations of the trait approach led some students of leadership to alter their approach to the study of situational-interactional factors. This approach focused on the interaction among group members rather than on the leader himself. The leader's traits were regarded as merely contributing factors in interaction with other relevant variables, such as group environment, the nature of the group task, characteristics of other group members, etc. This made it possible to get around the disturbing fact that the individuals possessing leadership traits were frequently not designated as leaders. Currently the situational-interactional approach is followed almost exclusively.

The concept of "leader" is not at all simple to designate, nor is there any closed consensus about it. A list of definitions might include:

1. An individual who exercises positive influence on others.

2. An individual who exercises more important positive influence than any other member of the group he is in.

3. An individual who exercises the most influence in goal-setting or goal-achievement of the group.

4. An individual selected by the group as leader.

5. An individual in a given office or position of apparently high influence potential.[2]

The multiplicity of definitions and approaches can be bewildering and frustrating to the social scientist who is inclined to study the phenomenon. Besides the variety of definitions of the leader and of leadership behavior, the understanding of leadership embraces a complex interaction between individual factors and factors that are at work within the group. The concept of leadership, therefore, opens up into a wide range of both psychological and sociological considerations.

## Interaction

Elaborating on the interactional concept of leadership, Gibb[3] focuses on several main points which he considers essential to the notion of leadership. First, leadership is always relative to the situation. Not only must the aggregate of individuals be united into a group with common goals by social interaction, but a certain kind of situation is required for the leadership relation to emerge at all. Further, the particular constellation of social circumstances existing at the moment determines which attributes of personality will be required for leadership status, and also determines which members of the group may be allowed to assume that role. Second, accession of an individual to the role of leader depends on the group goal and the ability or capacity of an individual to contribute to the achievement of that goal. Third, the basic psychology of leadership is that of social interaction. There can be no leader and no leadership without followers. Further, the leadership relation involves a mutual interaction in which the aspirations, ideals, attitudes, and motives of the followers are important determining factors along with the personality, individuality, or other leadership potentialities of the leader.

## Headship

Gibb goes on to an important distinction between leadership and headship. He says:

> When once the group activity has become dominated by an established and accepted organization, leadership tends to disappear. Even if this organization originally served the leadership role, any continuance of the organization as such, after the causal set of circumstances has ceased to exist, represents a transition to a process of domination or headship.[4]

The characteristics which distinguish headship from leadership are then listed:

1. The position of headship is maintained through an organized system and not by the spontaneous recognition of the individual contribution to the group goal.

2. In headship, the group goal is not internally determined.

3. Headship does not really involve a *group* at all, since there is no sense of shared feeling or joint action.

4. A situation of headship involves a wide social gap between the group members and the head, who works to maintain this distance.[5]

This distinction is important insofar as it parallels the distinction between leadership and authority. Authority is analogous to headship, although it is fairly obvious that Gibb's notion of headship is more on the authoritarian side.

It is interesting, however, that Gibb should note in passing that it is not at all necessary that headship should preclude the exercise of leadership. The remark might be confusing, were it not for the fact that the superior in a formally structured organization exercises legitimate authority (headship) within the formal structure. But the group is constituted not only by its formal structure, but by its informal structure as well. On this level, the superior's influence must be in terms of leadership. These distinctions may contribute some clarification to the relations between authority and leadership, but they are too neat. In terms of this distinction, the superior can only influence the group in virtue of his authority on the level of formal structure, and he can only influence the group in virtue of his leadership on the level of informal organization. It is not at all clear that such is the case.

In regard to Gibb's dichotomy, Janda[6] notes that the leadership-headship dichotomy, for example, that leadership is predicated on the basis of spontaneous recognition in the group, that the group goal is always internally determined in leadership, that leadership never involves a social gap, etc., can easily be challenged and does not hold up to careful examination. It is more realistic, in fact, to recognize that the authority relation is not at all limited to the exercise of influence along rigidly formalistic lines. While authority is defined in terms of legitimate social power, it has a privileged access to other bases of social power. Therefore, its influence has an impact on the group and on individual members of the group in a multiplicity of ways.

## Leadership and Authority

There is no significant consensus among students of group dynamics on these issues. Janda comments: "Leadership phenomena can be distinguished from other power phenomena when power relationships occur among members of the same group and when these relationships are based on the group members' perceptions that another group member may, with reference to their group activities, legitimately prescribe behavior patterns for them to follow."[7] Here leadership is based on legitimate power. Yet other theorists refer leadership to any power base operative within the group. Bass, for example, holds that "leadership may be viewed as influence occurring among members of the same group."[8] The position being taken here is somewhat more flexible. Authority and leadership are distinct forms of relation; one derives from formal group structure and the other does not. But the superior who exercises legitimate power, whether elected or appointed, is not thereby excluded from the exercise of other forms of power within the group. In fact, his position by reason of authority gives him a more or less privileged position which facilitates his more diversified influence over the group. I have treated in some detail elsewhere some of the dimensions of leadership within the religious group.[9] I was more or less inclined at the time to treat leadership in terms of legitimate power, but there is obviously no inner exigency to limit the term in that fashion.

If we may refer to a leadership function of authority, this may be more useful in calling attention to the diversity of the bases of influence on which the effective exercise of legitimate authority must rest. The group process and the exercise of authority are implemented at a dual level. The level of formal structure, at which the exercise of legitimate authority rests on legitimate power, is continually interacting with, determined by, modified and influenced by the level of informal organization. At this latter level, whatever one may conceive the structure of authority to be in formal terms, the actual functioning of authority is carried out in terms of social interaction, group processes (which operate at both task and emotional levels), and personal motivations (both conscious and unconscious).

From the point of view of effective exercise of authority, the superior cannot afford to prescind from the exercise of his leadership function. The mere communication of an order from the legitimate superior does not guarantee obedience. The response of the group to a command of legitimate authority, other things being equal, will be more favorable than otherwise. But to the extent that other processes are at work within the group acting to disqualify the superior's command or to diminish the forces which motivate members to comply with the command, obedience to the command will be mitigated.

## Identification

As I have already suggested, the basis of power which is most distinctive of leadership and which, as far as I can see, lends it its unique quality is that of referent power. The concept of referent power rests on the identification of the subordinate with the leader. The implications and overtones of this aspect of the leader-follower relationship are almost inexhaustible. Moreover, it is an aspect of the problem of leadership that has not received the attention it deserves.

Freud[10] had originally related the concept of identification with that of leadership. His ideas, however, were not very clearly thought out, and the current of thinking about leadership took a more sociological bent that carried them in a much different direction. One attempt to develop this notion was that of Redl.[11] He referred to "group emotions" as the "instinctual and emotional events taking place within persons under the pressure of group formative processes." These can probably better be conceived of as the (largely unconscious) emotional aspects of the group process.[12] He designated the group member around whom the group formative process takes place as the "central person" (leader). The central person can adopt a variety of roles for the basic processes of group formation. This gives rise to a number of types of group formation. It may be of some help to summarize these briefly.

1. "The Patriarchal Sovereign." The relation of members to the central person is based on the member's desire for the central person's approval. This is a loving relation which leads to identification with the central person's values.

2. "The Leader." The central person here appeals to the narcissim of the members in the sense that they wish to become like him. Identification here is based on the narcissistic wishes of the members.

3. "The Tyrant." The central person here dominates the group and produces a form of identification based not on love, but on fear —identification with the aggressor. Identification in this instance serves a protective function in the sense that the subject implicitly joins up with the aggressor through identification.

4. "The Central Person as Love Object." The members choose one and the same person as a love object. The central person is here an object of libidinal drives.

5. "The Central Person as Object of Aggressive Drives." The group unites in hostility to a central person.

6. "The Organizer." The central person renders an important service to the members by providing the means for satisfaction of their drives or needs, thus reducing conflict.

7. "The Seducer." The central person renders a service to the members by committing an initiatory act which cuts through guilt feelings, anxieties, and conflicts and permits the open manifestation of latent drives.

8. "The Hero." The central person again resolves the members' conflicts by committing an initiatory act and thus organizing the group action toward a desirable or praiseworthy goal.

9. "The Bad Influence." The central person resolves the members' conflicts over undesirable drives by the influence of his unconflicted example.

10. "The Good Example." The central person serves a similar function but in the opposite direction, resolving conflicts in favor of moral behavior rather than in the service of undesirable drives.

While this typology is not very useful in categorical terms, it seems to throw some light on the relation between identification and leadership. With the exception of those relations in which the central person serves as the object of group hostility or group affection (types 4 and 5), the organization of the group in relation to the central person involves some form of identification. In all of these types, the central person is also a leader. He is not performing a leadership function in serving as an object of love or hostility, although it must be admitted these latter instances also represent forms of influence on the group. Leadership is not, therefore, coextensive with influence.

The concept of identification is a complex one which has rich implications for psychic structure and functioning. Adequate discussion of it would go far beyond the scope of this chapter, but it is taken up later. On a more or less descriptive level, however, identification represents a fundamental and primitive way in which people relate to each other. It is essentially unconscious and therefore can be expressed on the level of conscious awareness in a variety of ways. In terms of the leadership relation, it can express itself in terms of admiration, imitation, liking. It can be put in terms of the adoption by the subordinate of the interest, attitude, intention, and objectives of the leader. The identification of ego-interest with leader-interest is a major unconscious component of the willingness of the subject to be influenced by the leader. The formula is serviceable even in reference to identification with the aggressor, for even here the threat is allayed by the formation of an alliance. Identification provides the unconscious substratum for cooperative and unified action. The leader is generally accepted by the group insofar as he is perceived as contributing to group goals, because of a prior identification of members with the group and its goals. This raises the further point that identification need not always be considered as occurring between individuals. It is also a feature of the individual's involvement in the group, and the necessary identification with the leader may be secondary and derivative from the primary group identification. We can, therefore, raise the further question whether even legitimate authority does not in some sense depend on a prior group identification.

## Referent Power

In terms of the bases of social power, referent power based on identification is not only the broadest but also the most advantageous of the forms of social power. Reward power is effective within limits, but it achieves effects only as long as the reward is forthcoming. Coercive power also has limited application and has the added disadvantage that it increases resistance in the group and tends to mobilize hostility. When the style of supervision is punitive, aggression is directly expressed against the supervisor (at least verbally) and indirectly expressed through diminished production.[13] Expert power is effective, though again limited; and one can reasonably inquire, I think, whether such power is really exercised exclusively of referent or legitimate power.

The relationship between legitimate power and referent power is fairly complex. Translating referent power into terms of positive attitude toward the leader, two major theories have been proposed. A theory based on types of power would predict that the leader's legitimacy results in a positive attitude of the subject toward the leader, as contrasted with a more negative attitude which would develop in illegitimate power relations.[14] The second theory, called the power-distance reduction theory, would predict that the smaller the power difference between leader and subject, the more positive would the attitude of the subject be toward the leader.[15] When these theories were tested experimentally, it was found that the power-distance determined the subordinate's attitudes whether the power basis was legitimate or not. However, when the power-distance was large, subjects showed greater resistance to illegitimate than to legitimate power. The power difference would seem, then, to be the more crucial variable, although legitimacy would also seem to have some positive effect.[16]

## Applications

Applying this to the religious group, increasing the power distance between subject and superior should decrease the degree of identification. This effect would presumably be mitigated by the superior's legitimacy which may, as we have suggested, be mediated through group identification. The balance of the superior's influence rests on the interplay of his legitimate and referent power. The higher a superior in the organizational structure, the greater will be his legitimate power and the less will be his referent power.

It is apparent from these considerations that the effective exercise of the leadership function of authority is very closely related to the internal processes of the group. Implicit in the approach we have adopted here is the suggestion that the influence of the leader over the group and the correlative coordination of goals and purposes between leader and group ultimately rest on relatively unconscious and emotional processes. The effectiveness of the group's task orientation is contingent on the organization of inner emotional workings, and these in turn are reflective of and derivative from often unconscious strata of the individual psyche. The concept of identification is an operative one here, but we have only touched the surface of it. The exercise of leadership in any effective sense, then, requires a basis in the identification of subject with superior and/or of subject with the religious group. It also involves (but does not require) a decrease in the perceived power-distance between subject and superior. The latter consideration is most pertinent at lower levels of the power structure, where legitimate power is less effective and influence depends more on referent power.

If we were to think about the power structure of the religious group in more or less absolute traditional terms, increasing the effectiveness of leadership becomes a rather limited possibility—it begins quickly to run into built-in mechanisms of resistance. If we shift the basis of our thinking to a more interactional framework and remember that power is not only legitimate and that leadership can be exercised at all levels of the structure—not only by legitimate superiors—the diminution of power-distance and the increase in identification becomes quite feasible. More effective leadership, then, might take the course of a broader distribution of participation in the leadership function of authority—without any change in the distribution of authority itself.

If one looks carefully at the structure of business organizations, a similar phenomenon is observable. If the corporate structure is viewed in terms of group process, the employees can be considered as participating members of a group organization which has specific economic and business goals. The degree to which employees become identified with the group and thus become active participants in processes directed to the accomplishment of group goals determines their value to the company. It is a generally accepted principle in labor-management relations that the more workers feel a sense of active participation, belonging and sharing in the company effort, the more productive and satisfied they are, and the more congenial is the course of labor negotiations. This kind of work climate is a function of identification.

Such identification becomes possible only where the power-distance between employer and employee is decreased. The history of the labor movement in this country developed out of an almost pure power basis. The legitimate right of the owner to own and direct his business was accepted and served as the basis of labor relations. The liability to abuse of that legitimate power gave rise to the labor union movement and the institution of collective bargaining. The basis of power had to shift, and as the power-distance diminished the role of referent power based in identification began to emerge. The vestiges of the older power structure remain active. Labor negotiations at this point in their history are cast in the role of the two great contending forces, two independent, contending and opposing loci of authority, each seeking to maximize its own advantage regardless of the advantage of the other.

The historical roots of conflict die out slowly. The labor movement has a long and bitter history which has generated a mythology that lives on. What seems apparent on the whole is that the interests of both labor and management are mutually dependent. They are participants in a shared process, the promotion of which is to their mutual advantage. What is required is a sense of mutual involvement, of shared goals and objectives, of mutual support and understanding—in a word, a sense of community within the business organization. Profit-sharing plans are a step in this direction. Such a development is not possible unless the bases of referent power are broadened and unless the power-distance between levels of the business organization are diminished. This requires changes in the authority structure of the organization and creation of new structures of authority in which meaningful dialogue between superior and inferior in the organizational hierarchy becomes possible.

In an analogous sense, the student rebellion on the campuses has the direction of not only disrupting older authority structures, but of creating new structures in which the power-distance between administration, which runs the school, and the students, who merely go there, is lessened. It is in the interest of an institution of learning to have its students identify with it and concern themselves meaningfully and creatively with its welfare and development. The argument is often used that the university is a persistent structure, while the students are transient figures on the scene. The argument misses the obvious point that the student body is a constant part of the university structure. A university without students is not a university.

The university requires a reorganization of authority structures which allows for the lessening of the power-distance between various segments of the university community. This calls for the evolution of structures for more effective student participation in the decision-making processes by which the university is governed. This does not mean that the clear line between administration, faculty, and students becomes blurred; nor does it mean that the essential distinctions between the respective responsibilities of administration, faculty, and student body should be obscured. It does mean that the older structure based on legitimate power and the authority of office is no longer adequate. The balance of power is shifting, and if the university is not to be destroyed, it must evolve new structures and a new concept of authority to meet the demand.

The force of the argument flows over to the black movement in this country. It is not so easy to see or make clear what the power-distance or power-distances are which separate black from white. There is no doubt that the black man feels the distance. He feels himself deprived, disadvantaged, alienated from the society at large. The distance impairs his capacity to identify with that society and to identify himself as a participating and sharing member of the society. It is apparent that what constitutes the perceived power-distance in any social structure is extremely complex and relates to issues of economics, status, acknowledged social role, etc. Above all, it has to do with one's own self-perception as an accepted participant in the social process. Political structures exist in American society to allow for that kind of participation for any minority group. But the use of those structures is contingent on a variety of other social factors as well as psychological factors. The kinds of influence and prestige which interact with and influence the political process are well known. There are also deeper personal issues of self-esteem and self-respect which encumber the efforts of the black community to achive political maturity.

The problem for American society is how to diminish the power difference between the deprived and the affluent subcultures without sacrifice of political ideology or governmental structure. One can only hope that we shall be able to initiate forces to build a sense of community in which differences are minimized, and in which the black community can recognize that it shares in and commensurately benefits from the social structure in which we all participate. If there is an overriding role for effective leadership in our times, this should be its direction and impact. When the forces of leadership in both the black and the white community are brought to bear on this issue, then there is promise of progress.

*Part II*

# Mechanisms

Authority and Identification

Authority and Values

Authority as Role-Relation

Authority and Mutuality

Myth and Authority

*Chapter 3*

# Authority and Identification

Authority functions in relation to individuals and in relation to groups by reason of a variety of mechanisms. Some mechanisms are quite transparent and function at a more or less conscious or pre-conscious level. Other mechanisms are less potent, more subtle, more complex. Identification is one of the latter variety. I would like to spend some time developing the notion of identification and exploring its implications for the exercise of authority. We shall have occasion to return to the question of identification under a variety of subheadings, but it may be useful, in terms of our overall understanding of the psychology of authority, to spend some time with identification itself. There is hardly a single psychic mechanism of greater relevance for the understanding of authority relations and group processes in general.

We must credit Freud with the basic intuition into the place of identification in the workings of human groups. He was the first to develop the concept of identification and recognize its role in the group process. His insight took its origin from a somewhat remote context. Along about 1914-1915, he began to clarify some of his thinking about problems of narcissism and masochism. His thinking about narcissism involved a theory of withdrawal of libido from objects so that it could be redirected to the self. This was conceived of as a libidinal regression from object attachment to a narcissistic state which recaptured some of the primary narcissism of infancy.[1] Thinking along similar lines, Freud argued soon after that the masochistic aim of feeling pain was really a transformation of the sadistic aim of causing pain. The masochistic individual derives pleasure out of feeling pain by identifying himself with the suffering object. The pleasure derives not directly from the inflicted pain, but from its associated libidinal gratification.[2] This, too, was a form of narcissistic regression. He wrote:

> Similarly, the transformation of sadism into masochism implies a return to the narcissistic object . . . the narcissistic subject is, through identification, replaced by another extraneous ego. If we take into account our constructed preliminary narcissistic stage of sadism, we shall be approaching a more general realization— namely, that the instinctual vicissitudes which consist in the instincts being turned around upon the subject's own ego and undergoing reversal from activity to passivity are dependent on the narcissistic organization of the ego and bear the stamp of that phase.[3]

## Development

Freud advanced his thinking about identification considerably in his formulations about the phenomena of mourning and melancholy. Mourning was a form of depression which followed the loss of a loved object. The mourning process enabled the person to gradually free the libidinal attachments to the loved object so that they become available for direction to new objects. Melancholy, however, was a form of depression which had to do with the worthlessness of the self. Such individuals manifested their depression by a continual self-criticism and self-depreciation. Freud noted that such complaints, which on the face of it seemed to be directed to the self, were in reality aimed at someone else. He conceived of the process of melancholy as one in which the breaking of the object-relation induced a withdrawal of libido, but that instead of freeing itself from the lost object, the object together with its associated libido was brought inside the ego. The transfer was brought about by identification. The ego identifies itself with the lost object, and object-loss thus becomes ego-loss.

The preconditions of this phenomenon included a strong fixation to the object and a narcissistic object-choice to begin with. This permits or facilitates narcissistic identification and an equivalent regression to narcissism. The loss is a narcissistic loss, and the depression reflects the ambivalence originally held toward the lost object. Narcissistic libido is withdrawn and attached to the self, and the aggressive feelings (sadism) originally directed to the object (and often unconsciously so) are also withdrawn and directed at the self. Identification effectively translates the conflict between ego and object into an internal psychic conflict between the ego and its identified self.[4] It should be noted that the identification was in the service of instinctual needs. It satisfied narcissistic needs by a narcissistic withdrawal of libido, and it satisfied the need to deal with hostile aggressive impulses by directing them against the self. The solution was neurotic, but it satisfied neurotic needs. It should be noted, also, that the entire process was unconscious. Further, it is clear that Freud thought of it as a regression from one kind of object-choice to original narcissism and that identification was really a preliminary stage of object-choice. It reflected the primitive way in which the ego placed itself in relation to objects by wanting to incorporate them into itself (oral phase of libidinal development).

## Identification in Groups

The next significant development came with the publication of *Group Psychology and the Analysis of the Ego* in 1920.[5] Freud became increasingly aware of the importance and generality of identification. He expanded his use of the concept in two major directions: first, to the analysis of family relations and their significance for libidinal development and, second, to the understanding of group formation. Identification became a form of emotional tie to a loved person by which the ego assumes the characteristics of the object. The son identifies with his father—he would not only like to be his father, but he would like to be like his father. Identification may involve only a single trait or even a symptom; it may take as its object not only loved but not-loved persons; it can be partial and limited. It becomes a point of coincidence between two egos. The repression of an object-choice is compensated by identification. Identification is now seen as a primitive form of object-tie with an object which can become a regressive substitute for a libidinal object relation by introjecting the object into the ego. Thus it can arise with any perception of a common quality shared with another person, even though that person is not a sexual object. It is obvious that the concept of identification had evolved to a point where it had to be relevant to more than the libidinal loss out of which it had been derived.

Freud went on to apply the concept to the constitution of groups. He formulated the libidinal constitution of groups in terms of the identification with the leader, primarily, and identification of members with each other in virtue of their shared identification with the leader. The libidinal structure of groups was therefore based on emotional ties between the members. As he saw it, there was a double tie: (1) identification, and (2) substituting the leader for the individual's ego-ideal. Identification among the participating members was a function of the substitution for the ego-ideal. The latter was also a form of identification, so that the double tie is really a double identification. He illustrated the issues by an appeal to two group structures, the army and the Church.

> It is obvious that a soldier takes his superior, that is, in fact, the leader of the army, as his ideal, while he identifies himself with his equals, and derives from this community of their egos the obligations for giving mutual help and for sharing possessions which comradeship implies. But he becomes ridiculous if he tries to identify himself with the general. . . . It is otherwise in the Catholic Church. Every Christian loves Christ as his ideal and feels himself united with all other Christians by the tie of identification. But the Church requires more of him. He has also to identify himself with Christ and love all other Christians as Christ loved them. At both points, therefore, the Church requires that the position of the libido which is given by group formation should be supplemented. Identification has to be added where object-choice has taken place, and object-love where there is identification. This addition evidently goes beyond the constitution of the group.[6]

The mutual tie between the members of the group derives from an identification of an important perceived common quality. It should be noted that Freud's analysis was more seminal than complete, and we shall have to broaden his formulations to reach a more adequate basis for the analysis of authority.

## Identification and Psychic Structure

Freud's more or less definitive formulations on the question of identity came in 1923 with the publication of *The Ego and the Id*.[7] His emphasis is on the role of identification in the development of the ego. Identification is seen as fulfilling an essential function in the development of character. Beginning with infantile experiences, the giving up of sexual objects results in an alteration in the structure of the ego. Object-cathexes are replaced by identifications, and the character of the ego evolves as a precipitate of abandoned object-cathexes. The alteration of the ego is such that it draws more and more of the libido to itself as an internal love object. The transformation of object-libido into narcissistic libido is equivalent to a desexualization of libidinal energy. Thus ego extends its control over the instinctual forces of the id. Identification then assumes a developmental role in which it is a primary mechanism for the origin of those changes in the structures of the ego which derive from relations with significant others. The early identifications are the most important and the most lasting. Early identifications with the parents issue into the complex relationships of the Oedipal situation. The resolution of this complex of identifications is decisive for the organization of the individual character. As Freud remarks:

> The broad general outcome of the sexual phase dominated by the Oedipus Complex may, therefore, be taken to be the forming of a precipitate in the ego, consisting of these two identifications in some way united with each other. Then modification of the ego retains its special position; it confronts the other contents of the ego as an ego-ideal or superego.[8]

As the ego progresses in development, it gains in strength and becomes more resistant to such influences. But the process of identification remains operative. Ultimately, Freud conceived of human character formation as resting genetically on a complex of identifications. Fundamentally, the identification with parental agencies gave rise to the superego, but there was added to this further identification with the parents of later periods, identifications with other influential figures, identifications formed as precipitates of abandoned object-relations.

*Extensions*

As Freud envisioned and applied identification, it took the form of a common and frequently employed mechanism which was internally related to instinctual needs and contributed one of the major mechanisms by which a more permanent and more highly organized psychic structure was erected in virtue of the vicissitudes of these instincts. The gradual broadening of the concept initiated by Freud from the status of a substitute for abandoned object-cathexes to sharing of common qualities was extended in the neo-Freudian literature. Its meanings have become multiple. It has been extended to imitation of admired or respected models, to group adherence, to acceptance of a cause, or to any close sympathetic or unifying action with other persons.

Sanford[9] describes identification as a process in which "the individual may be observed to respond to the behavior of other people or objects by imitating in fantasy or in reality the same behavior himself." Classes of behavior which are related to identification because they lead to similarities in behavior between a subject and a model are imitation learning, prohibition learning, identification with the aggressor, and vicarious affective experience.[10] Imitation may be the behavioral offshoot of an identification, but imitation may occur without any identification. Imitation and identification provide two major ways in which patterns of social behavior are adopted from models. Following Parsons and Shils,[11] imitation assumes that the other is a model only for a specific pattern of learned behavior, whereas identification implies a model for general orientation to behavior rather than specific patterns. It is obvious that general orientation can generate specific patterns of behavior, but that they need not. Prohibition learning, adopting the prohibitions of parents and parental substitutes, is a part of superego formation and involves identification, as we saw above. Identification with the aggressor was originally proposed by Anna Freud. She saw it as a means by which the developing ego mastered the anxiety from an outside threat by identifying with the aggressor. She proposed it as a fairly common stage in the normal development of the superego. It serves to transform the threat of the passive position into a more active assault on external objects. It is interesting that Miss Freud felt that this more or less intermediate stage of superego development was normal insofar as it functioned in the context of conflict with authority.[12] Finally, vicarious affective experience refers to a variety of forms of positive or negative effect which are experienced in consequence of identification with a model.

These various forms of identification, variously described, have a common connotation in that they represent attempts by the ego to modify itself in relation to a model—in Freud's terms, the shadow of the object falls on the ego. Identification with a model may serve not only to reduce anxiety over anticipated aggression; it may also serve more positive adaptive ends as a means to obtaining certain goals or gratifications. The model may be perceived as capable of achieving certain rewards or objectives, and the desire for these same goals may induce the subject to adopt some of the characteristics of the model as he perceives him. As Freud commented,

> Identification . . . may arise with every new perception of a common quality shared with some other person who is not an object of the sexual instinct. The more important this common quality is, the more successful may this partial identification become, and it may then represent the beginning of a new tie.[13]

## Socialization

More recent applications of the concept of identification point to its centrality in socialization. It is generally agreed that identification with adult models is an essential mechanism in the socialization of the child. Much of the knowledge required for cultural participation is passed on from generation to generation by this means. Acquired patterns of social behavior are taken over from established social models. The distinction between imitation and identification is pertinent here since imitation is the vehicle for acquisition of specific elements of culture, such as social skills, technical skills, etc. Identification, however, pertains to the acquisition of more generalized patterns of orientation. Its most important role in the socialization process is the development of an acceptance of adult values and value-orientations. Attachment to the social object creates a sensitivity, not only to the object's behavior, but to his attitudes, beliefs, and values, for it is these that characterize the object as a person.

The subject seeks not merely to have what the model has, or to do what the model does; he seeks further to be what the model is.

Identification has additional significance since it provides a basis for further motivation to accept still more social discipline. The needs for approval and esteem which it fosters are primary for the functioning of the social system, and the ability of the society to gratify them is a measure of the success of the system. The system stabilizes itself by internalizing common patterns of value-orientation in such a way as to satisfy basic needs which are in part built up through the socialization process.

## Identification and Group Processes

The relevance of all of this to ongoing group processes has been increasingly appreciated in recent years. Socialization has its primary analogue in childhood development, but the process is continuing and extends to adult adaptations to social life and culture. Culture is never static. It is a dynamic process which requires constant assimilation and adaptation in its participants. The social system, in whatever group organization it operates, is in constant evolution and requires the adaptation of its members.

The original Freudian analysis was cast in terms of the relation between the group members and the leader. The analysis is more consistent with totalitarian groups where the concentration of total authority is extreme. In more democratic group structures, however, identification continues to play a primary, although more diversified, role. In such group structures, the individual identifies primarily with the group rather than with a leader. Here again the sense of solidarity both reflects and promotes identification. The identification pertains to the general value-orientations which characterize the group culture. The individual chooses and internalizes some selection of the constituent group values and thereby identifies himself with the group. This is a more or less basic orientation which permits the individual to gain a sense of community with the rest of the group. This basic sense of community is then consolidated by the other identifications with significant figures in the group, whether these be in the role of leader or whether the significant individuals are peculiarly influential for a given individual.

## Identification and Values

The complex of identifications answers very basic needs for recognition, acceptance, esteem, and belonging. Identifications not only serve this satisfying function, but also bring about an alteration in the ego of the identified person. We can conceptualize this alteration in terms of the value-systems and identity. Both of these dimensions have intimate relations to the problem of character. The whole complex of character, values, identity, and identification are interwoven in complicated ways which reinforce the impression of their mutual dependence. While identification is the common mechanism, these elements all point to more or less permanent structural formations in the personality which account for the general disposition to act consistently in terms of persistent standards and style.

The value-system is an autonomous structure in the ego (Hartmann's secondary autonomy) which is built, in part, out of elements assimilated by identification. Adult identifications pertain less to matters of style than to matters of standard. They are concerned little with the manner of action and more with the basic values and orientations imbedded in the model. Identification with the group is almost exclusively of this kind. Identification with significant persons is often an amalgamation of other elements, but it can reflect the assimilation of values. In many instances identification is a reflection of the perception of  shared values without any question of transmission. Values are assimilated, therefore, on many fronts and from many directions. These internalized precipitates of external relations demand synthesis into an integral psychic system. The work of integration is a form of active intervention of the ego through its own synthetic function.[14] The value-system is never to be regarded wholly as a precipitate of acquisitions from outside; it represents, in addition, a synthetic organization produced actively and creatively by the further intervention of the ego.

## Identity

The concept of identity has been developed extensively by Erik Erikson in a number of works. The notion of identity has many complex ramifications which embrace most of the relevant aspects of ego psychology. Identity is formed out of a complex of elements, not the least of which are the contributing identifications which the individual acquires in the course of the life cycle. But identity formation is never equivalent to the mere acquisition of identifications. It involves an inner sense of continuity and social sameness which enable the individual to reconcile his conception of himself with his community's recognition of him. The individual's need to be recognized, not merely as an achiever, but in the sense of being given function and status in the community, is an important aspect of his adaptation. The sense of inner identity is relative to and derivative from the expectations with which the community regards each individual. As Erikson remarks,

> *Identity formation,* finally, begins where the usefulness of identification ends. It arises from the selective repudiation and mutual assimilation of childhood identifications, and their absorption in a new configuration which in turn, is dependent on the process by which a *society* (often through subsocieties) *identifies the young individual,* recognizing him as somebody who had to become the way he is, and who, being the way he is, is taken for granted.[15]

## Authority Relation

To turn more directly to the problem of authority, it can be stated that the authority relation has its roots in identification. Beyond the sense in which socialization of any kind can be interpreted in terms of the internalization of social object, the exercise of authority gains its concrete legitimacy through identifications. We must add the usual caution that the argument presented here is not concerned with the philosophical roots of authority. It is not a question of whether an authority is legitimate or not, nor is it a question of whether the legitimacy of an authority can be defended or not. The question has rather to do with the fact that individuals accept an authority as legitimate. Identification then, does not legitimize an otherwise illegitimate authority. It does not offer the foundation in terms of which an individual accepts and responds with obedience to the legitimate authority. We have described the notion of authority as "a dynamic and reciprocal relation between two or more persons in which one claims to be a bearer of authority, and at least one accepts the claim of the bearer to be authoritative in some areas of his own existence."

The claim to authority does not establish the authority of the claimer, however formally legitimate that claim may be. The claim becomes existentially relevant and meaningful only when and insofar as it is accepted. The claim becomes functionally legitimate only through acceptance.

The acceptance is always personal and immediate. It depends on and derives from the acceptor's perception of himself as liable to this authoritative claim. The individual in a sense identifies himself as one to whom the claim is pertinent. This self-perception requires an inner alteration of the self by which the self merges with a community of others who accept an authority. Since authority is a functional part of any social structure, membership in any social group implies an alliance of self with others by which the ego identifies itself with those others. Acceptance of the authoritative aspect of group structure is correlative with identification as members. It should be obvious that identification as a member of a group does not end with card-carrying or any other mere form of extrinsic denomination. Becoming a member involves an inner psychic transformation by which group goals and value-systems are internalized.

The authority relation also involves an interlocking of reciprocal identifications. Both superior and subject find common ground in their respective identification with the group. Through that identification they become sharers in a more or less common value-orientation. This does not reduce them to a least common denominator, however, since their respective internalized value-systems may represent different assimilations of the group's values and are always integrated with highly personal value-orientations derived from divergent identifications. Consequently, the authority relation leaves room for more direct identifications between superior and subject. Subjects may identify with the superior to the extent that the superior is perceived as embodying values inherent in the group value-orientation. Reciprocally, the superior identifies with his subjects. He does not internalize an abstract set of values, but a lived reality which is embedded in concrete individuals rather than in a superorganic reality. The extent to which he identifies with his subject distributively and effectively internalizes their shared and relevant value-attitudes. It also measures the effectiveness and meaningfulness of the authority relation.

In this fashion the group is constantly evolving its value-orientations and, in consequence, is constantly modifying the character of its authority relations. The influences flow in multiple directions and with varying intensities. It is important to realize that the inner vitality of authority, the effectiveness of its inner organization and exercise—all matters quite distinct from its formal dimension—derive from the establishment and integration of these identifications. This proposition has fundamental relevance, not only for the functional aspects of authority, but for its formative aspects as well.

Identifications pertain to the alterations of the ego by internalization of aspects of social objects. The process by which group members are formed—whether in religious or other groups—involves identification as a major formative process. In those groups in which formation overlaps with identity formation—as in religious groups in which candidates are adolescents, even late adolescents—the establishment, maintenance and integration of these identifications are of primary importance. Religious identity is an extension of personal identity in which the individual's perception of himself as a religious person vowed to a life of religious obedience becomes a primary element. The assimilation of group values and the development of meaningful and mature identifications within the authority relation are the solid strata upon which autonomous religious life and obedience become feasible.

## Unconscious Aspects

It is important to remember that what is internalized in identification is some partial aspect of the object. Often the unconscious mechanisms are tuned in on wavelengths that escape conscious scanning frequencies. Thus what is internalized is often some unconscious or repressed aspect of the model. As many authors have suggested, that which tends to get transmitted more significantly by identification is an unconscious attitude or value-orientation. The impact of this dimension of identification on authority relations is considerable. It is pertinent to consider what is available in the model for transmission. In the context of authoritarian attitudes and conflicts over authority, the model which is presented is one of rigid respect for authority and adherence to the letter of the law at one level. At another level, however, the model presents conflict over dependency needs, impulses to irresponsible action, and attitudes of rebellious-ness and disrespect for authority. The former aspects of the model are conscious and are implemented in the effort to defend against the unconscious and repressed wishes for the latter. But both levels are in conflict in the authoritarian personality and are, therefore, variously available for identification. In the relation between superior and subject, therefore, the authoritarian superior may unwittingly foster either excessive conformity or excessive rebelliousness through identification. We shall have occasion to return to this aspect of identification in reference to the transmission of values.

The inner psychic building-up of the social system is dictated by the characteristics of the participating personalities. The predomi-nant role of the authority-bearing figure in the social system makes the contribution especially significant. It is widely documented that authority and the attitudes it involves are frequently the vehicle for residues of earlier relations with parental authorities. It is altogether easy for new neurotic identifications to build upon earlier uncon-scious residues and reinforce prior authority conflicts. But the au-thority relation need not play into and need not play itself out on precast and neurotic levels. That participation can be a corrective one insofar as the models for social internalization are maturely con-stituted and display themselves effectively in the works of authority. Where authority functions through persons secure in their identity and identification as responsible authorities, the basic premises are provided for the reciprocal identification of responsible subjection. It is at this juncture, then, that the mutual regulation implicit in the authority relation is evident—responsibility engenders responsibility, and each makes the other possible. Displacement at either end of the relation sets up parallel displacement at the opposite end. Excesses and deficits can only distort and pervert the relation and its con-sequences. There is, however, an equilibrium point at which the processes of mutual regulation can achieve an optimum balance of those personal and social dilemmas for whose resolution authority exists—I mean freedom vs. order, initiative vs. subjection, obedience vs. rebellion.

*Chapter 4*

# Authority and Values

The authority relation involves, as we have seen, mechanisms and patterns of human interaction and relatedness which are operative at the most intimate psychic levels. We have already explored the place of identification at the level of group and intrapsychic functioning of authority. It is apparent from these considerations that the implementation of the exercise of authority has far-reaching consequences for the functioning of individuals in the group, even though such influences are often operative well below the level of awareness of all the participants.

These influences have a special pertinence in the religious group, where they are not only central in concern but also can be given a developmental regard. Religious formation is a process which deals primarily with the formation of perduring value systems in adolescent candidates. Value-formation is a primary concern of adolescence anyway, but in the context of religious formation the problem becomes more complex in virtue of the need for some degree of congruence between the internalized values of the individual religious and the constantly evolving value-orientations of the religious group. The group has a distinctive culture characteristic of itself which includes a complex system of values as an integral, constitutive part of the culture. Formation of the individual religious is directed at the enculturation of the individual in such a fashion that the internalized values which he accepts and integrates as part of his own psychic structure are congruent with those of the group. Identification, of course, plays a major role in this process.

## Value Systems

The notion of value and the relationship between value-orientations and individual value-systems have been discussed by Parsons and Shils.[1] Patterns of value-orientation are primary and central elements in the organization of the group culture. This holds true of any group structure where the group process is at work over and above the intrapsychic dynamisms which support and substantiate group processes. The group culture is transmissible since it is constituted by shared meanings which function as symbolic controls for orientations of the sharers of meaning. Individual personalities have internal needs and expectations which can achieve some level of interpersonal generalization by control in and through a common symbolic system. The group culture answers to the needs and expectancies of its participant members by organizing shared symbolic systems which are concerned with specific group functions. Cognitive functions find an organization in systems of ideas and beliefs; cathectic functions find organization in expressive symbols; and evaluative functions find organization and expression in normative symbolic systems or values. Such value-systems represent a synthesis of cognitive and cathectic (affective) elements by which an agent commits himself to an orientation in terms of consequences and implications which are arrived at by a complex process of social interaction.

## Value Variation

Such value-systems, operative in the group culture, are independent of, but at the same time related to, systems of personal value-orientation. The personal value-system is ultimately unique to the individual personality. The value-system of the individual involves a selection of cultural value-patterns so that the group incorporates a spectrum of individual value-orientations. Through processes of selection, adaptation, and integration, new patterns of personal value-orientation which diverge significantly from preexisting cultural patterns can arise in the group. The group culture, therefore, embraces a certain spread of variant value-orientations which usually cluster around a dominant value-system which is generally characteristic of the group culture. Groups vary in their inherent capacity for tolerating variant values in their members. The range of tolerance is smaller in more authoritarian groups.

Stouffer[2] has offered evidence that the resolution of conflicting social norms follows a pattern consistent with the concept of social norms as ranges of permissible behavior rather than as narrow and rigid categories. In any social group there are both systems of evaluative symbols or standards and a certain strain in the direction of conformity. If the norms are clear, the individual has a choice between unequivocal conformity or clear-cut deviance. If this individual tries to conform to the norms of more than one social group, he can either conform to one and deviate from the other, insofar as the two norms are in conflict; or he can try to conform in part to both by seeking a viable compromise. In the exercise of authority, conformity is dependent on the compatibility of the directives of authority with the dominant values of the group and its constituent members. Variability in the group values arises from variability between individuals, each recognizing a somewhat narrow range of permissible behavior, thus creating a wide distribution of permissible behaviors; or it may arise from a group consensus as to a common broad spectrum of permissible behavior. In these terms, the effectiveness of the exercise of authority is a question of the degree of overlap between the value-system implicit in authoritarian directives and the predominant value-system of the group.

## Value Formation

I would like to focus on the role of authority in the process of value formation and integration. The thesis which I would like to advance and explore is that the authority relation provides a matrix within which values are communicated and reinforced. The process of value formation is considered as an ongoing and continuous process in which values are constantly and dynamically being evolved. The process can reach a certain level of developmental closure so that the value-system becomes a more or less permanent structure on the psychic economy. Such closure is normally found at the closing stages of adolescence. The closure is only relative, however, since a variety of postadolescent circumstances can loosen the structured articulation of the value-system and permit the ego to reconstruct and resynthesize its value-system in the interest of adaptive ends. It is also worth pointing out that the authority relation is not the sole medium through which values are communicated. This is also an active function of the group, which exerts a constant influence on its members to achieve a level of cultural conformity. The role of authority in this process is particularly prominent, and is especially important, both because authority exercises such a pervasive influence on the group and the individuals in it, and because the influence of authority reaches such significant psychic levels in those involved in it.

The group carries on an active process to insure its own internal coherence. This has been referred to as a "pressure toward conformity," but the label is not altogether appropriate. Some groups, especially those in which authoritarian attitudes are predominant, are particularly intolerant of variability and may employ direct pressures to achieve uniformity and conformity of submission to authoritative directives. But most groups, in fact, work to achieve conformity by more indirect and less coercive methods. The mechanisms I refer to are not deliberate or designed with any conscious intent. They are substantially unconscious, both on the level of the group process itself and on the level of the individual psyche.

The most successful tactic is that by which group pressures bring individual value-systems into some degree of congruence with the value-system inherent in the group culture as such. The question facing us, then, is how the group accomplishes this—or to put it less anthropomorphically, what mechanisms are at work to bring about congruence between individual and group values. What is always in question is a relative congruence, or as Stouffer might have it, a range of overlap in value spectra. In any case, the question which must be asked pertains to the degree of relative congruence in value which the group must attain in order to preserve its own internal organization and group structure and in order to achieve the group goals. Divergence not only fragments the group structure, but also impairs the effectiveness of group functions directed to group goals.

## Values and Identification

We have already given some consideration to the function of identification in the authority relation. As we have seen, identification is one of the major mechanisms by which authority can be meaningfully exercised. It constructs and preserves the foundation on which the relation builds. It also underlies the formation of values. Following Kluckhohn's lead, we can define values as explicit or implicit conceptions (distinctive of an individual or characteristic of a group) of that which is desirable and influences selection from the available modes, means, and ends of action.[3] The definition may not be entirely satisfactory, but it is serviceable. It points to the fact that values are internal regulators of behavior. The value-system provides the internal standards by which individual and groups select a course of action from a diversity of available possibilities. It also implies that values are operative only in the context of free choice, so that the standard is even more specifically internal.

When we appeal to identification, we are appealing to a mechanism which aims at making the subject like an object. The child aims at becoming like his father; the member aims at becoming like his superior. It is not always clear what constitutes this likeness. But it is probably safe to say that the likeness is different for different contexts of identification. The identification of the child is cast on the simple and straightforward level of behavior. The child acts like his father. It is immediately apparent that mere similarity of mannerism of action does not satisfy more adult needs to identify. Adult identification extends beyond action and mere imitation to a level at which the internal psychic organization of the subject begins to approximate that of the other. Adult identification has to do with the reorganization of the internal modulation of behavior so that they approximate the internal regulators of the object of identification. The subject becomes internally like the object when he has internalized the intrinsic norms of the object. These norms then produce by way of secondary effect a congruence of attitudes, beliefs and behavior which wears the face of identification. Implicit in many of the more sophisticated contexts in which identification plays a role is the fact that the essential dimension of identification or its primary resultant is congruence of value-systems. The individual becomes identified with a group by internalizing the group evaluative symbols and norms so that these norms become a functional and integral part of his own personal value-system. The subject identifies with his superior when a similar congruence or significant overlap results between the value-systems of each.

It is important to note that such identification and the value congruence are each implicit in the other, but the direction of development is from identification to value congruence. One does not realign values and thereby become identified. One is identified, largely unconsciously, and thereby realizes value congruence. We have already discussed elsewhere the workings of identification and its dynamic motivations. The point needs to be added in the present part of our discussion that the upshot of identification by way of implicitation is the formation of new values. The process is not static, but remains open-ended. There is an inner necessity for continuing process insofar as the ongoing adaptation of the group is continually modifying and evolving the group value-system. The individual member maintains his belongingness by constant adaptive modifications of his own internal value-system.

## Communication of Values

The authority relation, functioning as it does in virtue of a subtle identification, becomes the matrix of value-formation. In fact, we can think of the authority relation as having a major function in the communication of values. Communication and formation of values are formally different aspects of the same process, but it is obvious that they are intimately associated. Communication becames formation in virtue of the identification between subject and leader. Communication reflects the quality of mutuality in the relation [see Chapter 6, "Authority and Mutuality"]. Values are communicated from leader to subject, and it is this aspect of the communication that fits most easily into the power schema of authority. The leader unites, molds, and in an indirect sense, directs the subject by the communication of values. The subject internalizes these communicated values, and thereby the foundation is laid for more explicit directives from the leader, and the subject's obedient compliance and acceptance both of the directives and their legitimacy.

In terms of relationship, however, things are more complicated. The mutual reciprocity of the relation suggests that values are not only communicated from leader to subject, but that they are also communicated from subject to leader. Communication involves a two-way channel. Communication is achieved in one direction by the identification of the subject with both the leader and the group. It is achieved in the opposite direction by identification of the leader with the group, or more specifically, with the group's value-system. The group value-system undergoes constant change, and the leader, in order to maintain himself as de facto leader, must adaptively assimilate these changes just as the members must assimilate evolving group values in order to maintain their group identification. The communication of values, then, is a special case of the mutual regulation which takes place within the authority relation. The process cannot be thought of in terms of a purely developmental model, that is, as organized along the same lines as the formation of values or value precursors in the parent-child relation. The subject in any group structure is not merely subjected to modifying influences. He is caught up in a continual process of interaction between himself and group forces in which influences flow back and forth with mutually reciprocal modifications.

From the point of value-transmission to the subject the levels of communication are multiple. The substantial elements of communication are positive in the form of directives and negative in the form of prohibitions. The authority figure communicates many affirmations on many levels and with many degrees of significance and reinforcement. These are translated into verbal commands, written communiques, concrete actions, and a large spectrum of metacommunications. The authority figure also communicates prohibitions in a variety of ways. The consistency among these various levels and kinds of communication is not always complete. There may, in fact, exist significant gaps and contradictions between any two concrete communications. The contradictions do not often present themselves in the bright light of consciousness—for any of the parties involved. A communication in one context may contradict a communication in another context, and the contradiction may never be consciously adverted to. Or a verbal communication may be contrary to actions carried out in the same context, with the contradiction being unrecognized by all parties concerned. While the contradictory content is not consciously recognized as such, both affirmations are picked up and effectively communicated.

Behind such contradictory communications there is a division in the communicating agent. Where the superior or leader is communicating contradictorily, the communications reflect an internal conflict in his own psyche at an unconscious level. The influence of intrapsychic conflict on value transmission is immediately apparent. Values are transmitted at a conscious and an unconscious level. The formation of values in those receiving and responding to these communications goes on at conscious and unconscious levels. Where the communications are conflictual, the process of value formation and assimilation is obscured and obfuscated. What is, in fact, picked up is an amalgam of conscious affirmations and unconscious elements. The conscious affirmations are usually more or less congruent with the acceptable content of the group value-system. The unconscious elements are usually reflections of less acceptable impulsive and instinctually derived content which are divergent from group values.

The whole problem of how such conflictual elements are communicated and picked up is extremely interesting. Similar mechanisms are at work on a developmental level in the dynamics of juvenile delinquency. Johnson,[4] for example, has pointed out that:

> Identification with the parent consists of more than incorporation of the *manifest* behavior of the parent; it necessarily involves inclusion of the subtleties of the parent's conscious and unconscious image of the child. The healthy parent fantasies his child as capable of becoming law-abiding. The well-integrated, mature mother does *not* immediately check on a child following an order or request; she unconsciously assumes that the order will be carried out. The neurotic mother, who immediately checks or warns that if the job is not done dire consequences will follow, merely conveys to the child that an unstated alternative exists in the mother's mind. It is frequently with this alternative image in the mother's thoughts that the child more strongly identifies. . . . The child internalizes, then, not only the positive, socially consistent attitudes of the parent but also the frequently unexpressed, ambivalent, antisocial feelings.[5]

What is more simply detectable in the parent-child relation is analogously operative, often in more subtle ways, in the authority relation. To cast the present analysis in terms of our consideration of the authoritarian personality, the authoritarian leader communicates his own inner conflicts regarding power on different levels. The subjects of such a leader pick up both the unconscious dependency as well as the more conscious and explicit exercise of power. When such communications become the basis for divergent action by individuals, the superior is likely to become excessively punitive precisely because the impulse present in the divergent action mimics his own unconscious and repressed impulses. The association of such divergent impulses with conflict in the leader or superior goes unrecognized by both leader and subject [see Chapter 8, "The Authoritarian Personality"].

## Instinctual Aspects

The subtleties and complexities of such communications and their implications for identification and the evolution of value-patterns and behavior in the group are considerable. The problems in religious groups are magnified by the institutionalized insistence on purified and highly moral behavior patterns. The complex behavior of the religious is programmed in a variety of prescriptions, rules, directives, customs, and the rest. The obsessive insistence on such prescribed behavior leaves open a large capacity for the more subtle communication of more impulsive and more instinctual elements. It is easy to be fooled, since more often than not, excessive insistence on institutional prescriptions is in the service of defense against instinctual pressures. An emphasis on love can be a defense against hate. An emphasis on chasitity can serve as a defense against unconscious libidinal impulses.

The interplay between impulse and control, between instinct and ego, between impulse and delay, between gratification and conscience is the stuff of our inner lives. It is also the stuff of our inner conflicts. These very elements can play into the ongoing processes of the religious group; and the generation and communication of values reflects these many levels of conflict and awareness. In the religious group these processes assume an added significance since the life of the group touches the life of each member so closely. Their significance is also magnified by the proximity and dependence of group goals on the value-system. The member participates in the group in order to share more intimately the system of values and in order to share them distributively and apostolically with other men.

## Organizing Function

Given the context of intimate and relevant value proximity, the authority relation assumes an important function vis-à-vis the integration of the group in terms of its inner organization. That relation provides the common ground or focal point at which the value interest of the community and its members meet. Authority functions, among other parameters of group organization, as the directive force by which group efforts are organized and channeled to achieve specific group goals. The authority relation does not generate values in the community, but by reason of its unique role in the structures and organization of the group, it serves uniquely to integrate a coherent and recognizable value-system for the community. This is in virtue of its organizing function on one level, but also in virtue of less apparent mechanisms of identification and value transmissions.

The importance of multiple levels of communication in religious groups cannot be sufficiently emphasized. The place of values in the economy of religious life demands that individual value-systems be sufficiently well integrated so that instinctual elements are meaningfully channeled, modified, directed, neutralized, or sublimated. While individual value-systems are generated intrapsychically, the process of formation reflects important extrinsic influences. The personality functioning and personal adaptation of individual religious depends on the mature integration of personal value-systems with the consensus of group values. We are forced to conclude that growth to personal maturity, development in spirituality, and ultimately the fulfillment of group goals and purposes are functions of the degree to which values are effectively transmitted and integrated through the authority relation.

*Chapter 5*

# Authority as Role-Relation

In our consideration of authority we have been using a primarily relational notion of authority. It seems appropriate at this point to focus more deliberately on the concept of role and to try to explore some of its implications for authority. Role theory has taken its place as one of the more substantial contributions of contemporary social psychology, even though most of those who use it and write about it complain that it is really less of a theory than a set of descriptive generalizations. In any sense, it has demonstrated its usefulness often enough to serve as a profitable tool of analysis. The limits of our present concerns exclude a full exposition of the ramifications of role theory, so we shall content ourselves with a few basic notions.

## Role Theory

Role theory really derives from both psychological and sociological roots and consequently serves as an articulating construct between the personal level and the level of social interaction. In any social system or group, each individual has a status or position. Status is necessarily relational in the sense that it locates the individual multidimensionally in relation to the other participants in the system. Status is characterized by a set of rights and obligations which regulate the individual's interaction with other individuals and other statuses. The social system involves a number of status systems in which positions are allocated in terms of different standards. Positions may be allocated on the basis of what a person is (age, sex, religion, etc.); these are "ascribed statuses." Or they may be allocated on the basis of what a person can do, and these are "achieved statuses." Every individual concurrently occupies positions in a number of status systems, and the aggregate of these positions defines his "status set."

Each such position or status carries with it a set of norms or expectations. These expectations specify a range of behavior which the individuals occupying other positions "expect" of the person in that position. It defines the range of behavior appropriate to the position in question. The set of expectations defines the roles. There is no generally agreed upon definition of role as such, but it can be taken to refer to the set of expectations in the social context surrounding the occupant of any position (prescribed role), or it can refer to the specific expectations which the occupant of the position perceives as applicable to himself (subjective role), or it may refer to the occupant's behavior when he interacts with occupants of other positions (enacted role)[1]. Generally, the term "role" is used to refer to the behavioral enactment of the prescribed role.

As Merton[2] pointed out, each social status is associated, not with a single role, but with an array of roles. These roles constitute a "role-set" which he defines as the "complement of role-relationships in which persons are involved by virtue of occupying a particular social status."[3] There are forces at work in any social structure which generate conflicting role-expectations. The members of the role-set occupy different social positions from that of the occupant of the status in question and consequently have different attitudes, values, and expectations. Merton offers the example of a school board which is composed of a diversity of members from differing socio-economic backgrounds than the teacher. The teacher's role can, thereby, be complicated by the conflicting role-expectations generated within the role-set.

Other mechanisms are operative, however, to stabilize such role-sets. Some statuses are of greater importance than others in the set of role-relations, so that the associated role-expectations have a greater or lesser significance. Power and authority are also unevenly distributed in the role-set. Not all the members of the role-set are equally influential in shaping the behavior of the status-occupant. Moreover, the status-occupant is not merely passively at the mercy of power coalitions. Variations in the role-structure can reinforce the relative power of the status-occupant.

In the interplay of influences and expectations involving a wide variety of role-relations, the individual may find himself occupying positions with incompatible role requirements. Such role-conflict may be generated by conflicting demands, either between status-positions, e.g., the doctor who wants to recommend birth control to a patient under circumstances which violate his religious convictions, or within the role-set itself. The beliefs, values, and attitudes associated with one role may come into conflict with the beliefs, values, and attitudes associated with another role. The more complex the social structure and the more fluid the situation of the involved institutions, the more likely are such conflicts.

It should be plain that the structure of the social system in any group is built up out of reciprocal role-expectations which stabilize the role-functions and role-relations by a process of mutual regulation. These reciprocal expectations are integrated into a functioning social system in virtue of shared value-orientations. The expectations of any role include what a person is expected to do both by himself and by others. Within a range of acceptable behavior consistent with the role-expectations as viewed collectively through its relation to a commonly achieved value-system, the actions of an individual meet social approval or disapproval. Insofar as the individual shares in the common value-orientation, or to put it another way, insofar as he is identified with the group, he has equivalently internalized the group standards. Deviation from role-expectations, therefore, meets with both internal and external sanctions. Such reciprocal and variously reinforced role-expectations tend to organize into a pattern of relations which is uniquely characteristic of a given social system. The interaction tends to stabilize the individual's role-set and thus provide a more or less consistent set of expectations and behavior patterns associated with each person. Social groups differ considerably in the degree of rigidity or flexibility in the pattern. The reinforcing mechanisms generally tend to encourage action within the range of permissible behaviors consistent with the common value-system. But it is apparent that individuals often deviate from the consensus of expectations. More flexible systems can tolerate or support a rela- tively higher degree of nonconformity, and this is both a channel of creative energy within the community and a socially instituted mech- anism for preserving current patterns of the culture. More rigid systems have less tolerance for nonconformity and bring sanctioning mechanisms more forcibly to bear in suppressing it.

## Identity and Role-Relations

While social interaction produces a certain consistency in role- configurations and role-sets, it is also apparent that this does not account for the total consistency observable, nor does it represent the whole of human personality. Man is more than a composite of role-relations. While this is indeed a truism, it raises a further ques- tion as to the relation between the individual's role-status and its more or less consistent role-set on one hand, and the individual's personality on the other. We can usefully turn here to Erikson's formulation of the concept of identity. As Erikson suggests,

> It is this identity of something in the individual's core with an essential aspect of a group's inner coherence which is under con- sideration here: for the young individual must learn to be most himself where he means most to others—those others, to be sure, who have come to mean most to him. The term identity expresses such a mutual relation in that it connotes both a persistent same- ness within oneself (selfsameness) and a persistent sharing of some kind of essential character with others.[4]

Identity is not merely a matter of inner self-continuity or maintained inner synthesis and awareness, but it has to do with a persistence of inner solidarity with the ideals and identity of a group.

The inner perception of continuity and sameness of self is parallel to and derivative from a consistent recognition of the social sameness of the individual by his community. Inner perception and social rec- ognition are interdependent. The formation of an identity as a devel- opmental task requires a resynthesis of preceding identifications into a uniquely new configuration which is at the same time congruent with a set of roles and expectations generated in the interaction between the individual and his community. It is a matter of "self-realization coupled with a mutual recognition."[5] Identity and its formation requires an inner integration of the consistent roles in which the individual relates to his community and receives the role-set itself and between the role-expectations of the status systems in which the individual is involved. It also involves a capacity within the ego for synthetic integration of roles and statuses in a consistent totality which issues in nonconflictual role-function. It also involves the capacity for integration and formation of a value-system or systems in which role-expectations are responded to and role-functions carried out. I do not mean to convey the impression that such complex integrations are all *sine qua non* prerequisites of identity formation. Value-conflicts or role-conflicts may or may not represent derivations of identity diffusion, but it is certain that such conflicts increase the strain upon the integrative capacity of the ego. And, to a certain degree, the strength of the ego can be measured in terms of its ability to tolerate a measure of role- or value-conflict—even as the capacity to tolerate a moderate degree of anxiety is a reflection of ego resilience.

All of these more or less theoretical formulations have relevance for the authority relation. The authority relation is a form of role-relation in which the status-occupant who lays claim to the position of authority is enmeshed in a system of role-expectations within a definite role-set. The limits of the role-set are the limits of the group, that is, the role-set includes all those who recognize the legitimate authority of the claimant. The members of the role-set generate a set of role-expectations which imply the range of acceptable behavior within which the authority of the claimant is recognized. This shared function of role-definition is operative regardless of the definition of legitimate authority provided by more formal and institutionalized sources. The range of legitimate authority is often defined in fact by formal documents, constitutions, customs, etc. The legitimacy of existent authority and the range of its exercise is always subject to an implicit redefinition through the group process. The redefinition takes place through the consensual articulation of role-expectations which pertain to the role of leader or superior. The redefinition may narrow or extend the range of legitimacy attributed to the superior's role. Often, in religious groups, the range of legitimacy is extended rather than narrowed. It is well to remember, in any case, that the process of redefinition is dynamic and constantly in change, while the more formal states are relatively static. There is always in some degree or other a recognizable gap between them.

## Reciprocity

The role-relation is reciprocal in that the role of superior is responded to by the role of subject—a common status shared by all the other group members. Just as the group process generates expectations which define the role of superior, so it also generates other expectations which define the role of subject. Here again, the role is sometimes formally defined, but it is equivalently redefined on an individual basis. The subject role is always optimally integrated in a unique personality scheme which differs from individual to individual. Such role-constituents are not integrated into the personality structure like immutable elements, like bricks in a building. They are transformed in the assimilation and become highly personal variants. The subject role has a much greater diversity and flexibility in any social system, the more so as the flexibility inherent in the system increases.

The reciprocal role-relation involved in authority is constantly engaged in a process of mutual definition. The defining is carried out through the impression of expectations from the members of the role-set. Subjects define the superior's role by the expectations which they generate in interacting with the superior. The subject's role is defined by the expectations generated by the superior and by the expectations generated at large in the social system. Undoubtedly the crucial interaction for the evolution of these respective roles is in the superior-subject interface. It is at this point that the exercise of superiorship and subjectship are achieved. It is also at this point that the continuing process of mutual regulation is realized.

It is well to remember that the status of each person in the group is characterized in terms of a set of rights and obligations which regulate the interaction between persons and statuses. The rights and obligations are, in a sense, constituent elements of the respective roles. These moral aspects of roles are derivations of the value-orientation of the social system, concretized and particularized in relation to a given role. The rights attributed to any given role by such consensus are always congruent with the range of values held in common by the group, since the same members and the same basic processes are at work in evolving both the value-system and the role-system characteristic of that group. The rights and obligations referable to both superior and subject are worked out through mutual interaction and regulation. The moral force of the superior's directive is not identical with his right to command as a function of his role. They are, however, very closely related. The superior's right to command is answered reciprocally by the subject's felt obligation to obey. This, in turn, depends on the extent to which the superior's behavior is perceived as congruent with the shared expectations regarding his role as superior. The moral force of the directive is something else. While the subject may recognize and accept the superior's right to command, at the same time he may not feel that he is obliged to respond to the command and obey. By implication, then, the role does not carry with it an automatic moral imperative. While the role with its attendant rights does imply a reciprocal obligation to obey in those who receive the command, the moral aspect of the subject's response does not derive solely from the role-structure but from the value-structure as well. The individual generally perceives the command as obliging to obedience with moral force only when the command is congruent with accepted role-expectations and when the matter of the command is consistent with the individual's internalized value-system. The presumption of congruence between the individual value-system and the communal value-system, while frequently enough inapplicable, nevertheless underlies the presumption in favor of the legitimate superior's authority.

## Dynamic Viewpoint

While the authority role-relation is part of a role-structure which characterizes the social system in which it is operative, we should not lose sight of the fact that it is concomitantly in itself a relationship on the interpersonal level. Consequently, it becomes the vehicle for a considerable loading of interpersonal dynamics. We shall have ample opportunity to explore the implications of this aspect of the relationship in terms of the implementation of the respective roles, but at this point we can well afford to focus on some of the theoretical aspects of the interplay of dynamic factors.

The dynamic theory of human interaction postulates that in any given relationship there are operative unconscious dynamic influences which ultimately derive from prior significant relationships. The most significant of these preceding relationships are those involved in the human being's earliest and most primitive relationships with the significant human beings in his environment. The newborn child is plunged into a prolonged period of intimate dependence on his parents. Those relationships determine not only the mere fact of his biological survival, but they are the controlling influences for the shaping of personality and the emergence of adaptive capacities.

It is important to remember that the human organism is raised from the beginning of life in a context of authority. His most fundamental needs and wants are attended to by all-powerful and dominant persons. He is required to submit to their demands and to show them obedience. The family is the matrix of authority out of which the roots of all authority spring. The psychological sense of this statement is basic. The child comes to the adult world with its more highly evolved and elaborate authority structure with a residue of attitudes and dispositions toward authority which were acquired and honed in his childhood experience. He brings that residue, largely unconscious and implicit, to those more adult forms of the authority relation in which he participates.

Entering into mature authority relationships is always a problem in adaptation. It is always a question of entering into an interpersonal relation which is specifically structured in a number of ways. The relation involves the implicit demand for acceptance of authority, for submission to the demands of authority in obedience, for acceptance of the legitimacy of authority, and for the involvement of the individual in the prior commitments of the community. Entering into such a relation requires that the individual have acquired or be able to acquire a fairly specific role or role-set. Adapting to the requirements of the role involves a very complex interaction which rehearses many of the elements of the infantile adaptation to authority figures. The patterns of response are not merely abandoned like so much useless baggage. They become built into the more adult response in ways that are very subtle and often difficult to recognize. The infantile residues become unconscious but still play a definite and often decisive role in the pattern of response followed by the adult. The issue of dependency, for example, is a perennial one in all authority relations. A mature acceptance of the subject role in the authority relation implies the capacity to be dependent without guilt or anxiety and to exercise independence of judgment and initiative without hostility or rebelliousness. Infantile residues, however, may carry along unconscious threats of loss of self-esteem, loss of control, subjugation, castration, etc., whch produce anxiety. The individual cannot enter into relations to authority figures without anxiety and is forced to struggle against the implicit and unconscious threat posed by such figures.

The issue of dominance and submission is another of the discontinuities in cultural conditioning pointed out by Ruth Benedict.[6] The child is raised in a matrix of authority within the family. The child is conditioned to one set of behaviors and expectations and then is expected to assume a different set of behaviors and respond to a different set of expectancies as an adult. On one level the subjection of the son must be transformed into the authority of the father. The individual must shift from one role in authority to another which is quite divergent and even opposite. Adult dependence, as is required in the religious community, requires traits and behaviors which are forbidden in children. It is never a simple matter to move from the patterns of adaptation which have served with success over many years, to abandon them and attain new, more appropriate and more adaptive patterns. Particularly where the situation evokes anxiety and conflict, adaptation is likely to be impaired; and the individual is more likely to fall back on more secure patterns of reaction in a kind of regressive adaptation.

Consequently, role-relations are never defined in any exclusive sense by merely social interactions. They are intimately involved in and influenced by the underlying strata of unconscious residues which every individual carries with him. The authority relation, therefore, is dynamic in more than one sense. It is dynamic in the sense that it is constantly in process. It cannot adequately be conceived as a static entity. It is continually evolving, changing, emerging, shaping itself through the multiple and complex influences deriving from the ongoing adaptive process within the group as well as from the constantly active intrapsychic forces within the individuals who participate in it. It is dynamic also in the further sense that it expresses and serves as a vehicle for unconscious impulses, attitudes, feelings, and drives which have their roots in the primitive and infantile residues of the human personality.

## Chapter 6

# Authority and Mutuality

In developing the concept of authority in Chapter 1, we arrived at a formulation of the notion of authority which shifted the emphasis away from the formal aspects of authority and from authority cast in terms of control or power. Traditional treatments of authority have tended to emphasize the more formal and power-based aspects of the concept. It seemed more to our purpose in trying to explore the inner significances of authority to approach the notion of authority through a formulation based on the relational aspects of authority. Authority in this perspective can be viewed as a dynamic and reciprocal relation between two or more persons in which one claims to be a bearer of authority and at least one accepts the claim of the bearer to be authoritative in some area of his own existence.

### Reciprocity

The definition, such as it is, underscores certain fundamental characteristics of authority. The relationship demands reciprocity. The claim of the superior must be recognized, accepted, and responded to by the subject. Authority must be answered by obedience. The superior's claim to authoritative status is not enough to establish his authority as a viable reality. It requires the response of obedience and acceptance within the group to which it addresses itself. The relationship is derivative in the sense that it derives from concrete existential human situations and real group structures. The group exists prior to the working within it of authority, and it gives rise to the reality of authority among its own members. Where the members are institutionalized, as in the Church or in a religious community, they have a perduring structure which generates a context of authority as relation. The context of authority as relation is anticipated by the formal structure of authority which perdures as a more or less consistent property of the established and institutionalized group. As the group prolongs itself by the induction of new members, the extension of authority rests reciprocally on the acceptance by the new member of its legitimate claim to authority. The new member's acceptance and obedience does not thereby constitute the authority of the group, certainly not as a formal property, but it does extend and re-create the concrete relationship of authority which serves as the real vehicle for the preexisting group authority. The new member's acceptance, however, does have the effect of bringing into being the fundamental authority relation in regard to his own person which serves as the medium for his authority-based involvements and interactions with the membership. Consequently, while the existence of authority is always ultimately dependent on and derivative from the group, the dependence is not always immediately contingent on the acceptance of individual members. If the group accepts the authority as properly its own, membership hinges in part on participation in this group acceptance.

The reciprocity of the authority relation, therefore, does not pertain so much to the formalities of authority as to its exercises. It is the overriding presumption of this discussion that the formal aspects of authority are of little pertinence when isolated from the exercise of that authority. The exercise is caught up in reciprocity. The effectiveness of authority depends in large measure on the readiness of inferiors in the group to carry out its directives. That readiness rests on more than an underlying dependency need or readiness to comply. It rests on more than the structure of power relations. It is not so easy to spell out what constitutes the basis on which it does rest, but it is clear that whatever elements of human motivation and striving are pertinent to the basis of authority, there must be some consideration given to the utility of the relation of authority in providing important positive supports to human personal development and self-fulfillment.

## Mutual Regulation

The relation of authority takes place between a superior and a subject, between one who lays claim to and bears authority and one who accepts and submits to it. Relating to other human beings is one of the basic needs of man and one of his most significant areas of adaptation. Psychoanalysts speak of this problem in terms of object-relations. The developing infant begins the process of relating to objects in the first moments of life. Man is in a state of object-relatedness from the very first. The child relates first of all to the primary objects of his initial environment, his parents and, most particularly, his mother. The quality of object-relations and the capacity for forming object-relations is deeply affected by these earliest experiences. The importance of this process for the course of personality development has been treated at length by Erikson.[1] He points out that the rudiments of basic trust are structured in the infant's earliest experiences. Trust refers to a reasonable trustfulness as far as others are concerned and a simple sense of trustworthiness as far as oneself is concerned. The establishment of trust evolves from the child's inborn need and ability to take in by mouth. This is coordinated with the mother's ability and intention to feed him and love him. As Erikson puts it, the infant "lives through, and loves with, his mouth; and the mother lives through, and loves with, her breasts."[2]

The first experience of friendly and giving otherness depends very centrally on mutual regulation between mother and child. The infant's biological demand must be met by the mother's psychological willingness to provide. Trust evolves out of the infant's continuing and stable experience of this warmth of giving, which enables him to place confidence in the other as the source of giving which can be relied on to remain giving. The mother is not only the source of relief from pain, but she becomes the relied on source of relief from pain. The success of this enterprise depends in part on the infant's developing ability to regulate his own need in the mutuality of his relation with the giving mother, so that his means of getting are coordinated with her means of giving. The mutuality of relation and regulation become the key to the founding of trust. Where mutual regulation and the mutuality of the relationship fail, the situation degenerates into attempts to control, either from the side of the mother or from the side of the child. The effect is to diminish the conduciveness to basic trust and increase the probability that the outcome will be a basic mistrust. This will stamp the child's evolving capacity to deal with and relate to other objects.

## Pseudomutuality

In the primitive relation of mother and child we can discern the rudiments of what becomes meaningful in other human relationships. The relationship is regulated by mutually interacting needs and expectancies. The pattern of the relationship can take the form of *mutuality,* of *nonmutuality,* or of *pseudomutuality.* The notion of mutuality is complex and is perhaps best approached by trying to clarify the less satisfactory forms of relatedness which represent the failure of mutuality.

Pseudomutuality refers to a form of relatedness with multiple elements. Where true mutuality develops out of a belief that one's own needs and expectations mesh with and are coordinated with the needs and expectations of the others in the relation, pseudomutuality rests on the strong need to maintain the wish for such coordination even to the extent of illusion. Every person has a need for relatedness and maintains an investment in sustaining a sense of relation. Isolation from other relationships or the recurrent failure to establish and maintain such relations can serve to augment the driving force of the need to relate. The quality of early object-relations, the underlying capacity for basic trust, and many other complex issues derived from experiences of separation and loss contribute to the power of the need to maintain a sense of relation.

It is clear that all forms of persistent interpersonal relation are structured in terms of some kind of complementarity. Pseudomutuality, however, involves a persistent concern with the complementary aspects of the relation at the expense of threatening the identity of the persons involved in the relation. Genuine mutuality is possible only between persons who possess a sense of their own meaningful and positively valued identity. Mutuality is based on the evolving and mutual recognition of the other's identity in the course of the experience of the other and interaction with him. In a genetic context, the evolution of personal identity derives from the prior experience of the identity of other significant persons. The rudiments of identity are laid down in infancy through the child's meeting of the mother's identity; or putting it the other way around, the mother's sense of inner identity as she participates in the intimate relation to her child is a precondition for the child's mastery of those important developmental tasks which form the foundation for the emergence of his own future identity.

On the level of interaction between adults, the sense of identity does not derive from the mutuality of the relationship; it is the prior condition for genuine mutuality. Without some measure of identity, the reciprocity of behavior and expectations becomes difficult, if not impossible. Identity implies difference and divergence among individuals. The individual who is secure in his own inner sense of personal identity can tolerate the divergent autonomy of the other, can respect and not violate his personal freedom, can recognize the individuality of his beliefs and values; and he can maintain a sense of respect for his person and rights. He is also capable of perceiving the other's changing expectations and needs as they present themselves. In any relationship, growth and situational change introduce changing expectations which must in part become transiently unfulfilled. The tension created by such circumstances can be tolerated in genuine mutuality, but in pseudomutuality it cannot. Pseudomutuality views the tension of divergent expectations as threatening to the relation itself. The possibility that such divergences may lead to a deepening or broadening of the basis of the relation is not entertained. Pseudomutuality cannot tolerate the divergence of self-interests. Genuine mutuality not only tolerates, but feeds upon the recognition of such divergent interests. The consequence is that emergent expectations are left unexplored, and the older and more comfortable expectations and roles are preserved even though they are no longer appropriate or adaptive.

The inevitable outcome of the relation of pseudomutuality is ambivalence and conflict. The relation on one level offers much, but on another fulfills little. The individual is drawn to it by the promise of meaningful relation and involvement, and is simultaneously repelled by its recurrent ineffectiveness and constraint. The failure of mutual perception and recognition continually empties the relation of its meaning and effectiveness. Its positive aspects cannot be examined and expanded; it becomes barren and sterile. The pseudo-mutual relation is caught on the horns of a characteristic dilemma: divergence begets disruption of the relation and must be avoided; but avoiding the divergence makes growth of the relation impossible.

## Nonmutuality

The alternative form of failure of mutuality is that noncomplementarity referred to as nonmutuality. Many relations are of their nature restricted to specific roles or specific functions. The relation of customer and bank teller, for example, hardly takes place at an interpersonal level at all and does not entail a strong investment in exploring the potentialities of the relation for the participants. There is some complementarity, but it is not reciprocal or mutual. In more persistent relations, nonmutuality represents a flight from mutuality. The relationship is depersonalized. It becomes predicated in terms of a specific role or function. It is a refusal to participate in an interpersonal relationship. The relationship is reduced to a set of functional interactions; it is, in a sense, mechanized. The customer who always goes to the same barber but never attempts to relate to him personally and never talks to him has a form of contact which is purely and explicitly functional and based on a specific role-function. The customer might just as well put the money in a machine—except that machines are not yet able to do the job as well.

## Mutuality

There is no question that genuine mutuality is often threatening. It is threatening because it involves intimacy, and intimacy of interpersonal relation is threatening to the neurotic personality. There is little ground to expect that the structure of relations among people would be predominantly formed along the lines of genuine mutuality. The neurotic fears and anxieties which are the common lot of human beings make that expectation too sanguine. Mutuality is as precarious as the identities on which it rests. It is distorted by the multiple interventions of transference, projection, repression, denial and other such devices which mask each person's perception of his fellowman. It becomes difficult to recognize and even more difficult to accept the other as he is.

The capacity to perceive the other, as he is, and to accept the other, as he is, is central to the notion of identity and and offers a major dimension to its social function. Identity is after a fashion formed in the social exchange between individuals. My own perception of myself and my own appraisal of myself is shaped and constantly modified by the perception of me held by those around me. I read myself in their eyes; I identify myself in terms of their reactions and responses to me. The developed sense of identity permits trust in self which provides a basis for trust in others. My own sense of trustworthiness and self-trust is a necessary precursor of my ability to trust in the trustworthiness of others. The developed sense of identity is secure in its own sense of autonomy to an extent that makes it possible for the autonomous person to grant autonomy to others around himself. The truly autonomous person can permit and tolerate other centers of personal autonomy without resorting to the defending and controlling devices of doubt, shame, guilt, and fear. These parameters and more are the constituents of a genuine sense of identity. These are likewise the parameters which underlie the possibility of genuine mutuality.

The failure of mutuality, it seems to me, has certain definite implications for the pattern of dynamics within the structure of a group. The reference to group patterns is meaningful here insofar as authority functions within a group structure and has relevance only in that context. While mutuality addresses itself to the authority relation between persons, there are further implications which can be brought into focus on the level of group function and which pertain to the interaction between intrapsychic and group processes. In a situation where pseudomutuality comes to predominate in the quality of personal relations, a sufficient degree and duration of pseudomutuality can induce the development of shared group mechanisms by which any deviations from the persisting role structure of the group are either not recognized or are recognized and given a delusional reinterpretation. These shared mechanisms, the so-called "social defense mechanisms," act in such a way as to shut out and exclude any meanings or communications that might enable an individual member of the group to differentiate his personal sense of identity within the group role-structure. We will discuss social-defense mechanisms in more detail in Chapter 9.

By referring the mutuality of relation to the group context, we have really opened up the implications of the authority relation to the broader issues of group process and group function. The group has an internal dynamic interactional process by which it modifies and shares its inner life.[3]

The group culture has, as one of its central components, a role-structure in which the specific role-function of individual members is being constantly defined. A patterning of pseudomutual relationships creates a role structure which works against the emergence of any individual member as an autonomous and independent identity. The subliminal perceptions and incipient communications which might foster divergent expectations and interests, and which provide the substrate of individuality, are instead distorted, diffused, made ambiguous, fuzzy, and vague. Persistent pseudomutuality has implications at the group level and, conversely, the group process becomes participant in the extension and prolongation of pseudomutuality at the interpersonal level. The entire structure serves fundamental needs for the preservation of relationship despite loss of a sense of personal identity and a capacity for mutuality.

## Mutuality in Authority-Relation

In the relation of authority the place of mutuality is central. The relation between superior and subject in whatever group structure it finds itself can take the shape of genuine mutuality, or it can assume a form of noncomplementarity, either nonmutuality or pseudomutuality. Nonmutuality serves to preserve the relation only on its most minimal functional grounds. It is more of a form of nonrelation. It depersonalizes and therefore destroys the relation. It permits no room for trust or identification. It is no more than a sham of authority. It is a refusal to enter into relation and therefore a form of rebellion against authority. Where the role of authority is pervasive in the group culture and touches the individual at very significant levels of personal existence—as is the case in religious groups—nonmutuality is symptomatic of some form of disturbance. It suggests an incapacity for relationship as a result of defect or diffusion of identity, either on the part of the subject, or on the part of the superior, or on the part of both. It is therefore disruptive, psychologically perilous, and destructive of the aims and functions of the group.

## Pseudomutuality in Authority-Relation

Pseudomutuality, in contradistinction to nonmutuality, aims at preserving the relation in authority—in fact, it preserves the relation at the cost of other important elements. In pseudomutuality the superior and subject enter into a relationship, but the interaction is such that the cost of maintaining the relation is paid in terms of a loss of individuality and personal integrity. Pseudomutual authority loses sight of the inherent dignity-in-relation of the respective persons. There is a failure of trust in a context which demands trusting submission and a reciprocal trust of the initiating other. There is a failure of autonomy in a context which demands autonomy of leadership and personal autonomy in function. In the religious group, authority is considerably more central to the group life and to the existence of individual members than in most other forms of group life. It is, in Turner's[4] terms, an identification group rather than merely an interaction or valuation group. It provides the individual with the major source of perspectives, attitudes, and values. Part of the individual's emergent identity is formed within and in relation to the religious group. His identity involves and includes a sense of inner participation in the life of the group. The sense of solidarity is particularly important in the life of the religious group, and that sense is in part a function of the religious subject's sense of identification with the group.

Where pseudomutuality predominates in the authority relation in these circumstances, the reverberations and implications are deepened and extended significantly. The authority relation is the hallmark of group participation, and the relation therefore assumes a centrality and significance which is peculiar in religious groups. There is an inner push to preserve and deepen the relation. Where the superior, however, is unable to enter into a relationship of autonomous trust and mutual respect; and the subject is unable to meet the superior with mutual respect and a sense of inner confidence, mutuality fails, and the relation lapses into pseudomutuality. The relation is preserved but at a cost. It becomes a vehicle for authoritarian attitudes and uncertainties [see Chapter 8, "The Authoritarian

Personality"]. It frustrates the mutual exchange of expectancies and needs which constitute part of the reward and satisfaction of submitting to such a relation. It creates disharmony, misunderstanding, anxieties, and dissatisfactions. It impedes that basic process of identification which enables individuals to intermesh individual and group goals, individual and group needs, individual and group purposes. It undercuts in a very profound sense the union of mind and heart which is a necessary prerequisite for that best form of obedience which St. Ignatius Loyola called "obedience of judgment."

The most devastating aspect of pseudomutuality is that it operates in effect to exclude those individuals who come to the relation with a mature and articulate sense of identity. It either excludes them or forces them into a position of deviance, since only in deviance can they maintain their sense of personal identity and autonomy. The relationship is preserved but in such a way that the confrontation of the relation with any differentiation is avoided. Individuality and differentiated identity is threatening to pseudomutuality precisely because the interaction with undiffused identity calls for a series of chained interactions which forces the involved parties to readjust in the direction of clarification of their own identities. The very mechanisms which bring the pseudomutual relation into being remain at work to preserve it in being. The diffusion and uncertainty of identity finds support and assuagement of anxiety in the mutual vagaries of the pseudomutual relationship. It finds a substitute form of relationship where genuine and intimate relationship is impossible and threatening.

The consequence is that mature and stable individuals tend to be excluded from the system, and this cannot but work to the ultimate harm of the group. This is particularly pertinent where continual pressures are being exerted on the group members for greater initiative and responsibility, as is often the case in contemporary religious and business groups. This results in a pressure toward remodeling the group culture to fit the needs of the diffusion in identity of its members. The group can subtly take on such a configuration as to support and foster pseudomutuality and banish genuine mutuality. Conversely, there is a constant process of internalization of group norms and expectancies which exercises itself on individual members to soft-pedal any deviant expectations or perceptions. The group pattern becomes a sort of internalized system of regulation which no longer allows the exploration and participation which permits deepening of relations. Members strive for a sense of relation by fitting into the role structure of the group with its role-expectancies for non-individuated participation. The social organization of the group takes on a pattern which gives expression to a subculture of myths (see Chapter 7, "Myth and Authority"), and an ideology which emphasizes the threatening aspect of any divergence from the fixed and limited number of roles available in the system.

There emerges from this pattern of interaction a set of shared mechanisms which excludes open recognition of noncomplementarity in pseudomutual relations and thus helps to perpetuate that pseudomutuality. They act at primitive and unconscious levels to prevent the emergence of any meanings that enable individual members to achieve some measure of differentiation. The implication for personal development and integration is simply that the taking of roles in such a group situation is not a function of actual participation or real experience. Consequently they cannot be integrated into the functions or values of an actively synthesizing ego. Rather, what happens is that the role structure of the group is internalized as part of the archaic self-regulatory principle, the superego, and functions unconsciously to determine behavior directly. Thus personal growth, emergence to maturity, and the evolution of a sense of an autonomous and responsible self is inhibited.

## Religious Implications

The upshot of these considerations is simply that authority is best exercised in terms of genuine mutuality. This demands that the religious superior recognize the autonomy, initiative, and individuality of his subject. It demands that religious subjects respond with respect, tolerance, trust, and responsibility. There must evolve that delicate process of mutual regulation wherein the superior's command is answered by the subject's willingness to obey, and the subject's initiative is answered by the superior's tolerance and trust. Only by a continual and mutual exploration on both sides of the relation does that emerging sense of identification come about which draws superior and subject together in a shared sense of mutual purpose and understanding. It is fundamentally through this relationship that authority, which touches so many facets and levels of religious life, can exercise a positive and maturing developmental influence. And finally, it is only through this relationship of genuine mutuality that the exercise of authority in the religious group can approach the purposes and objectives for which the religious institutions themselves exist.

*Chapter 7*

# Myth and Authority

The authority relation represents a basic human matrix within which there are displayed almost the full spectrum of human social and psychological processes. It is not only constituted by the interaction of the superior and subject in terms of the interpersonal interaction that takes place between them as individuals, but it also takes place in the broader, more transactional context of the life of the group. On an individual level, the authority relation becomes the vehicle for a host of intrapsychic dynamic factors which derive from the inner workings of individual psyches. On a group level, the authority relation becomes a vehicle for the dynamic processes that take place on the level of group interaction. The situation is further complicated by the fact that the two levels are themselves constantly in interaction. The individual influences the group, and the group influences the individual. And the authority relation is deeply involved in and reflects both of these interactional levels concurrently and often indissolubly.

## Myth

I would like to address myself for the moment to the formation and prolongation of myths within the authority context. This may seem a strange aspect to take up, since the study of myths is a prerogative of contemporary anthropology. Anthropologists are concerned with myths insofar as they reflect the culture of primitive people. Myths are concrete expressions which embody an abstract idea. They are story-forms which embody both ideas and the justification of those ideas. The effective myth is so constructed that it carries an emotional appeal which enlists endorsement of the ideas in terms of an acceptable justification of them. The reality of the story is beside the point; what is important is that the story and its inherent ideas are believed to be real.

Perhaps one of the most cogent, and for our purposes most applicable, formulations of the notion of myth was supplied by Malinowski in his classic monograph, *Myth in Primitive Psychology* (1926).[1] Malinowski proposed the thesis that there was an intimate conection between the myths, the sacred tales of the tribe, and the context of ritual acts, moral deeds, social organization, and even practical day-to-day activities from which they derived. He was reacting against the so-called nature mythologists who found in myths the primitive attempt to understand or explain the forces of nature, as well as the historical view for which the myth serves the function of a chronicle. For Malinowski, myth was something altogether different.

> Myth as it exists in a savage community, that is, in its living primitive form, is not merely a story told but a reality lived. It is not of the nature of fiction, such as we read today in a novel, but it is a living reality, believed to have once happened in primeval times, and continuing ever since to influence the world and human destinies. . . . Studied alive, myth, as we shall see, is not symbolic, but a direct expression of its subject matter; it is not an explanation in satisfaction of a scientific interest, but a narrative resurrection of a primeval reality, told in satisfaction of deep religious wants, moral cravings, social submissions, assertions, even practical requirements. Myth fulfills in primitive culture an indispensable function: it expresses, enhances, and codifies belief; it safeguards and enforces morality; it vouches for the efficiency of ritual and contains practical rules for the guidance of man. Myth is thus a vital ingredient of human civilization; it is not an idle tale, but a hardworked active force; it is not an intellectual explanation or an artistic imagery, but a pragmatic charter of primitive faith and moral wisdom.[2]

The myth has a sociological function which overrides its historical function. Whatever the reality of the past, the myth serves to cover the inconsistencies in historical events rather than to record them. As Malinowski saw it, the myth does not represent a past reality so much as a present reality which was active in the life of the tribe. Myth functioned particularly in the matrix of sociological strain, where differences in rank or power, of precedence and subordination, are in question, or where profound historical changes have taken place. Myth had a specific function, as he saw it.

> Myth, as a statement of primeval reality which still lives in present-day life and as a justification by precedent, supplies a retrospective pattern of moral values, sociological order, and magical belief. It is, therefore, neither a mere narrative, nor a form of science, nor a branch of art or history, nor an explanatory tale. It fulfills a function *sui generis* closely connected with the nature of tradition, and the continuity of culture, with the relation between age and youth, and with the human attitude toward the past. The function of myth, briefly, is to strengthen tradition and endow it with a greater value and prestige by tracing it back to a higher, better, more super-natural reality of initial events.
>
> Myth is, therefore, an indispensable ingredient of all culture. It is, as we have seen, constantly regenerated; every historical change creates its mythology, which is, however, but indirectly related to historical fact. Myth is a constant by-product of living faith, which is in need of miracles; of sociological status, which demands prece-dent; of moral rule, which requires sanction.[3]

We owe to Malinowski the crucial insight that the myth is born within a societal matrix and that it is in some sense derivative from the culture that embodies it. The myth is not just a story; it is a lived reality. It is a shared belief which is shaped by the ongoing dynamics of the life of the cultural group. It expresses the reality of beliefs, needs, and conflicts which characterize and determine the life of the group. At whatever level the organization of the group exists, myth exists as an indispensable dimension of its inner life. Myth is derivative from the group culture and reflects the profound psychic forces that work within that cultural matrix.

## Mythical Thinking

But the myth is more than a tale. Behind the tale with its embodiment of beliefs, attitudes, values, and the rest, there is a mentality.

The myth is generated and sustained not only as a thought, but as a form of thought. The mythical mentality has been analyzed profoundly by Ernst Cassirer. For Cassirer, mythical thinking could not be described in terms of mere invention. The myth had an objective significance, not in the content which it embodied, but rather in the significance and power which it held for human consciousness. The problem of the myth as a form of thinking was not its content, but rather the intensity with which it was experienced and believed. The dynamic force of the mythical consciousness was such that it could only be explained by a reality behind it.

But even the most primitive of mythic expressions are clearly not reflections of a reality only, but truly creative elaborations. The tension of subject and object, of inside and outside, is resolved in terms of an intermediary realm of conceptualization. This intermediary expression is not a freely creative act, but it has the stamp of necessity born of an underlying mechanism. There is an underlying necessity which requires the world of signs to appear to consciousness as objective reality. Cassirer comments, "Every beginning of myth, particularly every magical view of the world, is permeated by this belief in the objective character and the objective force of the sign."

Mythical thinking, therefore, stands in opposition to scientific thinking. Cassirer remarks that "myth lives entirely in the presence of its object." Science proceeds by a dialectical movement by which each particular event is linked with other events in a series and thus subordinated to a more general process and law. Science thereby achieves a certain abstraction and generality. Myth, however, proceeds by subjection to the impression itself and its momentary presence. It has no resources to extend that moment beyond itself to the past or the future. It cannot correct or criticize the present impression since it cannot measure it against what is not present, what is past or future. As Cassirer remarks:

> And if this mediate criterion is absent, all "truth" and reality dissolve into the mere presence of the content, all phenomena are situated on a single plane. Here there are no different *degrees* of reality, no contrasting degrees of objective certainty. The resultant picture of reality lacks the dimension of depth—the differentiation of foreground and background so characteristically effected in the

58529

scientific concept with its distinction between "the ground" and
that which is founded on it.[4]

The mythical mentality does not separate the ideal from the real;
it does not oppose the image to the object. Where the observing eye
sees only representation, the myth sees reality and identity. The
image does not represent the thing; it is the thing and thereby re-
places and substitutes for the thing's reality. And for the mythical
mentality, all images occupy the same plane of reality and force. The
image, like the word, has inherent in it real force.

Mythical thinking differs from scientific thinking not only in its
content, but in its concept of causality as well. Scientific thought
tends to isolate specific events and establish their relationship as
prior condition and effect. But this kind of abstraction and sequential
reasoning is alien to mythical thinking. Myth accepts every coexistence, every simultaneity and every juxtaposition or sequence as
representing real causality. By the principle of mythical causality, it
is the swallow that causes the summer. As Cassirer remarks: "The
principles of *post hoc, ergo propter hoc* and *juxta hoc, ergo propter
hoc* are characteristic of mythical thinking."[5] Mythical causality,
moreover, does not concern itself with general laws and the relation
of individual events with such laws. Rather it explains individual
events by an appeal to individual acts of purposeful will. Scientific
understanding requires that the event be reduced to a certain set of
universal conditions. It explains, for example, the death of a man by
an appeal to universal laws of physiology. Mythical understanding,
however, requires an explanation of this man at this time. Universal
causality does not explain on these terms. The individuality of the
event can be explained by something no less individual than the
event itself.

Finally, and most characteristically, there is little room in mythical
thinking for what Cassirer calls passive contemplation. Rather the
myth is a form of active contemplation which derives from a rich
matrix of feelings, attitudes, and purposes. The myth, therefore, becomes the vehicle of the implicit and even unconscious dynamic
forces at work in the community. As Cassirer puts it:

> Insofar as myth condenses into lasting configuration, insofar as it
> sets before us the stable outlines of an objective world of forms,

the significance of this world becomes intelligible to us only if behind it we can feel the dynamic of the life feeling from which it
originally grew. Only where this feeling is aroused from within,
only where it manifests itself in love and hate, fear and hope, joy
and grief, is that mythical fantasy engendered which creates a
world of specific representations. But from this it seems to follow
that any characterization of the mythical forms of thought applies
only to something mediated and derived—that it must remain inadequate unless it succeeds in going from the mere mythical form
of *thought* to the mythical form of *intuition* and its characteristic
form of *life*.[6]

## Defensive Function

The driving forces behind mythical thinking are multiple and
complex. The myth is formed and preserved in the service of far-
reaching sociological dynamisms, but it is also motivated and given
a sense of inner reality by profound psychological needs. One such
primary need is what Nunberg has called the "need for causality."[7]
Man is forced to deal with a variety of influences in the course of his
experience and living. He is confronted by the inner stimulation of
his own instincts, which serve as the inner psychic forces to whose demands he must continually adapt and whose energy must constantly
be channeled. He is confronted no less insistently with the infringements and demands of the reality that surrounds him, both physical
and social. The inner instinctual forces and the outer reality forces
are powerful currents which threaten the security and integrity of the
human ego. The ego has a basic need to seek mastery over such
forces in a continuing process of adaptation.

Cognitively, control is a matter of establishing causal relations in
the sequences of stimulating events. The association of facts in a
conditional relation is a preconscious activity which is part of the
fabric of everyday experience. When the ascribed relation of causality is fictitious the conditioning activity serves a defensive function
and we call it "rationalization." It is illusory because it gives the impression of fact where none exists. Thus conscious and preconscious
thought processes are brought into the service of profound, often
unconscious, wishes and needs. As a rule, increasing the degree of
anxiety created by the apparent disruption of the ego's control increases proportionally the tendency to rationalization. The more

such basic unrepressed and unconscious instinctual elements are operative in a given psychic situation, the more insistent is the need of the ego to defend itself, and the more intense will be the pressures for establishing such causal relations. The analysis of true and objective causality is a function of the reasoning ego exercising its critical faculty without emotional involvement. Where man is emotionally involved, as he is persistently in the course of his daily life experience, dynamic forces are at work which can, and often do, distort his causal judgment.

Arlow[8] phrases the argument in terms of the "faltering ego." The ego is caught up in the problems related to the impermanence and fluidity of its own boundaries. Its boundaries face the demands of external reality on one side and the pressures from the unconscious on the other. The fear that the boundary between the ego and the unconscious may be overwhelmed by instinctual energies is the basis of anxiety. The myth serves in this context as a mechanism for bolstering the faltering ego. The myth serves an important psychological function, therefore, as a vehicle for the discharge of instinctual drives. But it also serves the equally important, if not more significant, function of a mechanism for the mastery of external and internal reality. Anxiety is defended against by a displacement of it onto a symbol. At the level of shared meaning inherent in the symbol, the group is able to achieve some degree of mastery of the threatening reality.[9]

## Myths and Emotion

The emphasis that I would like to make in relating the functioning of mythical thinking to authority is simply that mythical thinking reflects certain more general characteristics of cognition which have a place in all human activity. Mythical thinking, while it has been explored and analyzed in terms of a primarily anthropological context, as deriving from the culture of a tribe or nation, can be related to the inner constellation of beliefs, values, and attitudes which constitute the culture of any functioning human group. The same psychic needs and dynamic forces are at work in shaping the patterns of interaction in contemporary groups, whether work groups or living groups like the religious community, as can be discerned in the examination of primitive myths. It is a myth to believe that modern man has abandoned mythical thinking. Rather I would suggest that it provides a significant portion of his day by day thinking and awareness.

To focus for a moment on the myth itself, the myth can be considered as merely a story; but it is important to remember that the story has relevance only in relation to a complex of attitudes, beliefs, and values which it embodies. However, the myth as story is of considerable importance. Part of its impact depends on the artfulness of the story and its narrative. The story contains either implicity or explicity a set of attitudes toward certain people or types of people and situations. It further enunciates a set of beliefs which serve to justify the attitudes. The beliefs do not always represent reasonable or objective conclusions, but may in fact be determined largely by emotional reactions to certain stimuli. Such emotive beliefs are usually expressed or formed in a rational form which lays claim to factuality and objectivity. This is the area where rationalization is most often recognizable. The myth also embodies a set of values which lie beyond the attitudes and their justifying beliefs.

It goes without saying that this complex set of influences has a great deal to do with the way in which individuals who give credence to the myth perceive reality. The need to cognitively structure the world of our experiences makes us see what our interests, values, and beliefs allow us to see. The constituent elements of myth play an important role in determining how it is that an individual will cognitively structure his world. The myth will often exploit the human need for structure by supplying what Fearing[10] has called "ready-made structuralizations" or stereotypes. The stereotypes reflect the appraisal of reality which interprets the reality in terms of the values, beliefs, and attitudes inherent in the myth.

Myths and mythical thinking are important aspects of human group activity, wherever it is found. Sykes[11] has presented some interesting documentation of the formation of myths in industrial settings. In different industries, workers have a different ethos and attitudes toward employers, trade unions, and fellow workers. In all cases, the groups had certain myths which justified their beliefs and attitudes. In one printing plant it was found that strongly hostile attitudes toward the company and management were transmitted and justified by stories about the behavior of a previous manager. The stories recounted his tough and rigid treatment of workers. They were cited as recent occurrences which justified the workers' currently hostile attitudes toward the management. Yet the director in question had died seventeen years before, and his active participation in the plant had ended more than forty years before.

Another case disclosed a violent antipathy on the part of the workers for the company's rate-fixer. His meanness was proverbial, and the workers were liberal in providing examples of the ways in which he tried to cheat them when fixing rates. This was a constant source of labor grievance, and the men blamed the company for keeping him. The foremen also complained about him because the workers would object even to good rates, since they were convinced that this would ultimately prove to be another attempt to cheat them. In fact, the original rate-fixer had retired many years ago, and the rate-fixing was now carried on by a department. The original notorious rate-fixer had been the first head of the department, and his well-deserved reputation spread to the department. The stories associated with the rate-fixer turned out to be an aggregate of all the worst experiences of the workers with a variety of rate-fixers over a period of forty or more years. Every new rate-fixer who appeared in the plant was fixed with the stereotype of the original rate-fixer, even though the majority of the workers knew that he was long gone. When discussing grievances, the workers always cast them in terms of the persistent myth of the cheating rate-fixer and repeated the standard stories about him. As Sykes points out, the myth persists because it has an emotional appeal. It is given an appearance of rationality in that the various stories had at least an indirect basis in reality. The myth is also straightforward and simple, while any rational analysis of the rate-fixing department would have been complex and difficult. The myth also served to establish a uniformity of attitudes and beliefs since the myth was passed on to each new worker and would evoke similar attitudes in him. The myth provided a shared perception of the work situation which tended to buttress the workers' organization against management.

What is interesting in such situations is that the mythical thought processes ignore, distort, and manipulate the complexities of the reality in order to bring into focus another fundamental reality. The myth is formed in the service of emotions. It creates structure and organization in the midst of real complexity and ambiguity. Its clarity and simplicity falsify the reality, which is neither so simple nor so clear. The reality it does effectively formulate is the reality of the hostile feelings which underlie it and find expression in it. Moreover, the shared perception which it generates actually justifies and gives a shape and substance to an object for the underlying hostility. The myth, then, in a sense gives substance and direction to a prior anger and resentment which is provoked toward the figure in authority. The origins of that hostility and resentment has deep unconscious roots that derive often from very infantile levels of experience. The myth equivalently lends structure, organization, credence, and justification to a complex welter of external and internal stimuli, which are in some degree conscious and in some degree unconscious, which are both objective and subjective, factual and emotional.

## Myth and Authority

In the light of the preceding analysis, however fragmentary and rudimentary it might be, it becomes easily apparent that authority is one of those crucial and central areas of group life which are highly susceptible to mythologizing processes. The lived reality of the myth constitutes a major aspect of the deployment of authority in the group. This is particularly true of the religious group, in which the function of authority is so central. I have rarely had the experience of participating in a discussion of the problem of religious obedience without hearing the recounting of a story which displays the foibles of a superior. The story is a part of the myth; the telling of it is a part of the process of mythologizing the authority relation. The stories are often a recounting of real events. I do not mean to contend that superiors and persons in authority do not make mistakes or are not saddled with the limitations and weaknesses that are the common human lot. There are true stories that document this reality. But even the true stories are recounted in such a way as to mythologize. The story does not inculcate the conclusion that this individual superior made an error of judgment or displayed some degree of ignorance. The story rather aims implicitly at the conclusion that this is the way one must expect superiors as a stereotype to behave. The unreasonableness of the superior in the story becomes the unreasonableness of superiors; the rigidity of the superior in the story becomes the rigidity of superiors. The mythologizing process and the mythical thinking that it embodies builds up a myth of the superior. There is evolved an image of the superior which is stereotyped and fits no individual superior in reality. The mythical image, however, is a major determinant of the individual subject's response and reaction to the individual superior.

The mythologizing process is a two-edged sword. It works in the opposite direction as well. Superiors recount the foibles and foolishness of their subjects. They form thereby a mythical image of the subject as irresponsible, foolish, and untrustworthy. The image fits no individual subject. But because of the influence of the myth, because of its structuralizing and clarifying character, it prompts the superior to perceive his subject in terms of the stereotype.

It is easy to see how mythical thinking in the authority relation can become the vehicle for emotional attitudes on both the part of the superior and that of the subject. It is easy to see that mythical thinking can readily become the vehicle for authoritarian attitudes and beliefs. The inner emotional needs of the authoritarian personality can find their way into mythical expression and, through the cognitive determination of the myth, influence the course of interaction in the authority relation. Beliefs influence perception and perception sets the course of action. It is further obvious that mythical thinking at this level can reflect the mutually supportive projective systems of defense which we have already mentioned in Chapter 6 [see also Chapter 9, "Systems of Social Defense"].

## Myths of Obedience

There is no area in religious life which is so delicate to discuss and difficult to talk about as religious obedience. Part of the difficulty is that there persists in every religious group a mythology regarding obedience. The mythology is in part formative. It sets forth an idealized attitude, belief, and system of values which are calculated to foster, support, and justify the actual demands of religious obedience. Even the more or less formal documents which certify the religious group's dedication to obedience are resplendent with mythical images. Ignatius' classic letter on obedience provides a striking example. Mythical thinking, therefore, embodying as it does the beliefs and values of the group, can serve a positive formative function. Psychoanalysts have suggested that at least one function of mythology was to support the ego in its organizing attempts to sustain stable value systems and beliefs in the face of disruptive forces. The function of the more or less legalized myths regarding religious obedience is not far removed from this. They serve to sustain the religious ideals and values in the face of disruptive influences.

The extent of mythologizing religious obedience does not end there. The process is continuing and incessant. The religious group is constantly forming the myth, constantly adding new elements to enlarge and support the myth. It provides a complex of stories and attitudes which in some degree reinforce the formative aspects of the myth and in some degree contribute to a negative myth of obedience and authority. One can critically analyze each separate contribution to the myth, one can dissect each story, whether factual or fictitious, or both, and whittle away the bases of the myth. But men do not live and respond in terms of critical analyses. They live in response to the emotional needs within and the perceived realities without. And it is the myth which embodies and displays these very elements.

The area of religious obedience and authority is one of the primary focuses for anxiety in the religious life. As such it becomes the object of rather intensive mythologizing activity. There is a traditional myth of religious obedience which is handed down and given a certain fixity by being incorporated in the official documents of the religious group. As I have suggested, this traditional myth is primarily positive and formative in emphasis. Thus Ignatius proposes certain mythic images in his letter on obedience—one thinks of the image of the staff in a man's hand, or the monk set to watering a dead stick, or the good monk who obliged his superior by bringing back a whole lion—images which represent mythic elements handed down by a long religious tradition. The question as to what these images meant to Ignatius, whether they were mere acknowledgements of such a tradition and not really pertinent to his own theory of religious obedience, or whether they were integral aspects of the argument, is really not our concern here. They represent in any case mythic elements which have a formative force.

Such traditional elements of myth are complemented by other mythic formulations which have a more local and proximate origin. Every novitiate and every province has its local lore, which sets forth a kind of locally adapted and amplified version of the ideal of obedi-

ence. The legend of a local hero of obedience is added to the traditional images and the mythic recountings of saints and men of virtue.
The mythologizing process is never at rest but is constantly adding to
itself new elements. Thus the mythic process is a lived reality and a
dynamic force in the ongoing life of the religious group. It contributes
to the group life precisely insofar as it serves to express and codify
the group's beliefs about obedience and authority. I would like to
underline the emphasis on the role of the group in such mythologizing. The beliefs which are represented and codified in this fashion
are not the beliefs of any individual, but they are the beliefs which
are accepted and consensually certified by the group itself. Thus the
mythic process derives from the culture of the group itself and also
contributes to formation of the culture of the group in that it conveys
the attitudes and values of the group and thus acts to establish and
interpret the inner morality of the group.

## Function in Religious Group

For the religious group, the inner morality is a matter of attitudes
toward and adaptation to the ideals of the group. The myth sets
forth a set of idealized and stereotyped norms which embody the
group ideals. This pertains to certain practices and behaviors, certain customs and attitudes which in combination make up a code of
behavior for the obedient religious. The mythic process at its best
may operate to serve an important psychological function. It codifies
beliefs and offers support in group consensus for the individual to
adapt to the normative demands for member participation in the
group. The myth serves an adaptive function, at least in part. It
simplifies and clarifies the group's present demands for obedient behavior. It embodies certain norms which represent the contemporary
expectation of the group for participation in the authority relation.
Thus the individual's relationship to the superior is in part predicated
against a background of mythic formulations which determine what
the character of that relation is to be.

The mythic process also generates *pari passu,* as has been suggested, negative elements which find their way into a myth of authority. What is extremely interesting is that the negative mythic elements
enjoy a certain isolation from the more positive elements. The positive elements are incorporated into an idealized mythic formulation

of obedience which remains more or less isolated from the negative elements. Positive and negative do not balance and modify each other as in the reality of authority they must; they remain independent of each other so that the positive myth becomes an unreal idealization, and the negative myth takes on an autonomy which plays itself out too often in determining the concrete attitudes and reactions of group members. It is the negative myth more often than not which is active in influencing the concrete perceptions of superior and subject. The myth in its various embellishments sees the superior as harsh, unreasoning, rigid, arbitrary, inflexible, and ungiving. It sees the subject as uncooperative, unreliable, undependable, foolish, immature, and selfish.

This dissociation of mythic elements is puzzling if we forget that the entire process is at the service of powerful unconscious forces and emotional influences. The dissociation within the myth is admirably adapted to serving two important needs. On the one hand, it serves the need for members of the religious group to have an ideal of self-commitment and dedication to the will of God and superiors. In this regard, the myth is supportive and offers reinforcement to unconscious narcissistic needs and important adaptive goals which are integral to religious life and enjoy the justification of that life with its religiously endorsed ideals. On the other hand, it serves the need for these same members to deal with the underlying, often unconscious, hostility which underlies attitudes toward the authority situation. The authoritarian personality is especially prone to this aspect of the mythic process. His inner need is to see the superior as harsh, demanding, rigid, and authoritarian. The negative myth in a sense is generated in part by such dependency needs and conflicts as we will see in discussing the authoritarian personality [Chapter 8]. The myth can be said to be functioning in the service of such authoritarian conflicts.

The unfortunate part of the mythologizing process is that it does serve these needs so well and that in consequence the reality of the problem of authority is obfuscated by mythic elements. It would be more accurate perhaps to say that these mythic elements are an integral part of the problem of authority. The mythic influence is to promulgate an altruistic ideal which tends to be cast in unrealistic terms. The result is that this positive notion of obedience and authority loses its relevance to the day to day realities of religious obedience and the exercise of authority. It tends to be displaced to the level of an unattainable ideal which has little relevance outside of the merely formal context of authority. This is no service to the reality of religious obedience, whatever gain it may bring to less apparent needs.

The other and more obvious drawback is that the negative myth creates obstacles to the ongoing exercise of authority. The difficulty is complicated, as always in such matters, by the fact that perceptions tend to shape the reality of social situations. It becomes difficult at times to draw a line between the mythical and the real, between mythically determined perceptions and real reactions which are the ultimate product and reaction to such mythical perceptions. As Thomas' classic law has it, if men define situations as real, they are real in their consequences. Myth which takes its origin out of some reality shapes the perceptions of participating members, and these perceptions give shape to a new reality which in some sense accommodates itself to the myth.

## Contemporary Mythologizing

If one looks at the contemporary scene in which crises, frustration, and anxiety abound on all sides, it is not difficult to see the mythologizing process at work. There is no surprise in this since the mythic process takes its origin from basic human motivations and answers to basic human needs. Where those motivations are at work and where those needs are operative, we can expect to find the stuff of myth. It is particularly in relation to the authority structure and the interaction of superior and inferior that the mythic process can be seen at work.

The pattern of mythologizing, in religious groups, which I have described at some length can also be seen in analogous form in the Church at large. One of the authoritative groups in the Church which has been the object of considerable mythologizing is the bishops, particularly in the United States. The bishops, of course, particularly in the post-Vatican II era, are in a peculiarly vulnerable position since they have become the focal points of practical renovation and reform in the Church. The implementation of the conciliar decrees in any given diocese lies almost exclusively in the hands of the ordinary. Thus the bishops have become the objects of intense public scrutiny. With increasing intensity since the last session of Vatican II, the American episcopacy has been cast in a rather derogatory stereotype. The bishops have been cast in the role of ecclesiastical "bad guys." They are regarded as reactionary, conservative, unsympathetic to any renovation or change in the Church, lacking in understanding of the needs of the contemporary Church, obstructionistic, etc. There are undoubtedly some members of the hierarchy who fit such a stereotype, but not all—and very few could fit all the elements of such a stereotype. But every action of a bishop which can be incorporated into such a stereotype is caught up and built into the myth. The mass media are contributors to this process in that it is precisely these mythopoetic elements which enjoy some degree of sensationalism and make "news." The mythologizing process goes on at a massive level. Every mistake, every misjudgment, every reactionary stance of a bishop is turned from that into a faulting of the hierarchy itself. Instead of one man's mistake born of human limitation, it becomes a characteristic episcopal position—a stereotype. What else can you expect from a bishop?

The upshot, of course, is that there is generated through such mythologizing the expectation that every bishop can be expected to act in such a fashion. There is also the explicit expectation that every bishop shares the attitudes, insight or lack of it, conservatism, and even theological naiveté that the stereotype demands. There is always an historical core to every myth. There is a reality that in some part corresponds to elements of the myth. These are unfortunate circumstances which lend conviction to the myth. For example, the widely-publicized resignation of Bishop James Shannon willy-nilly created the impression that a reasonable and liberal man cannot remain in the ranks of the bishops. The episcopal stereotype is thereby confirmed and reinforced. The myth takes on a new vitality.

The mythic process can be seen almost anywhere one looks for it. The modern pastor is a special target, as any curate can testify. The student movement in this country is permeated with it. Universities must almost of necessity be mythologized before they can be attacked. The rhetoric of the SDS and other student radical groups represents an intense effort to mythologize the authority structures they revolt against. It is easy to recognize that the mythologizing is an expression of and a response to basic needs and conflicts. The authority must be seen as overly rigid, repressive, unyielding, unsympathetic, and reactionary before any attack on it can be justified. One can say that such mythologizing is unfair, that it distorts reality, that it is "dirty pool." It is that, but one should not overlook the core of reality that the myth represents. The myth mobilizes beliefs and convictions in the service of a felt need which must be acknowledged. One cannot stop the mythologizing process. But one can acknowledge the need and bring intelligent resources of the community to bear to resolve it.

The analogous situation obtains in the black movement. Mythologizing runs rampant on both sides of the debate. There is a black stereotype at large in the white community, and a white stereotype in the black community. Every black failure, every black inadequacy, every black rage, every black crime, every black sexual extravagance, every black rebellion confirms, reinforces, solidifies, and absolutizes the black stereotype. I have rarely had the experience of talking to middle- and upper middle-class Americans about the race problem without having to listen to some elements of the black myth. Prejudice feeds on the stuff of mythology. The black stereotype points the black man as lazy, stupid, careless, thriftless, promiscuous, prone to easy and immediate gratification, irresponsible, etc. These qualities are undoubtedly distributed through the black community. But massive mythologizing has built them into a stereotype which identifies these undesirable qualities with the color of a man's skin. There is no room in the myth for the good qualities and the resources of talent and cultural capability so readily evidenced in the black man. The intelligence, moral courage, integrity, and spiritual strength of so many black leaders are discounted as exceptions which prove the rule. They cannot find their way into the myth because they do not answer to the deep emotional and instinctual needs that the myth requires.

There is myth at work in the black community as well. The image of "whitey" has been sketched in the minds of Negroes in all of his worst attributes. The hateful image is scorched with all the bitterness of hundreds of years of repression and prejudice. There is a bitter reality to this, but there is also an intense mythologizing process which erects and maintains a stereotype of both the white man and the black man. The mythic process works both ways. Interestingly enough, it both reinforces the stereotypes of white repression, injustice, and prejudice and contributes to the maintenance of the white stereotype of the Negro as deprived, lazy, stupid, and irresponsible. There is a tendency to redefine prominent Negroes who have made it in the white man's world as no longer belonging to the black community. I remember talking to a black woman about Senator Brooke. Her comment about his successful political career was: "Him? He jes ain't a Nigger anymore!" To exclude such successful figures from the black community serves to maintain both stereotypes, black and white, for the one cannot exist without the other; and both answer to deep emotional needs in the black and the white communities.

One of the directions of the black power movement is to change the black man's stereotype of himself. It must be recognized that such a change cannot be wrought by slogans and rhetoric. Slogans and rhetoric are a start, but they must be attended by some hard realities. The black community must begin to overcome the hard realities of poverty and cultural deprivation. The undertaking is massive. The black community realistically will not be able to accomplish such a task without massive amounts of outside assistance from the white community. But outside assistance is not enough. The elements of the myth have to be tested out against the realities of the situation. The substantial effort must stem decisively from the black community itself. There is no other way to self-respect, self-esteem, and an emergent sense of social participation and identification. The effort at demythologization can be realized only by testing out the elements of the myth against the hard reality. But man cannot live without myth. We can only hope that by effective action within the black commuity itself and within the community at large, black and white, demythologization will yield to remythologization in more human and more hopeful terms.

*Part III*

# Distortions in Authority

The Authoritarian Personality

Systems of Social Defense

*Chapter 8*

# The Authoritarian Personality

The inner face of authority is much more complex and diverse than its outer face. By this I mean simply that the formal structure of authority is mirrored in the internal dynamics of the group by an incredibly diversified pattern of complex dynamic interactions. The influences which determine and shape the pattern of these inter- actions are many. They are both social and psychic in the real sense. Our understanding of them requires the relative isolation of some of the more salient influences and an attempt to bring the isolated aspects into clearer focus.

## *Background*

In looking at the authoritarian personality we are equivalently crystallizing a more or less common constellation of personality fac- tors. The concept of the authoritarian personality was born out of re- search on German anti-Semitism in the 1930's. Jaensch's work in particular[1] sets forth contrasting personality types. The S-type was declared to be liberal, an adherent of the view that behavior was shaped by education and environment, individualistic, effeminate, and generally unstable. Such for Nazi Jaensch were Jews, Orientals, Communists, and other anti-types. The ideal J-type, however, emerged as tough, masculine, reliable. His behavior was fixed by birth, blood, and national tradition, and he was intolerant of ambiguity. The J-type was anti-Semitic and a potentially ideal Nazi. Jaensch's findings were apparently politically contaminated.

Interest in anti-Semitism was extended into the research carried out at the University of California which finally issued in the massive study published under the title *The Authoritarian Personality*.[2] The concept of the authoritarian personality was here based on the co-variance of a variety of test data. A single test measure was constructed to identify the constellation of characteristics which corresponds to the authoritarian personality—the so-called F Scale. The characteristics associated with the authoritarian personality are as follows:

1. Conventionalism: rigid adherence to conventional middle-class values.

2. Authoritarian submission: a submissive, uncritical attitude toward the idealized moral authorities in the group.

3. Authoritarian aggression: a tendency to be sensitive to, condemnatory and punitive toward those violating conventional values.

4. Anti-intraception: opposition to the subjective, the imaginative, the tender (as opposed to tough-minded).

5. Superstition and stereotype: belief in mystical determinants of individual fate, and a tendency to think in more or less rigid categories.

6. Power and "toughness": preoccupation with control, power-submission, strength-weakness; tendency to identify with power figures: exaggerated assertions of strength and toughness.

7. Destructiveness and cynicism: generalized hostility.

8. Projectivity: tendency to believe that dangerous things are happening; projection outwards of unconscious emotional impulses.

9. Sex: excessive concern with sexual fantasies.

What the California study has demonstrated is that these characteristics tend to vary in relation to each other. The relevance of this fairly consistent finding in terms of its relevance to politics or to the understanding of the workings of authority is an entirely different question. We will try to explore it in what follows.

What is not clear from research of this kind is what the implications of such covariance might be. Can we postulate an underlying personality dynamism to account for the covariance, or are we dealing with a set of socio-economically determined variables covarying in response to other influences? The answer is not immediately forthcoming. The empirical finding of covariance creates a problem in understanding that leads us into the heart of the concern over the problem of authority. While it is not clear that we can postulate an underlying personality structure to unify the data, the possibility remains that such does exist or that the pattern tends to express itself in varying degree in individual personalities. While this basic question remains unanswerable on a scientific levels, much of the thinking about the authoritarian personality has proceeded as though the question were answered in favor of the existence of such a personality. The concept of the authoritarian personality is nonetheless a construct and a typology. The temptation is to stop reminding oneself of this fact and to analyze the authoritarian personality as though it were a real personality. As a consequence, the discussion has tended to run to a caricature which is rarely if ever recognizable in the real order. This is more of a caution than a criticism as we enter on a consideration of the implications of the authoritarian personality.

## Escape from Freedom

The other major formulation of the authoritarian personality is that of Erich Fromm, especially in his *Escape from Freedom*.[3] Fromm postulates man as a freak of nature, embedded in nature yet transcending it. Man alone has the capacity to create himself, to expand his own life and fulfill his own potentialities. He does this through freedom. There is not only *freedom from* but *freedom to*. Contemporary man has won negative freedom, the freedom from the forces of constraint. But the victory has left men isolated, alienated, anxious, powerless, and eager for new submissions. Salvation must come through the achievement of positive freedom, which for Fromm is the freedom to realize oneself, to achieve the expression of one's intellectual, emotional, and sensuous potentialities. Freedom carries with it a threat. It is a burden. One of the major neurotic motivations is to escape from freedom.

A primary mechanism of escape from freedom is the tendency to surrender one's own independence and to fuse oneself with something outside in order to acquire the strength which the individual lacks. This is most commonly found in strivings for submission or domination, the normal counterparts of neurotic sadomasochism. Masochism usually appears as feelings of inferiority, powerlessness, or individual insignificance. The masochist often shows a marked dependence on powers outside themselves, other people, institutions, or even nature. Sadistic tendencies are found hand-in-hand with the masochistic, often in the same personality. They involve tendencies to make others dependent on oneself, to have absolute power over others, to rule others in such a way to exploit and use them, to see or make others suffer. These latter tendencies are usually less conscious and are often covered over by reaction formations and rationalizations of excessive concern for and goodness toward others. "I rule you because I know what is best for you."

## Dependence and Domination

A prominent issue in these kinds of relationships is that of dependence. The dependence of masochism is obvious, but the dependence of sadism is not. The dominating one seems so strong and secure, and the objects of his sadism so weak and submissive, that the dependence of the stronger one on the weakness of the weak one is often overlooked. The strength and power of the sadist, however, depends on the submission of weak subjects for its subsistence. Where such sadism wears the face of love, it must be remembered that the sadist does not dominate the lives of others because he loves them; he loves them only because he can dominate them. The very essence of the sadistic drive is the pleasure derived from complete domination over the other.

It is paradoxical, therefore, that the need for power is rooted not in strength, but in weakness. It is an expression of the individual's inability to stand alone and of his need for others to sustain him. As Fromm points out, power can mean either *domination*, the power over others, or *potency*, the power to make and do. He remarks:

> Far from being identical, these two qualities are mutually exclusive. Impotence, using the term not only with regard to the sexual sphere but to all spheres of human potentialities, resuults in the

sadistic striving for domination; to the extent to which an individual is potent, that is, able to realize his potentialities on the basis of freedom and integrity of his self, he does not need to dominate and is lacking the lust for power. Power, in the sense of domination, is the perversion of potency, just as sexual sadism is the perversion of sexual love.[4]

Fromm uses the term "authoritarian character" to refer to this sadomasochistic type of personality on the grounds that it is consistently characterized by its attitude toward authority. Briefly, the authoritarian character admires authority and tends to submit to it, while simultaneously wishing to be an authority and have others submit to him. In the authority relationship, when the relation is benevolent, the authority serves also as an object for identification. Fromm uses the image of the teacher who by the exercise of his authority nourishes the growth of the subject. Authority in this type of relation tends to dissolve itself insofar as the student gradually approaches the knowledge of the teacher in virtue of the teaching relation. In an authoritarian relation, however, the authority is resented. Inhibiting authority is, therefore, either hated, or by way of repression and reaction formation, overestimated and admired. The hatred and/or overestimation, however, tends to increase as the relation becomes more intense.

## Power

We have discussed the relationship of authority to power elsewhere (Chapter 2, "Leadership and Authority"), but it is particularly relevant in the present context. The authoritarian personality is especially characterized by its attitudes toward power. Fromm puts it in graphic terms:

For the authoritarian character there exist, so to speak, two sexes: the powerful ones and the powerless ones. His love, admiration and readiness for submission are automatically aroused by power, whether of a person or of an institution. Power fascinates him not for any values for which a specific power may stand, but just because it is power. Just as his "love" is automatically aroused by power, so powerless people or institutions automatically arouse his contempt. The very sight of a powerless person makes him want to attack, dominate, humiliate him.[5]

It is also characteristic of the authoritarian character to see himself as submitted to fate. His fate may be rationalized as destiny, natural law, duty, or more religiously, as the will of God. The essential thing is that there be a higher power outside of the individual in regard to which the individual can do nothing other than submit. The authoritarian does not lack courage, activity, or belief. But the root of his existence in powerlessness adds a definite quality to these characteristics. Activity becomes action in the name of something higher than oneself. Courage becomes courage to suffer what fate or a superior will has destined him for. To suffer is the highest virtue. His heroism is to submit to fate, not to change it. His belief is rooted in doubt and functions to compensate for it.

## Critique

While Fromm's formulation of the authoritarian character has a certain dynamic consistency, it is susceptible of criticism on a number of grounds. Methodolgically, the formulation is not supported by a shred of scientific evidence—beyond that provided by the impressions of literateurs and the wise men of many ages. The roots of Fromm's thinking in psychoanalysis have never been solidly clinical. His argument is therefore basically philosophical. The authoritarian character as he presents it is more caricature than character. It is never present in reality as a pure type. Moreover, his deployment of the character is more in the service of ethical ends than in the interest of understanding human behavior. The major conclusion to which his argument tends is that all forms of irrational authority—tradition, superstition, convention, authoritarian monotheism, propaganda, charismatic leaders, bureaucracy—must be abolished. The real error is that in producing a caricature of irrational authority, Fromm is unable to bring into focus the real functions and existential roots of authentic authority.[6]

The point, however, is not to evaluate Fromm's formulation. Even as a caricature, it provides us with a clearer view of certain decisive issues which are intimately related to the question of the authoritarian personality. Whether or not the authoritarian character can be found in reality is for our purposes beside the point. What is to the point is that the mechanisms which can be seen in clearly etched fashion in the authoritarian character and the underlying dynamisms from which they derive are common human stuff. In this sense authoritarian traits are endemic. They are derivative from sadistic and masochistic drives which can be found at large in human beings.

The refutation of Fromm's social theory, then, rests upon a rather simple possibility. The possibility is that of the coexistence and coherence of authority with maturity of personal function. Fromm's analysis, however, puts us on our guard. It should put us on the lookout for those traits which mask the underlying sadomasochistic needs for dominance or dependence. The relationship of superior and subject, from whichever term it is considered, lends itself all too easily to the expression of sadistic and masochistic drives. Where they are operative, they act to the detriment of those involved and simultaneously to the detriment of the authority relation. Sadomasochism undermines and destroys the effective operation of authentic authority.

## Aggression

The roots of the problem lie in the rather primitive conflict over aggression. It is difficult to write about aggression. It is universally denied and universally expressed. Good people are appalled by the prospect of themselves as creatures endowed with aggressive and hostile drives, and as expressing these aggressive tendencies in countless ways in the course of their everyday lives. There is something offensive to the less realistic posturing of the Christian ethic of love in the concept of man as inherently hostile, aggressive, and hating. But the evidence is overwhelming and all about us. We do not need to appeal to the refinements of clinical experience to document the ubiquity of such expressions of aggression. We need only look at the rage for football, the epidemic of violence in the streets, the hot breath of the boxing arena waiting for the finishing punch, the punishment of children by parents, and a host of other common, and as the saying goes, "culturally acceptable" forms of the expression of aggression. It is important to recognize in all of this that the deployment of aggressive drives is culturally valuable and enriching. Aggression provides the force behind many a competitive effort. It can be refined to the highly polished skill in the artful mutilation of the surgeon's knife—which in fact employs the means of aggressive cutting and wounding in the service of a humane end. The angry demonstrator may destroy and lash out in the service of what he feels to be higher ideals.

Aggression, therefore, finds its way into human affairs in sinuous and insidious ways. We should not in the least be surprised to find it intimately entwined in the operations of authority. This is indeed what happens across a wide spectrum in the authoritarian character. The conflict over aggression is primary. The conflict is often operative at quite primitive levels of the personality. It is more often than not unconscious. The individual is caught between the press of hostile impulses, conscious or unconscious, and the restraining mechanisms which have been elaborated through a succession of developmental efforts. The restraints are elaborated through successive identifications, ethical standards, social mores, religious beliefs, and other civilizing influences of society and culture. The inner psychic drama at this level is a tale of the constant effort to come to terms with, handle, and live through the vicissitudes of aggression. Each man must come to terms with it in his own style and to his own degree. The question, therefore, can never be whether aggression is or is not present; the question must be how and in what degree aggression is operative.

Our objective, then, is to explore the sense in which the authoritarian personality involves and derives from such basic and often unconscious aggression and to illumine some of the implications of this insight for the inner workings of authority. We must keep in mind that aggression is a kind of basic given in the structure of every personality. In the interaction of personalities which constitutes the relation of authority, there is inevitably injected in some degree an element of aggression. Where aggression becomes determinative of the quality of the relation, the relation becomes authoritarian.

A basic conflict over aggression implies a developmental defect in the formation of mechanisms for effectively dealing with aggressive feelings. Aggressive feelings are poorly controlled, and the sense of mastery over them in inhibited. Where the maturity of the mental apparatus has reached such evolution that it is able to utilize the energic potentialities of aggression for more constructive purposes, the conflict is minimized. Psychoanalysts speak of this as "neutralization" of aggressive drives. When the development of this capacity is impaired, however, neutralization is limited, and the aggressive drives retain their primitive and hostile character. Such forces are threatening to the integrity of the ego. The more frail the ego, the more threatening is aggression. Control is, therefore, a matter of deep concern, whether it be the inner control of destructive energies or the outer control to angry impulses. It is no surprise, therefore, that authoritarian individuals are preoccupied with the problem of control and power. The often unconscious activation of aggressive impulses reflects itself in the generalized hostility, suspicion, lack of trust, and critical cynicism which they display. By projection of these impulses they are brought to view their environment as riddled with dangers and hostile threats. These threats are frequently projected onto the behavior of the people around them, and these people are reacted to under various conditions as threatening, hurtful, dangerous, and untrustworthy.

There is another side to the working out of these aggressive impulses and their handling. The inner resources of the individual are strained in his efforts to deal with aggression. He seeks support and reinforcement in his struggle for control by identification with the sources of power around him. It is as though by psychic alliance with the power centers which surround him, he is able to bolster his inner sense of wavering control. His submission to the moral authorities in his milieu tends to be rigid and uncritical. His anxieties are aroused whenever the security of the prevailing power alliance is threatened. If he wields authority, he wields it insecurely and is threatened by any occurence that raises questions about the absoluteness of his power and the security of his control. His anxiety is alleviated by unquestioning submission from his subordinates. If his subordinate should question or challenge his authority, or even worse take initiative independently of it, his control is weakened and the status of his power challenged. None of this need be present to his conscious mind, but may well run on in the deeper recesses of his unconscious thought. His authoritarian behavior is then rationalized on some other grounds, while the real motives rooted in the conflicts over inner aggressive impulses are untouched. Nonetheless, the anxiety implicit in any threat to his control drives him to embrace and cling to the elements which support that control. He clings therefore to conventional values and becomes punitive toward those who violate them; his thinking is constrained into more or less rigid categories and stereotyped concepts.

## Freedom and Order

The combination of these dynamic forces makes it very difficult for the authoritarian person to be flexible, to admit mistakes or fallibility. While Fromm overdraws the portrait, he is nonetheless "on target" when he speaks of this manner of life as an "escape from freedom." Freedom is threatening because it allows for the unpredictability of spontaneity. Freedom is threatening because it cannot be controlled. The inner dynamism of the authoritarian disposition is to suppress freedom—in the name of any other noble investment —but unequivocally to suppress freedom. This is very interesting, of course, for the concerns of authority. In whatever its guise, authority concerns itself with achieving a balance between the demands of order and the demands of freedom. We can think of it as a continuum in which order is maximized at one extreme or limit, and freedom is maximized at the other limit. While authoritarian extremists may find themselves driven to one limit where order is supreme and freedom minimized; and libertarians may surge to the opposite extreme of complete freedom to the detriment of order; the real world of functional authority finds itself operating somewhere between the extremes. There is no one optimal point on the continuum at which maximal freedom is guaranteed along with the requirements of order. There is an optimal point, however, for each authority relation, each operating within the distinctive requirements for order and commitments to individual freedom that characterizes the relevant group structure within which that authority functions.

We will have occasion to describe the operation of social defense systems as they apply in relation to the operations of authority, (Chapter 9, Systems of Social Defense"). It is evident that the dynamics underlying the authoritarian personality contribute to the institution of such systems. The social authoritarian system arises through the coalition and collusion of interacting postures between authoritarian personalities. The more authoritarian the tendencies of those participating, the more evolved does the social defense system become. The superior becomes punitively aggressive towards his inferior, and the inferior becomes masochistically submissive to his superior. Both these postures are characteristic of the authoritarian personality. Thus the pattern and structure of the system derives from and in a sense depends on the dynamic interaction of intrapsychic forces. The social and the psychic are intertwined and mutually determinative.

## Dependence

The whole question of the authoritarian personality has implicit in it the further issue of dependence. Someone has cogently remarked that contemporary civilization has exchanged the problem of sexuality for the problem of dependency as the staple of neurosis. This is untrue, of course, as well as misleading, since the two problems are in fact correlated. But it serves to bring the issues of dependency into the limelight.

Dependency cannot be lightly dispatched. It is a decisive and ubiquitous issue. Every man is situated at the very beginning of his life in a dependency relation. His submission to that relation assures his survival. Dependency creates an alliance with the powerful figures who feed, house, clothe, warm, and love him. The lack of dependence or independence, the throwing off or rejecting of that dependent relationship, carries with it the threat of the loss of love, rejection, abandonment. But, to grow is to mature, and to mature is to withdraw in gradual evolution from the restraints of that infantile dependence. Man must achieve independence if he is to become himself. This is the difficulty, then, that man must mature to independence, while his maturing carries with it the residues of his infantile experiences. His becoming independent includes the inherent threat of loss of love of the powerful one, abandonment by the leader, rejection by the superior. The threat is an infantile one; it is more often than otherwise unconscious; it is a reactivation of fears entertained at one time in regard to the parents.

The revival unconsciously of infantile fears in the authority relation derives from the original authority relation in the family. It is interesting, therefore, to reflect on that original relationship in which the primary relation of authority is experienced. We have already spoken of the problem of the child who is born into a situation of necessary submission, and who must live through the vicissitudes of moving through the stages of development from the submission of the child to the mature independence of the adult. But authority in the family also presents a problem for the parents. The birth of the child forces the parents into a relation of authority within which they must exercise authority appropriate to their responsibilities as parents. Thus a biological event precipitates a new social constellation in which the young parent is called upon to exercise authority. The situation may or may not activate basic conflicts over authority in the parent. Where such conflicts exist they contribute to an imbalance in the relation between parent and child in which parental authority becomes authoritarian. The authoritarian posture of the parent demands continuing submission from the child. This serves to create that set of circumstances in which conflicts over dependence and submission flourish in the developing child.

Authority figures in general can be meaningfully compared to the plight of the parent. When a member of the religious group, for example, is appointed to the position of superior, he is forced into a position of authority. This may activate latent conflicts over authority. The resulting insecurity and anxiety may be alleviated by an authoritarian response. The question is often raised as to why individuals often seem to become surprisingly rigid and demanding when they assume the office of superior. In the light of the foregoing analysis, this is not surprising. But it requires that we postulate in such an individual unconscious conflict over the fundamental issues of dependence and hostility. Being forced into the role of superior and being called upon to exercise the functions of authority serves as sufficient stress to bring the underlying authoritarian tendencies to light.

## Tendency to Submit

One of the moot points in all of the treatments of the authoritarian personality is the extent to which authoritarian tendencies can be identified in any given population or in the population at large. Conclusive data are lacking, and it is difficult to argue from the fragmentary studies available. The research conducted by Milgram and his associates at Yale is nonetheless suggestive. He aimed at evaluating the extent to which his subjects would tend to obey commands to inflict punishment on a third person. The subjects were ordinary professional, business, and working people. They were instructed to inflict a punishing electric shock on another fake subject who was supposedly learning a list of paired associates. For each successive error, a stronger electric shock was administered. The subject was provided an electric shock generator consisting of 30 levers which were labeled from 15 to 450 volts. The "learner" provided many wrong answers so that the subject was brought quickly to the highest shock levels. The victim's responses to shocking were programmed on tape. At 75 volts he began to groan. At 150 volts he demanded that the experiment be terminated. At 180 volts he cried out that he could not stand the pain. When the shocking subject tried to end the experiment, the experimenter merely said, "You have no other choice; you must go on!" The overwhelming conclusion of the experiment was that the tendency of these ordinary subjects to submit to authority and its demands, even in the face of severe conflict over what they conceived as inhumane behavior, was considerably greater than anyone might have suspected. The subjects continued to shock their victims to the point of excruciating pain and beyond without any other compelling force than the experimenter's order.[7]

There are many questions involved in such research which must for the present remain unanswered. The point is that significant numbers of these subjects tended to submit their judgment and personal principles to the demands of an authority. We can infer that the need to submit was strong enough to bring these subjects to perform acts which they would not otherwise perform and which they would otherwise strongly condemn. These results have been confirmed and extended in subsequent research. The disturbing features, of course, are the extent to which such submissive tendencies are found and the intensity which they sometimes manifest. Milgram concludes, "A substantial portion of people do what they are told to do, irrespective of the content of the act and without limitations of conscience, so long as they perceive that the command comes from a legitimate authority."[8] From the point of view of scientific psychology, it is of great interest to know what factors are at work in producing such tendencies. It would also be of great concern to understand what it is that persuades or enables other individuals to resist the tendency to submission and to act with independent judgment and conscience. From the point of view of the understanding of authority, it raises fundamental questions.

## Religion

The relationship between authoritarianism and religious conservatism is also somewhat provocative. Studies of authoritarian trends have consistently pointed to its higher incidence in adherents of

Roman Catholicism. This may not mean much since it is also significantly correlated with increased religious attendance in all religious groups. However, high authoritarian scores are correlated with less education, greater age, rural dwelling, membership in disadvantaged minorities, and poorer socio-economic status. The theory has been advanced that the degree of authoritarianism is negatively correlated with the number of social roles mastered by the individual. It may reflect on the psychic level a limited capacity for mastery of social roles.[9] This may explain the apparent association with a variety of such sociological categories.

From the point of view of religion, however, the significant association seems to be with religious conservatism.[10] One can speculate that the religious dogmatism of the Church's teaching exercises a basic attraction for the individual with authoritarian tendencies. One must be careful of overextending such a conclusion. One wonders at times whether the contemporary scene is not marked more by antiauthoritarianism than anything else. It is, however, worth questioning whether authoritarian tendencies do not answer to the appeal of an infallible dogma underscored by the authority of a divinely established Church. Such a posture might, though it need not, lend itself to a significant degree of religious conservatism. It seems inescapable, at any rate, that the Church's dogmatic magisteriality and its derivation from the Christian tradition and revelation makes it inherently and theologically conservative.

A parallel question can be raised directly for the religious group as such. Here group affiliation and submission to authority is supported by an appeal to the will of God. The authority is ultimate and the individual's dependence on it explicit. The analysis of authoritarianism and its inherent need to submit to a supporting and strengthening authority must at least raise the question whether the formal structure of the religious group does not lend itself to the fostering of authoritarian trends. We may also ask whether the religious group does not tend to assimilate and maintain in its ranks to a significant degree individuals who share authoritarian tendencies in some measure. The questions are provocative, but they are no more than questions. There is no necessary relation between affiliation with a religious group and authoritarianism. In fact, the best ideals of religious formation would point in a different direction.

It may be that the authoritarian personality is incompatible with religious obedience. Whether that brief can be made formally and ideally is one issue. Whether the religious group does in fact assimilate and foster authoritarian tendencies is quite another issue. If, however, the latter question could be answered in the affirmative (to any significant degree), it would suggest that the issues involved in the authoritarian personality may be acutely relevant to the understanding of the inner working of authority in the religious group.

## The Fate of Authoritarianism

It seems clear from what we can see on many fronts in the contemporary world that the death knell of authoritarianism is being sounded. In many different contexts in which authoritarian attitudes and postures were formerly regarded as tolerable, if not acceptable, these attitudes are no longer being acceded to. The vertical structure of authority, in which power was concentrated in a single source, is being gradually and sometimes abruptly and violently overthrown. The alternatives are no longer to exercise power or to submit to it. The nature of acknowledged power has been diversified and the bases of power have been distributed within the social structure. This is happening at many levels of social organization. It is happening in the churches, in education, in the political realm, and in society at large.

The old structures of authority were well adapted to the implementation of authoritarian attitudes. Superiors were the absolute source of decision and command. Subjects were the absolute sources of submission and obedience. The respective roles were clear and decisive and needed no questioning. But the shift in attitudes has made these attitudes obsolescent. The authoritarian attitude can be maintained in neither superior nor subject. In the shift of authority structures, the continuance of authoritarian attitudes in either superior or subject is a violation of the nature of the authority relation and a denial of the respective responsibilities which each brings to the relation. The authoritarian stance, moreover, is admirably congruent with the formal structure of authority. This applies to all organizational structures which are hierarchically or bureaucratically organized. But as we have pointed out before, the formal structure does not take into account the variety of forces and influences which alter and transform the exercise of authority as it finds expression in the practical and existential order. The authoritarian attitude, therefore, condemns itself to an exercise of sterile formalities which does not meet the demands and exigencies of the real order. In its attempt to exercise itself against the real order, it must work against fundamental human tendencies and needs, and it must ignore basic psychological facts. In order to translate itself into real terms, the authoritarian attitude must ride roughshod over basic human concerns and must contend against the resistance of any forces which deviate from its own presumptions. The cost is told in human unhappiness, misery, frustration, lack of initiative, and ultimate inefficiency.

There are unquestionably islands in contemporary society where the ideal of authoritarian bureaucracy and efficiency can advantageously be preserved. By a process of socio-cultural selectivity analagous to biological selectivity these islands may be preserved. It is a matter of their ultimate adaptive value. They are not to be found in religious groups, where concerns with individual freedom and responsibility are emerging with increasing urgency. They are not to be found in the Church, where the structures of authority are being decentralized and the role of individual freedom and conscience increasingly acknowledged as an integral part of the Catholic tradition. They are not to be found in the other Christian churches, where democratization and concern with individual conscience has been prominent. They are not to be found in the universities, where teaching has given way to learning and where initiative and participation at all levels of the university community have become staples of the educational process. They are not to be found in government, where the emphasis on individual freedoms and rights has become a recurrent feature of contemporary political processes.

It is hard, therefore, to say where authoritarianism can survive. The structures which gave it a vehicle for expression are being gradually transformed. That does not mean that the authoritarian character will not continue to function as a basic human typology. Man will never transcend the fundamental conflicts over aggression and dependency. But the social structures which foster and give expression to authoritarian trends can be changed and are changing. It is the work of intelligent and perceptive human beings to understand the processes of change and to shape the evolution of the structures of authority.

*Chapter 9*

# Systems of Social Defense

In the preceding considerations of the subject authority has been presented in its formal and informal, as well as its structural and functional perspectives. I have tried to suggest in terms of a sociopsychological analysis that traditional models of authority, which were generated in relation to the legitimate yet highly restrictive context of a philosophico-theological problematic of authority, have served as the basis of our pragmatic day-to-day functioning in the authority context. The traditional models, however, emphasize the formal and structural aspects of authority. I have tried to suggest that many of the contemporary problems which focus on authority issues reflect conflicts and ambiguities more specifically at the level of the informal and functional aspects of authority.

In this present phase of the consideration of authority, we can turn our attention to an important and functional dimension of the exercise of authority. It should be said at the outset—and the caution is necessary at nearly every step of a consideration of this kind—that the matters under consideration do not directly concern themselves with the formal structure of authority. Questions of the legitimacy of authority, its nature, its locus, its role and function in the organization of social structure are simply not at issue. What is at issue is a set of psychological problems which are involved in and evolve from the practical exercise of authority in the concrete existential order.

## The Role of Anxiety

The role of anxiety is of central importance in the following discussion. I would like, therefore, at the outset to discuss some relevant points about anxiety in more or less general terms before entering into more specific considerations. Anxiety is one of those concepts that are difficult to define and impossible to agree on and which elicit multiple connotations. Consequently, the definitions tend to multiply, and the understandings become as diffuse as the contexts and users of the definitions. I will return to some of the more classic usages. In his early approaches to the problem of anxiety, in his *Three Essays on Sexuality* (1905),[1] Freud tended to view anxiety somewhat restrictively as an overflow of libido. His more mature thought on the subject, expressed in the complex and provocative *Inhibitions, Symptoms and Anxiety* (1926),[2] produced the concept of anxiety as a signal of impending threat or danger. One could thereby distinguish realistic anxiety from neurotic anxiety. The former was a reaction to external threat, a fear determined by some object or situation in which life was threatened or harm implied. The latter, however, was not proportioned to any external threat; rather it was a response to some form of internal threat.

In dealing with anxiety, one of the fundamental questions to be considered has to do with the character and sources of the inner threat that produce it. Needless to say, the question is exceedingly complex, and there is much to be said about it—as well as much that cannot yet be said about it. It can be said, however, that signal anxiety involves a threat to the integrity of the ego. The sources and specifics of that threat can be multiple. The ego is the agency of conscious autonomy and control. Anything, therefore, that threatens the autonomy, security, control, and stability of the ego is perceived as threatening. This is relatively easy to understand in relation to external sources of threat, but it becomes difficult in the consideration of internal sources of threat.

To begin with, the internal sources of threat are not always conscious. Contemporary psychology has demonstrated, if nothing else, that the dimensions of psychic life reach beyond the boundaries of consciousness, that man has a complex life of wishes, needs, drives, and instincts which operate beyond the reach of his conscious mental life. The crucial problems of development and adaptation evolve out of the continuing and constant problem of organizing, integrating, and harmonizing the evolving organization of the more or less conscious mental apparatus with the persisting and continuously vital activity of the less organized and dynamic strata of the mind. This creates a concatenation of developmental tasks at every level of the life cycle from earliest infancy into advanced old age.

The fact that the vital stratus persists at an unconscious level effects every aspect of human life and activity. There is no room here to elaborate a total psychology of this aspect of man's inner life. I only wish to point out that its existence complexifies the understanding of anxiety. For it is in this aspect of psychic functioning that anxiety often finds its source. Anxiety can accompany the unleashing of libidinal drives, of aggressive impulses, of forbidden or proscribed impulses of all kinds. Such impulses can be disturbing when they are unconscious. They produce anxiety, as a rule, when consciously or unconsciously they pose a threat to the integrity of the ego.

I will focus on only one aspect of the threat which I think can serve as a basis for our further analysis. One of the significant elements of threat to the ego is the destruction of self-esteem or the diminution of self-value. The disruption of libido produces anxiety because the associated wishes are inconsistent with the self-image the ego maintains and which is essential to its psychological survival. Such impulses are therefore threatening. Similarly, the arousal of aggressive and hostile impulses can be threatening insofar as they violate the maintained self-image. Without going into the basis of the self-image and its genesis, the self-image is teleologically calculated to support and maintain self-esteem and self-valuation. It is an essential component of normal adaptation and mature psychological functioning. It is as essential psychologically as oxygen is physiologically. There is no substitute for it. When it is threatened or in danger, human beings instinctively defend it and struggle to preserve it. When it is damaged, men suffer the agonies of masochism, depression, guilt, and suicide.

An important aspect, then, of this state of affairs is that the occurrence of anxiety requires a certain degree of ego development and a matured self-image. The more evolved one's sense of personal self-esteem and the more matured the sense of personal value, the more vulnerable is the person to anxiety. This is, of course, if taken without proper qualification, not an altogether defensible statement. But within limits it has a degree of applicability. There are obviously other factors which influence the occurrence and intensity of anxiety. The more realistic the self-image, for example, the more flexible can the ego be in the face of the threat of impulse—and consequently the less threatening is the impulse. The point to be stressed is that perfectly normal and well adjusted people are subject to anxiety. Anxiety is part of human existence, because it is the common lot to have impulses, conscious and unconscious, which threaten the intrinsic sense of value linked with every man's personal self-image.

The threat to self-image and its concomitant sense of personal value is in fact a far-ranging and significant aspect of human motivation. It is of extreme interest psychologically to explore the roots of this very general and all too little appreciated aspect of the mental life. But I will content myself here with merely stating the fact. We may return to it in further considerations, but for the moment the focus of our concern is on the broader interactional issues which derive from it.

## Anxiety and Authority

A basic psychological fact about authority is that for most men, if not all, it constitutes an area of conflict and anxiety. The reasons behind this phenomenon are multiple and can hardly be exhausted. I would like to separate the exercise of authority from the reaction or response to authority. Both aspects have their conflictual and anxious elements. It is perhaps easier to grasp the element of conflict in the response to authority. The psychological relationship which is inherent in the response to authority on the part of the members of a community or organization recalls and reactivates attitudes and dispositions to authority which reach back through the life history to the earliest and most primitive such relationships. The issues that are implicitly raised, therefore, in the response to authority are issues of dependence, submission, and obedience. These issues and their correlative postures are characteristic of and perhaps caricatured by infantile relationships. The child is preeminently dependent, submissive, and obedient. But his dependence is adulterated by ever-increasing impulses to progressive independence from parental control and limitation. His submission is increasingly modified by the innuendoes of revolt from parental demands. His obedience is continually and increasingly tempered by resentment and resistance.

There is no question that along the course of the individual's developmental history there is an accretion of such formative influences. The residues of such influences remain operative, but they remain operative in a manner quite removed from the conscious intent of the person responding to authority in the contemporary moment. The residues of prior experiences remain active in an unconscious manner so that the individual finds himself responding with emotions and attitudes which do not fit the reality of the immediate situation or relationship. The total response to authority in the present situation is colored and modulated by the activation of parallel unconscious fantasies which derive from earlier and primitive levels of experience rather than from the present context. As a result, the response to authority may incorporate emotional and attitudinal overtones which may derive from unconscious fantasies. Thus, the conflictual aspects of the authority relationship which derive from more infantile and primitive levels of the psychic organization can become active in partially determining a present response.

It is, of course, obvious that conflicts over authority are not only unconscious. But the key issue is whether conscious conflicts do not imply and reflect less conscious conflictual aspects of the total psychic response. A convincing case can be made that such is the reality. While we are often taken up by the conscious aspects of conflicts with authority figures, with the apparent motives and arguments, we so often remain sublimely unaware, i.e., unconscious, of the basic motivational elements. Proof is always difficult to come by, but on clinical grounds evidence can be mustered to support the position that such basic conflicts are the fundamental human lot. We all fall heir to them, since we are all victims of the infantile experience of restriction and submission to the overpowering significant figures (parents) in our most primitive experiences.

The activation of such primitive and infantile conflicts and their attendant emotions is associated with the arousal of anxiety. Anxiety is a derivation of the arousal of infantile residues which carry within them an inherent threat to the integrity of the ego. The unconscious conflictual fantasies aroused in the authority relation embody very basic and instinct-dependent forces whose activation constitutes a danger to the integrity and control of more organized aspects of the mental apparatus. It is important, therefore, to try to bring into focus the basic concept that anxiety is built into the authority relation, not by reason of its formal structure, but by reason of its informal process.

Thus far, we have considered only the roots of anxiety in response to authority. What about its exercise? Here, too, authority carries within it an inherent anxiety. It is sometimes difficult to appreciate, but the fact remains that those who exercise authority and those who must respond to it experience similar conflicts. It should also be remembered that the number of those who exercise authority but who are not required to respond to it is indeed small.

We can go further. The exercise of authority implies and imposes responsibility. The superior accepts and strives to fulfill that responsibility. Psychologically speaking, his acceptance of the role of superior carries with it the implicit role expectation that he act and function as the responsible one. He achieves a sense of his own identity as embodying the ideal of responsibility. His self-esteem and sense of value are tied up with his idealized self-image as "the responsible one." The catch is that, like all human beings, the one who exercises authority, "the responsible one," is also subject to irresponsible impulses. These irresponsible impulses reflect the activity of the less organized and dynamic levels of his personality. Such impulsiveness is inconsistent with the demands of his self-image. It contradicts and erodes the image of "the responsible one." It therefore constitutes a threat to the integrity of his self-image. This threat becomes manifest as anxiety. The basic insight in this approach is that men are constantly subjected to the influence of impulsive, ill-controlled, disruptive, and threatening and often unconscious stimuli which elicit anxiety. The purest heart carries within it the seeds of impure impulses and wishes that disturb its equilibrium and cause it to feel the sting of anxiety. The gentlest soul has within it the fire of anger and hostility that produces the searing pain of anxiety. And so, too, the most reliable and responsible man has within him an ever-active source of impulses to irresponsible action which pose for him the threat of anxiety. Characteristically, the impulses—libidinal, aggressive, irresponsible, or whatever—are not felt as such. They do not reach the conscious in their true colors. They are masked and distorted beyond recognition, but they leave their telltale mark in anxiety.

## Social Defense Mechanisms

Common knowledge in our age of psychological sophistication gives credence to the role of man's psychological defenses in allaying anxiety. The defense mechanisms as commonly conceived are erected and utilized by the individual psyche to ward off the threat implicit in anxiety and to modulate and modify the pain associated with such a threat. Such mechanisms are intrapsychic; they come to life in the individual psyche and maintain the psychic functioning of each individual, exclusive of his interaction with his fellows.

On the level of social interaction and transaction within a group, however, it is possible to consider other defense mechanisms which also alleviate anxiety. Particularly where the anxiety flows from the structure and characteristics of the group, individual intrapsychic mechanisms have a limited utility. The members of the group have needs to use the organization in their struggle against anxiety. Psychologically, individual members of the group externalize their characteristic defense mechanisms, and there arises within the group a collusive interlocking of defensive postures which constitutes a massive socially structured defense system.

To focus our analysis more specifically on authority, we can begin with the postulate that the group is composed of individuals who carry within them the basic conflicts about authority which we have already discussed. Each individual carries within him the roots of a conflict which revolves around the generation of irresponsible impulses. The conflict arouses anxiety and puts into operation defensive functions which are aimed at preserving the integrity and adaptation of the ego. The mechanisms are largely unconscious and take the following form. The first step consists in the denial of the conflict itself and of the associated anxiety. The ego uses denial in a purely repressive fashion in this first step. The conflict and the threat of its associated anxiety are simply denied and deprived of admission to the consciousness. The mechanism is totally unconscious and operates at a fairly primitive level. The ego cannot tolerate any conscious recognition of the existence and operation of such a detrimental conflict. Nor can it deal effectively in any way with the threat of anxious disruption which attends the existence of such a conflict. Consequently, the conflict and anxiety are almost automatically masked out, blotted out and repressed from consciousnes.

The second step in this defensive movement is the splitting or separation of the two aspects of the conflict. Responsibility and irresponsibility are divided and isolated from each other. Thus, the two elements which are mutually involved with each other in conflictual opposition can be dealt with in isolation without any regard to the inherent conflict. The third step involves the projection of the repressed and isolated elements outside of the psyche to objects in the environment. This last step, also largely unconscious, completes the essential steps of the process. Thus, the basic conflict and the associated experience of anxiety are driven out of consciousness by repression and denial and become unconscious, and the sting is disengaged. Next, the denied conflictual elements are separated from each other and regarded in isolation i.e., without conflict. Finally, the denied and divorced elements are separately projected to disparate portions of the social system outside of the individual and can be dealt with separately.

The first two steps, denial and splitting, set the stage for and make possible the third step of projection. It is through projection that the socially structured defensive system arises. The projection works in the following way. The individual member of the group of organization projects his own feelings of responsibility to authority figures above him in the structure of the group. At the same time, he also projects the separated feelings of irresponsibility to his subordinates in the social system. Since his responsible attitudes are really reactions against his irresponsible impulses, the more unruly the impulses to irresponsibility, the more harsh, restrictive, and demanding must his responsible attitudes become. Consequently, the more intense and persistent his own unconscious impulses to irresponsibility, the more restrictive and punitive does his responsible self become. The projection of these separated and basically conflictual elements results in a perception of superiors as harsh, repressive, demanding, and punitive and in the perception of inferiors as carefree, impulsive, lacking in any sense of responsibility, and unable to be trusted with any commission or responsibility of consequence.

The result of this unconscious set of operations within the social system is or can be rather far-reaching, both for the individuals involved and for the operation of the social system. The point should be made that the mechanisms proposed here are general and widely operative human mechanisms for dealing with the disturbing effects of conflict and anxiety. The basic economic principle involved is that it is easier and more tolerable to deal with conflict projected into the interpersonal realm than to deal with it on the intrapsychic level. Conflict between individuals is undoubtedly painful, but it is less painful than the internal conflict, anxiety, and erosion of self-esteem that overwhelm the ego's defenses in the intrapsychic arena. The projection of repressive and strict attitudes to superiors creates difficulties in the interpersonal adjustment to superiors. But it also makes it possible to objectify and identify this aspect of the authority conflict and deal with it as though it were an external conflict. The superior can be blamed and struggled against in the external order, thus one aspect of the underlying conflict can be dealt with and the anxiety partially alleviated. Similarly, projection of irresponsible impulses to inferiors permits one to deal with the second member of the underlying conflict and further modify anxiety. Anxiety, then, is alleviated; but it is alleviated at the price of distrust, hostility, external conflict, and disorganization and disruption, not in the individual, but in the social system. The externalization, as it were, of the individual's characteristic defenses and their projection to the social system is intrapsychically adaptive; but it is disruptive on the level of social interaction.

The result of this way of handling conflicts of authority is that individuals at all levels of the social organization perceive those above them as harsh, repressive, demanding, and imposing unnecessarily strict discipline. Conversely, individuals at all levels perceive those below them in the social organization, their inferiors, as wanting in responsibility, careless, untrustworthy, etc. The result is that there is an unconscious but collusive redistribution of responsibility and irresponsibility within the social system. Responsibility is ascribed to certain roles, and irresponsibility is ascribed to certain other roles. In consequence, the functional exercise of authority is modified. Responsibility at lower levels of the organization is diminished, and responsibility at the upper levels of organization is increased. The tendency is reinforced by the perception of superiors that they are more responsible and that their inferiors are less than responsible. It is also confirmed by the tendency of inferiors to believe that they are, indeed, incapable of responsibility, and that their superiors are excessively endowed with that esteemed virtue. The whole is elaborated and evolves out of a collusive and interlocking system of denials, splittings, and projections which reconstructs the organization of functional authority in the social system. It redefines the task and role expectations at all levels of the system, and it does so in complete isolation from the formal organization of the system. The driving force is the internal conflict over authority and responsibility which arouses anxiety.

The further complication of this system is that, as a rule, people tend to act as others perceive them. People act objectively according to the psychic roles assigned them by others. And so the projective system, unconsciously derived as it is, begins to take on the cast of reality. Inferiors become, in fact, less responsible than their position and capabilities would dictate. Responsible tasks are forced upwards in the hierarchy of authority so that responsibility for their performance can be disclaimed at lower levels. Responsibility must therefore be assumed by (more responsible) individuals at higher levels, and the perception of those at lower levels as irresponsible is thereby substantiated. The impact of responsibility is diminished by a subtle form of delegation to superiors. The result, of course, is that superiors exercise too much authority, and inferiors share less and less in the responsible action of the group.

## A Social System

The process which we are discussing depends upon very basic and general human reactions and mechanisms. The arousal of anxiety in the authority relationship is a fundamental human experience, and it is through the mobilization of universally operative defensive mechanisms of denial, splitting, and projection that the socially structured defense system comes into being. The mechanisms can operate in any social structure in which authority functions.

I would like to turn attention to a specific social system which has been carefully studied and in which many of these mechanisms have been identified and their influence on the group and its functions traced. The study, made in the nursing service of a general teaching hospital in Great Britain, was conducted to help resolve a crisis that had arisen between the demands of patient care and the teaching obligations of the nursing service.[3] The level of anxiety and stress generated in this system was reflected by dissatisfaction, high absentee rate, high rate of illness among the nurses, and a very high dropout rate. The latter was particularly distressing, since fully a third of the nurses initiating their training did not finish. With rare exceptions, the dropouts were those women who were most highly regarded as potential nursing candidates.

The study of this social system revealed that it constituted a highly organized and tightly authoritarian system. At the bottom of the pile were the student nurses in their first year. They were responsible to and took orders from all other nurses. The other nurses were part of a pecking-order which was determined by years in training or service. Second-year nurses were responsible to third-year nurses, etc. In this tightly structured system, the stress and anxiety were handled by a variety of social defense mechanisms:

1. Depersonalization, categorization, and denial of the significance of the individual were achieved by the use of task-lists. Each nurse was assigned to perform a certain task for many patients and the supervisors imposed an ethic of equivalence according to which it must not make any difference to her which patients she nursed. She was also required to wear a uniform which became the symbol of expected inner and behavioral uniformity so that she was regarded as an aggregate of nursing skills rather than as an individual. This depersonalization was reinforced by frequent shifts of the nurses from one service to another, with an attendant increase in stress and emotional disruption associated with the disruption of interpersonal relationships among members of the nursing staff. The system thereby refused to recognize the importance of warm interpersonal relationships as an aspect of the nurses' work adjustment.

2. Detachment and denial of feelings. Nursing supervisors stressed professional detachment, control of feelings, and the avoidance of any disturbing identifications. The good nurse, they said, remains unattached ("detached") and does not mind moving from ward to ward at a moment's notice. This was reinforced by a variety of interpersonal repressive techniques ("stiff upper lip") which underscored feelings as professionally unacceptable. The students felt that this was evidence that they were not understood by the members of the staff directing them. This seems not to have been the case. The nursing supervisors recognized the problem and understood it, but they regarded sympathetic handling of emotional stress as inconsistent with traditional nursing roles and relationships.

3. Idealization of nursing candidates and denial of possibilities for personal development. Because of the nature of nursing tasks and the anxiety associated with their performance, the nursing service constantly seeks assurance that the candidates it is accepting are mature and responsible people. There is a consequent idealization of the nursing candidate, who is presumed to be mature and competent. The further consequence of this presumption is that the training program focuses on training in the facts and techniques of nursing and pays minimal attention to the needs of nursing students for personal growth, and the needs of all nursing students to grow in a sense of personal maturity and identification in a professional role.

4. Social redistribution of responsibility and irresponsibility. By

the mechanisms previously discussed, juniors are regarded as irresponsible, and seniors are regarded as excessively strict and repressive in discipline. Decisions are avoided at lower levels of the hierarchy. This is accomplished by excessive ritualization and standardization of nursing procedures. As a consequence, however, responsible tasks are forced upwards in the hierarchy. The general effect is that nurses at all levels are performing tasks below their level of ability and also below the level of their position. Another consequence is that all initiative and exercise of discretion are discouraged and avoided. It is not surprising, therefore, that the more gifted students would find this situation intolerable and would drop out.

5. Avoidance of change. Any significant social change implies an alteration in the social system as a defensive system. Change therefore implies an exacerbation of anxiety and at least a transient weakening of the defenses against it. The greater the anxiety in the system, the greater is the need for reassurance and reinforcement of the existing social defense system. The adherence to the existing system can take on the aspect of rigidly compulsive adherence to the demands of the system and an inability to tolerate any change. Efforts to introduce change are resisted by conscious and unconscious means.

The steps in the evolution of this defense system were arousal of anxiety, mobilization of defenses to allay anxiety, and finally the institutionalization or organization of individual defenses by unconscious collusive interaction into a rigidly functioning social defensive system. This serves the purposes of reducing anxiety, but it quickly becomes apparent that the prize is won at a tremendous cost, since it creates other stresses which tell on the participating members. It compels individuals to fit the demands of the system without any recognition of or provision for the normal human needs for warm, emotionally stable relationships, for the demands of self-esteem, for responsibility and the exercise of initiative and judgment. It moves the conflict into the social area where it can be less threatening and more easily dealt with, but in so doing it creates a rigid and repressive social system. The price is rather high—dehumanization and depersonalization.

## Implications for Religious Communities

The present analysis is calculated to illumine some of the informal aspects of implementation of authority in social structures. The religious community is such a structure, and it is a structure in which authority plays a primary role.[4] It is not overly bold to assume that religious are human beings and that they share with other human beings conflicts over authority. It seems safe, therefore, to assume that if we look carefully we shall find many of the elements of such social defense systems operative in religious communities. Generalizations, however, are difficult, because so much depends on the existential factors and on the level of maturity inhering in any given community. We can also presume on good psychological grounds that where individual and group maturity is high, anxiety is minimal and social defense mechanisms play a minor role in the group process.

It may be worthwhile, even so, to reflect on some characteristic postures of the religious group to find out whether they may not reflect the operation of defensive systems. I will follow the previously indicated points. The denial of the significance of the individual has been a cardinal point in the spirituality of religious groups and is still often proposed as a sort of ideal. The place where this emphasis is most clearly made is in relation to obedience. The good religious is ready to do whatever is asked of him, wherever and whenever. This implies that one religious is as good (or as bad) for the performance of a given task as any other. There is no question that an extreme adherence to this posture is less and less common, but one is sometimes prompted to wonder whether it does not cling to life as a kind of agrarian ideal, whimsically clutched, but enjoying little realistic application. The other side of this posture, which used to be ignored but is becoming more and more of an issue, is that obedience required depersonalization and a degrading of the person. One could perhaps justify such a posture in terms of sacrifice to the common good in some fairly primitive contexts, but the modern context more and more often requires judgment, initiative, and responsibility in members of religious communities in order to accomplish the purposes of the community. This means that not only the individual but also the community must pay a price. It is difficult on such terms to justify a posture which denies the significance of the individual.

Religious groups have a curious cult about feelings. They think that feelings are suspicious and undesirable. Detachment and control (denial?) of feelings is so much more virtuous. One often senses an avoidance or denial of feelings as if everyone was agreed that somehow they did not belong and so they collusively attempted to avoid them. Avoidance of feelings is often inculcated both intrapsychically and in the context of interpersonal relationships.

A striking parallel to the nursing system is the idealization of candidates that is often seen in religious groups. Selection of candidates, tests, interviews, and other screening devices are employed to assure the religious group of the best available candidates. One can raise the question whether the consequence does not also involve a presumption of maturity. There is no question but that religious groups are embarrassingly impoverished when it comes to provision for the handling of developmental emotional problems in their members. This has particular application to formative years in which young adolescents are received as candidates and then subjected to spiritual formation over a long period of time. Unfortunately, the emphasis is all too frequently on subjection to institutionalized patterns of behavior, including the matter of prayer, rather than on developmental and emotional problems and their proper working through. I maintain the importance of the former, but I must also insist on the importance of the latter. The current provisions for such problems are generally discouraging, if not nonexistent. Those who appeal to the institution of spiritual fathers as adequate for these needs point directly to the existing inadequacy.

By far the most serious and far-reaching implication for the religious community is the redistribution of responsibility and irresponsibility. Over the long haul of life in religion, this aspect of the defensive system can have a continuing and far-reaching attrition. The toll is taken by forcing the individual religious into an overly submissive and irresponsible position in which through an appeal to "obedience" he avoids responsible action and mature judgment. He too easily can resign his responsibility to his superior, and then, embittered by this situation, blame the superior for this state of affairs. This is all too easy since the superior is already perceived as repressive and demanding. There are a good many delicate issues that can be explored here, but they lie beyond our present scope. It can be said, however, that the avoidance of responsibility, however it comes about, is an immaturity. True obedience does not tolerate the avoidance of responsibility. Disobedience is of two kinds. One can disobey by deviance and rebellion. One can also disobey by submission and passivity. The latter form of disobedience is too often not recognized as such.

A further effect of this redistribution is the slow, gradual, almost imperceptible erosion of the individual's sense of personal value and self-esteem. This effect is also contributed to by mechanisms for de-personalization. The result is a form of self-depreciation which produces indifference, depression, an unwillingness to exercise initiative or imagination, a lack of spontaneity, and an inability to function effectively and efficiently. We forget, as I have already suggested, that self-esteem is necessary for any kind of responsible and successful activity. If the system erodes self-esteem, it also erodes the capacity for productive and creative activity, whether it be in teaching or preaching, or learning, or whatever. One often hears the complaint over the apparently large numbers of religious who become unproductive and lead their religious lives without active involvement with others with whom they come into contact. If the present analysis has any merit, it at least raises the question whether in such a circumstance we are not witnessing the attrition of a social defense system.

A final point is the matter of resistance to change. I think that little need be said on the matter here. It is easy to say that religious groups are resistant to change and to adopt a critical attitude, as many do. But there are unanswered questions as to what change really is and how much change is appropriate for the religious group. I have suggested elsewhere[4] that change and adaptation are necessary for the survival of the religious group. Change must be measured relatively That change is good which improves the effectiveness of the religious group in its common objectives and purposes. Resistance to change is therefore a matter of degree. Religious groups are changing, but the question can still be asked whether the change is enough, or fast enough. It is also true that there is resistance to change in religious groups. Where there is resistance, we can honestly ask ourselves whether it is derived from the operation of unconscious motivations and reflects the compulsive rigidity of a socially organized defensive system.

The present analysis is directed toward a particular aspect of the authority relation. Whether it is operative in a given community or to what extent it is operative can only be judged by evaluating the observable effects produced by such a system. It may have on over-whelming influence on the life of a community, or it may have a minimal effect. It is, however, I would think, always identifiable. If it does loom large enough to present a problem, what does one do about it? The question is a sort of automatic response of concerned religious. Solutions are hard to come by and I will avoid giving one. It can be said, however, that dissolution of the defensive system requires the willingness and capacity of those involved to tolerate the inner anxiety which originally motivated the generation of the system to begin with. The capacity to tolerate such anxiety and conflict is one measure of individual and group maturity.

## Other Implications

While it would be difficult to demonstrate the organization of such collusively supported social defense systems in other areas of society, I think it is immediately and transparently obvious that the mechanisms of denial, splitting, and projection are serious elements in many of the social areas we have been considering in this study. The reciprocally divergent attitudes in these areas provide a clue that something of the sort is up. Priests see their bishops as repressive, strict, and unsympathetic; bishops see their priests as rebellious, impulsive, and irresponsible. Students see administrators as unconcerned, remote, harsh, and rigid; administrators see the students as impulsive, uncontrolled, demanding, irresponsible, and lazy. Blacks see whites as repressive, unjust, unsympathetic, and prejudiced; whites see blacks as lazy, stupid, promiscuous, irresponsible, and criminal.

The overlap and congruence with the respective stereotypes as related to the mythologizing process should be noted. We remarked in discussing the mythic process that it expressed and responded to powerful and basic human motives and emotions. One can only wonder whether the reciprocal stereotypes are not the products in part of mechanisms of denial, splitting, and projection on a massive social scale. The interlocking perceptions can then be seen as, in part, projections of repressed aspects of deeper intrapsychic conflicts. The social stereotypes and mythologizing serve an ulterior function of handling deeper conflicts and alleviating the burden of individual anxiety by projecting the elements of conflict into the arena of social interaction.

*Part IV*

# Applied Aspects

The Role of the Superior

The Role of Subject

Authority and Community

*Chapter 10*

# The Role of the Superior

It is appropriate at this point, I think, to try to bring into clearer focus some of the concrete implications of the more or less theoretical considerations of authority which have gone before. I would like to deal with the role of the superior first and then discuss the implications of the subject role later. This separation of subject matter so closely related in reality may have its disadvantages, but it may serve to clarify certain issues. The following reflections are in no way intended to set down a set of norms for being a good superior. I would be at a loss to even attempt that ambitious undertaking. I am not even sure that I have any adequate idea of what a good superior is. Nor do I imply—I hasten to add—that good superiors are like the proverbial good Injuns. There exists many a good superior, but I do not know what makes them good or how to formalize their capacities and qualities. Any attempt to specify what a good superior is, or is not, is risky business at best, and I do not feel quite up to that. What I propose is a reflection on the implications of the role of superior. If I slip into certain practicalities, it will be through inadvertence.

On the contemporary scene, the role of superior has evolved into something considerably more complex than previous generations have ever experienced. The structure and function of religious groups has become incredibly more complex as time goes on. This reflects wide-ranging cultural patterns and forces, changing attitudes, new orientations, and the growing complexity and sophistication of the societal demands which press upon religious groups and upon religious persons in general. It reflects the emergence of professionalism in the religious group with its congruent attitudes and values. The professional orientation flies in the face of more traditional bureaucratic modalities from which persistent models of superiorship have derived. I have discussed these matters in greater detail elsewhere.[1] But it should be pointed out here that the shift from bureaucratic to professional mode of organization places additional demands on the superior to relate to and deal with the emergence of the stirrings of initiative and independence of judgment and action in his religious subjects. What is clear at the present moment in the evolution of things is that traditional models of authority are, in this regard, archaic.

## Becoming a Superior

The unfortunate thing is that no one is ever trained or schooled in the exercise of authority. No one is ever trained to be President of the United States. No one is ever trained to be a father. No one is ever trained to be a superior. When an individual is appointed to the position of superior, he begins to experience that species of transition between functional roles which we have come to recognize as cultural discontinuities.[2] He moves from the position of subject to that of superior. The insecurity of a new and unprepared-for role tends to pressure the individual to turn to the models of the exercise of authority which he has himself experienced. While those models may have served effectively within their own cultural context, they are more than likely to be inadequate for more contemporary circumstances. Thus, the perpetuation of traditional models of the superior's role have a limited value. The superior's role is evolving, and those who come to fill the role are faced with problems of adaptation and personal growth which traditional orientations and formulations do not satisfy.

When an individual is newly appointed a superior, he is faced for the first time with the responsibilities of authority and its exercise. He is faced for the first time with the necessity of responding to the expectations of the group which come to bear on his functioning as superior. The situation is calculated to arouse considerable anxiety related to issues of authority. Much depends on the superior's capacity to resolve that anxiety effectively. Being placed in a position of authority forces him to adopt a stance of authoritative function which is shaped by many subtle influences. The influences stem from his earliest experience of authority and his earliest identifications with authority figures. Every man is born into a context of authority and must relate to the problems of authority from the very beginning of his life. The first authority figures are his parents, both mother and father. His response to their authority is obedience, but it is often based on a subtle identification with the authority-exercising aspects of both parents. These aspects remain inapparent until the individual himself assumes a position of authority. This is no less applicable to the young parent who has been converted into an authority figure by biological circumstance than to the religious superior who has been cast in the role of authority figure by duly constituted processes of selection and appointment. Only in the face of the actual circumstance are the latent aspects of earlier identifications brought to light to become operative aspects of the functioning personality.

If these aspects are conflictual, the individual is likely to experience difficulty in assuming the role and function of the bearer of authority. The possibilities for ambivalence, insecurity, and uncertainty, as well as the conflicts over dependency which are found so characteristically in the authoritarian personality, become imminent. What issues out of this matrix of complex influences is either an excessive domination in the exercise of authority or a relative ineffectualness marked by excessive dependence and inability to exercise responsible judgment. It is of interest, of course, that the more or less traditional models of authority, particularly in the Church and the religious orders, are predominantly authoritarian. Authority is seen in terms of power, and power is restricted to the superior. The implication is that the superior alone is capable of judgment. Everyone else is capable of no more than obedience and obedience is mere submission. We are talking here about defects in development which can be accentuated by placing any given individual in the role of superior. But this is by no means the only pertinent consideration. Much to the point is the context in which authority must be exercised. The authoritarian model may have been quite reasonably applicable in a sociocultural milieu where an authoritarian stance on the part of the superior was in part a response to role expectations generated within the group. Where it is clear, however, that such expectations are not at all operative, an authoritarian stance is both inappropriate and probably maladaptive.

There can be little doubt that the superior's attitude is terribly important in this regard. Father Karl Rahner has pointed out that superiors can no longer act the part of Olympian papas. They can no longer act with the supposition that they are in a position to judge and decide with greater competence and qualification than any of their subjects. While it is true for the most part that the body of subjects which composes the community is generally increasingly knowledgeable and that individual subjects are equipped by endowment and training to offer professional judgment where the superior remains unequipped, even were this not the case we would have to argue that the superior errs when he acts autocratically in conducting his office. The superior ought not to comport himself as though he were superior. Pomposity, superiority, all the various forms of domination, imperiousness, intransigence, and all the trappings which tend to separate the superior from his community ought to be avoided. They are violations of the authority relation insofar as the accidental trappings become substituted in perception and inference for the essence of what the superior is and ought to be. In a sense, all such efforts can be regarded as defenses which the superior erects between himself and his community. They are unnecessary if the superior himself is free from the encumbrance of conflicts over authority and responsibility. If he is not caught up in such conflicts, such trappings are superfluous. And if they do not serve such neurotic purposes, they obscure the basic reality that the superior, more than other members of the community, is the servant of the community.

### Accepting Responsibility

What is of central importance is the superior's personal capacity to adjust to the responsibilities of his office with comfort and security and to remain responsive to the ongoing process among his subjects which forms the implicit expectations of the group for his role as superior. It would seem, offhand, that the assumption of responsibilities would be a straightforward and simple matter. It has often in the past been thought of in those terms. It was sometimes thought necessary only to read and assimilate the contents of a catechism of do's and don'ts for superiors in order to fulfill the responsibilities of the office. It is not that easy by any means. It is often difficult to define the superior's responsibilities. The difficulty has two sides. The definition requires a determination of what the superior's responsibility is and what it is not. This is not always clear, especially the negative element. But the negative element is of crucial importance. The negative element was often obscured in more authoritarian approaches, where most of the responsibility was aggregated into the superior's hands. But the negative element is most important in the preservation of the distribution of responsibility in the group. Responsible authority, therefore, finds itself within a limited area of application. It is sometimes a question when responsibilities are in fact being fulfilled.

I like to recount the experience of a physician of my acquaintence in this regard. He was appointed director of a large research project which employed several hundred personnel—doctors, nurses, orderlies, and patients. The project was conducted on an in-patient basis, and there was a considerable amount of interaction between participants on a continuous day to day basis. As director of the project, he found that every morning when he came to work he was besieged by complaints and difficulties from all levels of the project organization. He would be regularly presented with problems arising between nurses and doctors, between doctors and patients, between nurses and orderlies, between nurses and patients, etc. And every day he busied himself for several hours in straightening these little problems out. He became rather proud of his ability in this regard, and he got to be the Mr. Fix-it of the entire project. The difficulty was that he did not have enough time then to do his own work, particularly the important thinking required to keep the project moving. Moreover, he found that the complaints and problems did not diminish. Every day he would come to work and be met with an equally impressive list of problems. He finally realized that something must be amiss. He began to study the complaints and began to realize that in many instances it reflected some administrative failure on his part. He could recognize some failure in communication of his intent, some lack of policy decision, etc. So he began to realize that he had been looking in the wrong place. He had been looking for the source of the difficulty at the point where the difficulty manifested itself. But the source lay elsewhere. He began to analyze the fresh problems by trying to discern where he might have overlooked or omitted his own responsibility, or alternatively, where he had assumed the responsibility of someone else at another level of the organization. With his fresh approach, he found that the problems were analyzable and that little by little the number of new problems diminished. There came that wonderful day when he was met with no new problems. Not only that, but he found a growing spirit of cooperation and helpfulness in the project personnel. There was less rivalry, more helpful contributions and suggestions, an all-round better spirit. He felt, too, that he had achieved a much clearer recognition of what his own responsibilities were and where they ended. His own clarification of this limit made it possible for other members of the group to define their own areas of responsible action much more adequately. The result was an overall improvement of function along with an overall diminution of anxiety in the group.

The lesson in this parable is that the effective functioning of any group requires the recognition of the area of responsible action appropriate for each member of the group. It is important for the superior to recognize the extent of his own responsibility. If he is deficient in the performance of that responsibility, the group suffers. If he fails to recognize the appropriate authority of others in the group and if he interferes with the appropriate exercise of responsibility other than his own, he creates a situation of confusion and conflict. The important principle involved in this is that authority is distributed through the entire group rather than being concentrated in a single locus. The concept that the superior alone possesses authority is no longer tenable as soon as one abandons the restriction of authority to its formal aspects. Formally, of course, only the superior has authority. It is easier and probably less confusing here to speak of responsibility. The distribution of authority, however conceived, does not parallel the distribution of responsibility. The distinction is important since it was in part the ignoring of such a distinction that provided a weak point in the exercise of more traditional and authoritarian superiors.

## Responsibility in the Community

There is a new emphasis emerging in the Church of today which must force considerable change in the operative views of religious authority. The developments in and subsequent to Vatican II have altered the image of papal authority from that of ruler of the Church to that of the head of the Church who gives expression to the stirrings of the Spirit in the Christian community. The emergence of the notion of episcopal collegiality has been an important factor. Community is the operative notion. People see the Church more and more as a community of believers within which the Spirit works as a whole. The action of the Spirit is not restricted to some special subset of members. At the same time, the Church is an organized structure in which the responsibility for salvific action and promulgation of revealed truth is heterogeneously distributed. This latter aspect has often led to the restriction of the offices of the Church—teaching, preaching, administration of sacraments, etc.—in such a way as to suggest that only in the authoritatively appointed agents was this exercise of Christian responsibility permissible. The rest of the Church was permitted only passive acceptance and conformity. In fact, the Church is and should function as a community.

The life of a community requires that the participation of individual members be cast in terms of a share in the responsible action of the community. The community becomes an expression of a communal will and a communal responsibility. The superior functions most adequately when his decisions and actions are expressions of that communal will. Reference to our discussion of identification is essential here, since identification is a primary process through which the essential structure for such communal action is provided. It is well to emphasize that reciprocal identification is central. The superior must identify with his subjects individually and with the community as a whole. He must share individual and collective goals, attitudes, and values. There can be no conscious mimicry in this regard. The failure of identification will have its inevitable effect. It is difficult to draw the line between what is conscious and what is unconscious here because they tend to dovetail. The superior is concerned, caring, and helping insofar as he is identified with the group. He is trusted by the group to the extent that his underlying identification with the group and its concerns and interests is sensed and responded to.

It is apparent that the emerging emphasis on community and shared responsibility places increasing demands on the superior. He must be willing to run the risk of permitting subordinates to exercise their appropriate responsibility. His capacity to do this is a function of his own personal autonomy, since autonomy involves the capacity to allow autonomous action to others. There is always a risk in letting the initiative for responsible action loose in a group, but it is a risk taken in the interest of greater good. Unless the superior is willing to run this risk, he deprives his subjects of the opportunity for mature and responsible subjectship. The psychological harm is incalculable. The development of a mature sense of personal autonomy is an absolute requirement for a superior.

## Responsiveness

Another important aspect of the superior's role is trust. The superior must be trusted by the community as a whole and by individual members. The superior will be trusted only insofar as he is trustworthy. It must be plain to his subjects that their interest is his concern, that he offers himself as an ally rather than as an obstacle, that they can turn to him for help, advice, support, counsel. The superior must create a climate of relations in which it is plain that superior and subject are mutually supportive cooperators in the work of God's kingdom. The superior's inner identification and his sincere interest make the climate possible. The superior's inner sense of trust will make it a reality. That trust, as we have seen, implies inner trustworthiness and self-trust, as well as a capacity for putting trust in others. The superior must have a capacity to trust his subjects, and he must manifest that trust in a meaningful way so that a trusting relationship may develop.

The superior must strike a delicate balance between the responsible performance of his duties as superior and a sensitive responsiveness to the needs of the community. Part of the problem is the need for finding a fresh formulation for the role of the superior in the religious group. Yet, a fresh formulation need not be new. Our Lord said,

> You know that among the pagans, the rulers lord it over them, and their great men make their authority felt. This is not to happen among you. No; anyone who wants to be great among you must be your servant, and anyone who wants to be first among you must be your slave (Matt. 20:25-27).

Authority in its traditional exercise has too little modelled itself on these words. The authoritarian posture, whatever its other advantages, is un-Christian. There is no other place where truly Christian authority ought to be exercised more completely than in the religious group. The superior is therefore the servant of the community. He accomplishes that servantship when he exercises his directive power in response to the communal will of his community.

Recognition of the will of the community is never easy. Moreover, the superior's obligation is not only to his community, but to his community as a functioning part of the larger community of the religious order or further, of the people of God. He must respond, therefore, to directives from superiors higher in the organizational structure. But responsible superiorship requires judgment. It is of great interest in this regard to read the many letters of Ignatius of Loyola to various local superiors. He counsels, advises, and directs but constantly with the qualification that the local superior, who knows better than Ignatius the immediate situation, should use his own good judgment in deciding what finally is to be done. We can see there the principle of autonomy and responsible superiorship. Ignatius fulfills his responsibility and gives his own judgment, but at the same time respects the autonomy and responsibility of his subordinate.

Currently, some efforts are in process to organize individual religious communities along lines which would make the communal will more explicit. More and more, community meetings are being held to enable the community to come to a clearer consensus on matters touching it. This is a new phenomenon in religious life and seems to be fruitful in many ways. It should be noted that such communal participation was unheard of even a few years ago. It has the advantage (and disadvantage) that it institutionalizes and explicitizes a communal process. It makes it much more difficult for the superior not to take the wishes of the community into account. As the servant of the community, the superior must be responsive to its wishes. But responsible superiorship always requires autonomous judgment from the superior. His is always the problem of keeping everybody happy, and this, as Abraham Lincoln was wont to observe, is impossible. He must pass autonomous and responsible judgment of the best course of action taking into consideration and weighing directives of higher superiors, communal will, practicalities, and contingencies.

## Subsidiarity

More and more, in contemporary society, it is becoming apparent that decision processes are beyond the capability of individuals. The superior cannot know all that he needs to know in many instances in order to make a responsible judgment. He must, therefore, rely on the informed judgment of others. The superior's effort, then, must be in the direction of organizing the widest range of the best available opinions for preparing the groundwork for significant decisions. The mobilization of the resources of the community in arriving at decisions affecting the community is not only advisable on a variety of counts, but from the point of view of information gathering and effective decision making it is essential.

The basic principle which is at work in this liberalization or democratization of the exercise of authority is that of subsidiarity. The superior is faced with the problem of fostering greater autonomy in his subordinates and thereby avoiding the dangers implicit in infantile dependence. Autonomy and responsibility can never be expected where the psychological substratum does not exist. One must presume mature individuals. But even mature individuals will not respond with responsible and autonomous action where the climate of authority does not permit that. The principle of subsidiarity requires that individuals at all levels of organization of the group be permitted the exercise of their own free and responsible initiative. Pius XI's formulation in *Quadragesimo Anno* is classic:

> Just as it is gravely wrong to take from individuals what they can accomplish by their own initiative and industry and give it to the community, so also it is an injustice and at the same time a grave evil and disturbance of right order to assign to a greater and higher association what lesser and subordinate organizations can do. For every social activity ought, of its very nature, to furnish help to the members of the body social and never destroy or absorb them.

Subsidiarity requires that the superior should serve the community by supplementing, not supplanting, the freedom, initiative, and personal responsibility of those under his authority.

There is a great lesson to be learned in the matter of functioning as superior from the model of parenthood. Comparisons of the superior to the image of a parent is often misleading since it calls up old ghosts of paternalism. But the comparison is useful insofar as there are some interesting parallels between the exercise of parental authority and its effects and the exercise of authority generally, as well as in religious groups. The parent may react in a variety of ways to the demands of his parenthood. The exercise of his parental authority may take the form of domination. He may hover over every move and decision of the child. He thus restricts the child's exercise of his own proportional judgment, denies him the opportunity for adequate self-differentiation, represses the child's natural spontaneity, and fosters resentment. Such domination usually channels latent hostility, whether the outer face of the domination wears the trappings of open hostility or masks itself in the more respectable riggings of over-solicitousness. Usually such loving hypersolicitude is a substitute for hostile feelings which remain unconscious and generate ill-defined guilt feelings as well,which must be compensated by a show of love. In either case, the child reacts to the underlying hostility with resentment, anger, and hate. The relation of parent and child becomes tense and conflictual, with guilt abounding on both sides. It is also possible for the parent to be excessively permissive, vacuous, and weak. The child suffers because he lacks the ingredient of paternal support and discipline which is essential to his development. The child needs that support in order to come to deal with and master the internal and external threats to his emerging ego. He feels that the weak and permissive parent has let him down and has no care for him as a good parent should, and he resents that. He grows up to despise the parent. The patterns of reaction to ineffectual parents are quite complex and varied and share the common note of impaired personality development.

The extremes of parental adaptation to the demands of parental authority are paralleled on the level of the exercise of religious authority. The superior adapts to the demands of his position by some mode of exercise of authority which will find its way between the extremes of excessive domination and permissiveness. Either extreme is a renunciation of responsible authority. Either extreme creates a vacuum of authority which disrupts the balance of authority relations through the entire social structure of the group. The resulting structural imbalance creates uncertainties and doubts which issue in conflict. The conflict may reveal itself between levels of the structure, or it may erupt between individuals. More often than not it is likely to manifest itself in intrapsychic terms as anxiety. This was the lesson that my medical friend had to learn in becoming a responsible project director. It is perhaps the most difficult lesson for any authority figure to realize. Keeping in mind the relational structure of authority and the conception of authority relations as organized into a system, we have the theoretical tools at hand for appreciating this aspect of the exercise of authority and its implications. Imbalance at one point in the system is reflected in imbalance at other points. If the superior exercises his authority in a dominant manner, he invades the autonomous authority of others and deprives them of the proportional and appropriate exercise of their own personal authority. If the superior exercises his authority in a nondominant and permissive manner, he creates an area of ambiguity in authority relations which permits the subject or subjects to enlarge the scope of their own responsibility. Remembering that we are talking about an excessive withdrawal from the exercise of his proper authority on the part of the superior, the extension of the subject's exercise of responsibility exceeds legitimate responsibility and places him in potential conflict over the implied limits as defined in terms of the authority relation, and in terms of the consensus of distribution of responsibility within the group. This can in turn generate inner conflict and anxiety.

Thus, the basic problem of more traditional and authoritarian models of the exercise of authority is that they abrogate responsibility to the superior and correspondingly deprive the subject of his proper responsibility. We have already given consideration to the question of social defense systems which arise precisely out of the imbalance in the social system we have been considering here.

The principle of subsidiarity has broad applicability in many areas in which concern for the functioning of authority structures has arisen. But subsidiarity becomes merely an empty shadow if those who work within and with it are unable to assess its intrinsic value. For the superior, the demands placed upon him by subsidiarity can be quite taxing. Subsidiarity brings about a redistribution of authority. That has advantages, but it also carries with it definite risks. It loosens the superior's control over decision-making and direction. It creates large areas of ambiguity and uncertainty. The superior must be able to tolerate these anxiety producing aspects of subsidiarity, or else he will unconsciously be forced to undermine and destroy it.

Subsidiarity brings larger segments of the community into the actual workings of authority. There is a great advantage to this that needs to be stressed. The community has tremendous resources and energies which can be directed to the solution of its problems or the attainment of its goals. This is relevant to all forms of community or social structure. The active participation of larger segments of the community in the workings of authority brings these resources to bear in a manner which otherwise would be impossible. Such active involvement draws upon creative wellsprings and sources of initiative which must be regarded as essential to the welfare of the community.

In the religious community the tasks of adaptation and continual rethinking of the role and function of the community demands a continual reworking of community ideals, objectives, and purposes. It is impossible for a superior to carry out this effort without assistance from many other sources of information and attitude. There is also a relevant question of the age levels of the people involved. Superiors tend to be older and less responsive to contemporary concerns and values. Younger members of a community can provide that information and can offer a more contemporary point of view to the working and thinking of the authority process. Older members of the community, conversely, have a better feel for the important traditions and more persevering attitudes which are necessary as a modulating and controlling influence in the flux of change and new directions of thought and action.

In the parish, whatever its denomination—Catholic, Protestant, or Jewish—the pastor who does not permit active participation of his parishioners in the running and decision-making for their parish deprives himself not only of a useful and helpful working force but also of the skills and talents of the parish community. It is one thing for a pastor to decide what is good for his flock. It is another for the flock to take counsel with the pastor for what is good for them. So often one hears the complaint of pastors that this or that activity or parish function has not received the support he expected from his parishioners. Or one often hears complaints about money—usually the lack of it. It is possible in such matters that if the parish community had had a say in deciding what activities or functions it were willing and interested in supporting, the problem would fall not so much on the pastor's shoulders as on the parish community (of which the pastor is the leader). Likewise, if the parishioners had a say in deciding how much money would be spent and for what purposes, they would have a sense of personal interest and commitment in seeing to it that enough money and support were available. It is one thing to give money for the pastor's objectives; it is another to give money and support to a project for which I am in part responsible.

In the current university turmoil, students are clamoring to be heard, to have a voice in the affairs of the university. Often enough, they have to find a cause about which they can clamor. The choice of causes does not always seem significant or inspiring—but the underlying message is clear enough. The basic attitude of a university administrator is of central importance. He may see students as rabble-rousing, trouble-making adolescents who are having difficulty growing up. Or he may see them as an important source of creative energy and imaginative adaptation for the university community. The point of view has always persisted in the educational system that students come to school to be educated, and it is the business of educators to educate them. The options on what is to be taught and by whom were matters to be decided by educated men—not by ignorant students. This keeps the lines of authority clear and unambiguous. But it not only misconstrues the reality of the situation; it distorts the nature of the educational process. Education, particularly at the undergraduate level, is a matter of formation as well as information. It is a matter of dialogue and stimulation of ideas rather than merely passive assimilation. Students must be actively involved in the educational process. To expect students to become actively involved without allowing participation and commitment to the university as a community is to ask the impossible.

The other important aspect concerns what it is that students have to contribute to the university. To say "Nothing!" is to ignore some important social realities. The university is not merely an academic ivory tower in which learning is preserved by scholars and communicated to those who wish to submit themselves to its discipline. The university is deeply enmeshed in the influences and concerns of the community at large. The culture of the community—a term which embraces needs, demands, values, attitudes, and objectives— is continually evolving. In order to remain relevant the university must also evolve. That evolution requires a constant feeding in of information in an ongoing process of feedback control. Such control is necessary to give the university and the educational system of which it is a part a sense of direction and bearing. The age segment of the community which is represented by the students is one of the major forces for the generation of cultural change in our society. It is a segment that must be listened to, that will be listened to whether anybody else likes it or not. The current campus turmoil is part of the process by which this segment of the community is getting itself listened to.

The confrontation within the university is substantially a confrontation of values. The values embedded in the university structure, which characterize its mode of functioning, stem from a shared consensus of standards of a previous generation. Those values were the products of an historical and cultural process of great complexity. The historical and cultural context has changed, and a new generation is forming new values, new attitudes, new beliefs. They are divergent and must be so. If there were not a generation gap, at least in this regard, we would have to be concerned for the vitality of our culture and society. So there must be confrontation and there is! The important question is whether there can in addition be dialogue, mutual modulation, regulation, and eventual integration of divergent value systems. The process is never static, but always dynamic and open-ended. Students are creating new values. These can be seen as disruptive and destructive, but they can also be seen as breathing new life into what has gone before.

Erik Erikson has written with admirable perception that:

> It is for adult man to provide content for the ready loyalty of youth, and worthy objects for its need to repudiate. As cultures, through graded training, enter into the fiber of young individuals, they also absorb into their lifeblood the rejuvenative power of youth. Adolescence is thus a vital regenerator in the process of social evolution; for youth selectively offers its loyalties and energies to the conservation of that which feels true to them and to the correction or destruction of that which has its regenerative significance.[3]

The business community is no exception to this general law of generations. A new generation of young, university-trained executives brings, with its complement of technologically sophisticated skills, a new awareness and a new social consciousness and conscience.

There is an awareness of social problems and a desire for social responsibility that young people want to implement in their personal lives and in their work. They no longer accept corporate incentives and values. Doing a good job and making a living is no longer enough. They want to feel that their work has an impact on social processes and social issues. This brings a new and vitalizing set of values to bear on the values extant in a business organization. It means that corporate procedures may well be entering a new era in which social responsibilities and social commitment will become a vital focus of business enterprise.

The problem of the role of the superior in these areas is as clearly stated as in any other. It is a problem of leadership. It is up to the leader to find a way to establish dialogue, to bring divergent segments of the community together in meaningful and constructive interaction. Leadership cannot be conservative and reactionary or repressive without vacating its leadership function. Unfortunately this has happened to some extent. The vacuum of leadership has created the circumstances in which new forces of leadership are being generated from the community. Part of the campus problem, then, is the failure of legitimate authority to exercise its responsible leadership. One might suggest that the direction of effective leadership lies more toward utilization and integration of the powerful motivational forces that have been loosed rather than in their repression and exclusion.

## Autonomy

The ultimate issue from the point of view of the superior's exercise of authority is that of respect for the dignity and intrinsic personal authority of those who are his subjects. If the superior regards them as incapable of responsibility, then all responsible action must rest in his own hands. If, however, he is capable of maintaining a proper estimate of and respect for the responsible autonomy of all members of the community, it becomes possible for responsible action to arise elsewhere. The optimal milieu arises when at each level of the structure of the community responsible action is both impeded and spontaneously accepted. This state of affairs cannot be legislated or compelled into existence. It will arise spontaneously where it is given the opportunity to come to life. Insofar as the superior is in a more or less unique position in this regard, the realization of it depends in large measure on the extent to which he gives it opportunity. He does so by mature acceptance and fulfillment of his proper responsibilities as they take shape through the evolution of role-expectations which enunciate his own area of responsible action. His functioning in that position gives the authority structure a stability which allows the other exercisers of responsible action to mutually define their respective positions and expectations to fill out the rest of the system. The superior must depend in a sense on the estimate of personal dignity and worth that he accords his community as individuals and as a functioning group.

While there is much written these days about subsidiarity, delegation of authority, and sharing by the community in the decision-making process, it is my feeling that there is something more basic and fundamental which underlies these organizational approaches and without which they are doomed to frustration. True subsidiarity can be realized only as an offshoot of mature acceptance of personal responsibility and only insofar as real autonomy is achieved by superior and subjects alike. We can speak here of an inner authority which belongs to every man and which serves as the basis for his social participation in the authority relation. That inner authority derives from and reflects the maturity and mastery of his own personality. He becomes capable of the mutual regulation and meaningful interaction of the authority relation insofar as he is capable of inner mastery and autonomous action.

It may seem as though the complexities and intricacies of the superior's role defy accomplishment. It is true that it would be most difficult, if not impossible, to accomplish what I have set forth. The point is, however, that this is not a matter of accomplishment at all. It is a matter of human reaction and interaction. Mature men, acting intelligently and responsibly in a spirit of mutual respect and charity, tread this path more or less automatically. Maturity, respect for the other fellow, recognition of the inherent dignity of one's subjects, acceptance and recognition of the autonomy of each and every subject, these are all casual accompaniments of the person who has developed and brings with him to the superior's office a sense of his own identity and a sense of authentic relatedness to his fellowman. Without effort or strain, he is capable of autonomy, of trust, of responsible action.

It is appropriate here, perhaps, to make an important point. I am not one of those who believe with Rousseau that the less authority one sees the better. Authority is an important and necessary constituent of human social life. Authority, conceived as a relation with its concomitant interactions, is a stabilizing force in human life which supports the ego in its attempts to maintain inner stability in the face of instinctual threat. Authority provides a social structure which regulates individual expression and reinforces the capacity for autonomous action which is required for the stabilization of inner autonomy. It provides the necessary social regulations which make individual free action possible, since real individual freedom is correlative with real personal autonomy, both internal and external. In short, human beings are not saddled with authority. They need it in order to participate as fully human beings in a social system.

Thus, the authority relation directly consolidates external autonomy and indirectly consolidates internal autonomy. It has the highly specific function of maximizing both order and freedom. Authority directs itself to the achievement of the maximum of order consistent with a maximum of freedom. It is constantly preoccupied with the concerns of both these political goods, whether its concern is projected in terms of large political groups or small community groups. In a more profound and less obvious sense, authority likewise directs itself to the maximization of both order and freedom in the intrapsychic realm. We have seen already that the intrapsychic and the extrapsychic bear some interesting relations and parallelisms. The authority relation has important functions in the intrapsychic integration of those institutions of the mind which are responsible for intrapsychic order. I refer to those structures of the mental apparatus which contribute to the ordering of experience, the ordering of inner mental processes, the ordering of affective experience and which maintain consistency and organization in the interests of adaptation. There will be opportunity to discuss this concept more appropriately elsewhere. But the function of authority also extends itself to the support and reinforcement of the capacity of these same mental institutions to integrate their respective functions to achieve maximal autonomy and the capacity for independent self-determination and self-direction. This latter capacity comes close to what we are inclined to call freedom.

It is apparent then that the role of the superior or the bearer of authority has far-reaching implications for the functioning of the community and for its participating members. This is relevant for any social system, but its relevance for the religious group where the group life and the impact of authority are so extensive and so central is of considerable import. If one cannot say with any great assurance what a superior should do in order to be a good superior, one is at least entitled to hope that good men, well motivated and unencumbered by the impediments of infantile dependencies and conflicts, may profit themselves and their communities by their growing awareness of the implications and mechanisms by which their less obvious, indeed often unconscious, influence is extended.

## The Role of Superior in the Authority Relation

It is often difficult to bring the complex of qualities which characterize the superior's role in the authority relation into any kind of focus. It is a difficult role which varies considerably in emphasis and function in its many analogous contexts. The superior is the bearer of authority, but his authority is an authority based in and derived from the relation.

I have recently been working as a psychiatrist in an open ward of a mental hospital. In that position I was responsible for the combined therapy and administration of a number of severely disturbed, mentally ill patients. This meant that I not only had to carry on treatment of these patient's illnesses, which required intensive psychotherapy, but that I was also responsible for deciding what restrictions they would be put under, what privileges they could enjoy, whether they could eat in the cafeteria or not, whether they could leave the ward and under what conditions, whether they could leave the hospital and for how long, etc. I was, in short, responsible for a large number of decisions which had a profound effect on the patient's life. I was in a position of very nearly absolute authority, and the patient had to submit to that authority in order to gain the benefit of continued treatment. I was not particularly aware of it as I went through the experience, but as soon as I began to reflect on the authority relation, I became aware that all the complexities and subtleties of the authority relation were embedded in those relationships. The patients and I were caught up in a very intense way in an authority relation. As far as the formalities went, the structure of the situation was unambiguous. The authority was mine and not the patient's. The decision-making was mine and not the patient's. But in the working out of decisions the process was quite different. It was conditioned first of all by the fact that there was a relationship between us. The relationship was in its own way personal. It was friendly to the extent that such professional relationships can be friendly. I liked the patients. I was concerned for their welfare. What I communicated to them was a sense of concern, interest, helpfulness, a sense of commitment to what was in their best interests—regardless of their resistance to it or unwillingness to accept it. I also think that I communicated a willingness to listen, a conviction that what they felt and had to say was somehow important. Implicit in that was a deep respect for them as persons and an acknowledgment of their inherent dignity as human beings. Regardless of the formal structure of the situation, there was an implicit operative principle that no decisions were going to be made, no course of action followed, until they had had their say, until their concerns and anxieties had been heard and recognized, until their point of view had been listened to and taken into account.

The decision-making process was irrevocably mine. But in such a relationship the decision-making that I had to do was carried out in a context of collaboration. Decisions were never made arbitrarily or one-sidedly. They were, whenever and wherever possible, discussed, explored, considered together. The patient was never left out; he was always listened to, consulted with. There were, of course, times when decisions had to be made quickly and consultation was impossible. Patients could tolerate such exceptions because they were exceptions. They knew and understood that circumstances prevented the usual dialogue, but they also knew that any decision affecting them or the ward community was always open to discussion and reconsideration at any time. They also knew from the context of all other discussions and decisions that the decision was in the hands of someone they trusted, someone who was committed to their welfare and well-being.

There were also decisions that had to be made in the face of bitter and vociferous opposition on the patient's part. This was particularly true of adolescent patients. There were some direct, angry confrontations with several of my adolescent patients which they and I now recall with a sort of humorous reminiscence. But such decisions were always discussed, always kept open for reconsideration. It was clear both to me and to the patients that the decision-making was my responsibility and that I would exercise it according to my best judgment. I felt very strongly about that responsibility and never sidestepped it. The patients knew that and respected it. There was a certain consolation and security in the fact that they could rely on me to make a responsible judgment when it needed to be made. They were in this regard a little like children who need the security of knowing that a caring parent will prevent them from doing what may be harmful to them. This would have been impossible unless they knew that I cared about what happened to them, and unless they could trust me to be responsible even when they could not.

When I say that the relationship provided a context for dialogue, I mean that very seriously. Part of the objective of the relationship was to enable people who were unable to accept and exercise mature responsibility in their lives to begin to take responsibility for what they thought, felt, and did. The formal structure was such that it removed all responsibility from the patients and was therefore essentially infantilizing. But the concrete real relationship was quite the opposite. It carried within it a constant invitation and stimulus to increasing maturity and responsibility. The patient was invited to speak his attitudes and feelings and to share them. The very invitation in the context of such a dialogue was at the same time an invitation to objectify, evaluate, compare, and reflect on his own position. He was forced to take responsibility for it. He was forced to look at it objectively and evaluate its relative immaturity. There was a pervading invitation to make it more mature and more responsible. That dynamism was sustained by my own willingness to listen, consider, and take into account what the patient had to offer. The patient had little choice but to move gradually and often imperceptibly toward greater objectivity, greater realism, and greater maturity. But that movement would not have taken place if I, as the other participant in the dialogue, had not been committed to taking seriously and respectfully what he had to say. If I had not taken his opinions as a real contribution to a basis for forming my own judgment, the exercise would have been empty and meaningless.

There had to be a delicate balance in the relationship. There had to be an inherent respect for the patient's present capacity for responsible action and an acknowledgment and respect for his personal autonomy and freedom. That had to be balanced by a sense of the patient's limitation and need, of his immaturity and irresponsibility. Even when the former had to yield to the exigencies of the latter, there was always operative an implicit expectation that the patient would act more maturely and more responsibly. The expectation was generated in part by my own expectations of myself that I act with maturity and responsibility. The patients came to expect it of me also, but in so doing they could not avoid generating the same expectation of themselves as participants in the dialogue. Responsibility for me sometimes came to the point of making unilateral decisions. For them, it sometimes came to accepting and abiding by such decisions. There is a curious chemistry in such relations. Responsibility begets responsibility.

I am proposing my experience as a sort of paradigm of what the authority relation comes to be. It displays, I think, most if not all of the elements that characterize the authority relation wherever it exists. The relation is not univocal; the elements are displayed analogously in different contexts. Many contexts of authority are less personal, less involved, more task-oriented and formal. The relationship between officer and soldiers in the armed services would certainly be quite different. Or the relationship between a bishop and his priests would be something else again. Whatever the context, the elements are there in some degree, and the balance must be worked out on its own terms.

But I sincerely hope that the reflection on my own experience will bring into somewhat better focus the role, the attitudes, the values, and the overall stance of the one who serves as superior. To be a superior is to enter into a relationship with other human beings. To be a good superior is to exercise one's own responsibility in such a way that others who share that relationship are brought to exercise their responsibilities as well. That is, indeed, very close to a definition of leadership.

*Chapter 11*

# The Role of Subject

I would like to take up some of the implications of the role of subject. The consideration of this role touches on a variety of substantial issues, and it occurs to me that material which is quite pertinent to the consideration of the role of subject is scattered through almost every section of this present work. I will try at this point, however, to bring some of the essential aspects of the subject role into focus and thereby clarify some of the issues related to subjecthood. I have the feeling that it is no less important for the understanding of the workings of authority to form a conception of the subject's role than to have a clear conception of the workings of the superior's role. The latter is in some ways easier to accomplish in that superiors are much in the limelight, and the implications of their performance is at once more apparent and more available for criticism. The subject role tends to remain somewhat obscure and is certainly accorded less attention in general. If the conception of authority which we have been in labor to bring forward in these pages has any impact, it must be that the concrete working of authority is as much a function of one of the reciprocal roles as of the other.

## Distribution of Authority

One of the implications of the authority relation is that authority is inherent in every individual and in every member of a community.

This authority is derivative from and therefore correlative with the individual's inner maturity and capacity for responsible action. Authority is resident in the individual in virtue of his participation in the authority relation. Authority is also exercised in and through the community. We must have in mind both an existential authority on the individual level and a communal authority on the level of group consensus when we speak of subjecthood. Subjecthood, then, is a form of authority, and when we come to speak of responsible subjecthood we are speaking of an important form of the exercise of authority.

One of the overriding problems in dealing with the problem of authority is that we are traditionally lacking in any formulation or model for the authority of subjecthood. Traditional models of authority leave no room for it since they tend to aggregate all authority into the role of the superior. But just as we were faced with the correlative problem of evolving a conception of the role of superior which answers meaningfully to the connotations of authority as relation, so we are also faced with the problem of forming a concept of the role of subject which brings the inherent authority into clearer focus.

It is immediately apparent that traditional modes of conceptualizing formal authority had a marked imbalance built into them. There was no sense of the balance and interplay of multiple sources of authority. Authority was resident in one locus in the group structure and was to be sought nowhere else. There was no consideration of the possibility of distributed authority in the group. The reason, of course, was that the concept of authority was essentially univocal and based on a theological model according to which all authority derived from a single source. The model was also substantially monarchial in structure. The implicit assumption, however, was that the bases of authority were not to be sought in men but in offices. And by further implication, this conception of authority rests on the basic immaturity of those participating. Decisions, direction, and responsible action could not be permitted except in the hands of the superior, who alone could be regarded as mature.

It is also apparent that as soon as we move off the basis of the more formal aspects of authority and begin to think in terms of the exercise of authority, we are confronted by entirely different problems. Mature men do have a capacity for independent thought and decision. The capacity of maturity carries with it a fundamental human right to be taken into account, to be listened to, to undertake and share responsibilities, to initiate independent action, and to share in some sense in the decisions and actions that affect and pertain to oneself. This fundamental right has always been present and operative. It has also been recognized implicitly in traditional formulations of authority in terms of a persistent respect for the inviolability of conscience. But its status is unquestionably incidental. It has never come into focus as an integral part of the notion of authority itself.

It seems apparent that the contemporary world is witnessing an upsurge of a demand for the recognition of such authority. It permeates religious life and the life of the Church. There is a growing willingness on the part of subjects to judge independently and to accept the responsibility for their own judgments and actions. There is a growing force in the Church which is forcing a gradual decentralization of authority and its exercise. The voice of the layman is being heard with ever greater clarity and emphasis. These are authoritative forces which are assuming larger portions of the burden of explicit and formal authority, but even more importantly are having an incalculable influence on the patterns of the exercise of authority.

The same urgent demand is being heard in almost all segments of modern society. It is being heard clearly on the campuses, where students are demanding to be listened to, to be taken into account, to be given a voice in the making of decisions that have to do with matters that affect them and their lives. It is being heard in the civil rights and Negro movements in this country. People are willing to take to the streets and demonstrate for what they feel to be their right. They will demonstrate nonviolently as long as there is some hope of accomplishing something by nonviolent means. And they will demonstrate violently when it becomes clear in the face of intransigence and a reactionary clinging to the status quo that their demands will not be met. Whatever else may be legitimately or illegitimately embodied in the demands that are being heard in so many segments of our society, there is at root the demand to be acknowledged, to have a say in the direction of events. The demand is being made in many ways and with many voices for a place to be given to that fundamental right of mature and free men—to have a meaningful voice in the determination of decisions and actions that pertain to oneself and one's own interest.

To many this pattern of events may seem to have the face of revolt against authority. To see it in these terms is to fail to perceive what lies beneath it and what motivates it. The contemporary unrest over authority has more the shape of an attempt to redress the imbalance of more traditional authority structures and to bring into proper emphasis the other bases of authority in its existential sense which are in fact operative in the social structure. Authority structures in our time are undoubtedly in evolution. Rigid adherence to the older conceptions of authority has become an archaism, but the archaism is in many ways unavoidable. The fact remains that the working forms of authority are not really sufficiently clarified to permit secure adjustment. Authority, after all, as we have observed any number of times, has specific intrapsychic functions in allaying anxiety and stabilizing inner autonomy and control of basic instinctual drives. The flux in authority structures loosens that stabilizing influence and creates new anxieties. The attempt to deal with such anxieties will undoubtedly lead many to fall back on the security of clearer and more comfortable modes of the exercise of authority. But the fact remains that forces are at work which will not permit such outmoded models to function with the same reassurance as in a former day. The movement of evolving structures, therefore, creates its own archaisms. Given the mature capacity to tolerate the unavoidable anxieties, the better course would seem to be that of trying to evolve a more refined and inclusive notion of authority which is more responsive to contemporary demands and at the same time more consistent with persistent notions of human dignity and Christian responsibility.

With the emergence of broader bases of authority, the importance of communication for the viability of the community becomes increasingly apparent. Effective communication is not merely a matter of establishing more or less formalized and institutionalized means of communication between levels of the group structure. The imbalance of authority actually impedes communication, sometimes to the detriment of superior, subjects, and community. Meaningful communication becomes possible only in a group structure in which the balance of interacting authorities is achieved. Only when truly autonomous individuals are interacting in the context of the authority relation is the free flow of information feasible. Such operative autonomy implies mutual respect, trust, and the capacity for independent thought and judgment. Otherwise, the relationship tends to an imbalance of domination and submission, and automatic screening devices are set in operation which distort the channels of communication. One cannot ignore the fundamental reality that communication will not take place unless the essential bases for it are in existence.

## Responsible Subjecthood

The problem that we face is essentially one of defining what I propose to call responsible subjecthood. In a way, responsible subjecthood is merely looking at the authority relation from the other end— responsible superiorship. But it is not simply that. Responsible subjecthood is a reflection of responsible selfhood. It arises out of the inner matrix of mature personality functioning. It requires a sense of basic trust which permits the individual to have a sense of his own inner capacity for trustworthy action and to be capable of placing trust in the decisions of others which may play upon his own interests and actions. It requires in a unique sense the development of basic autonomy. Autonomy and responsibility in this context are almost synonymous. The responsibility of responsible subjecthood merely emphasizes the esssential role of inner autonomy in the interplay of the subject with the other sources of authority around him. He must be capable of independence in thought and action, and his response to the demands of authority must display that capability. His response must take place in terms of an inner set of values, convictions, and judgments which are uniquely his. Otherwise, responsibility is abandoned, and we are left with mere submission.

Responsible subjecthood makes an important contribution to the stability of authority structures in terms of its capacity to accept its proper responsibility. As we have noted previously, the distribution of authority in any group is worked out by the ongoing process of authoritative interaction. The superior's role is undoubtedly of greater import in this regard because his acceptance and exercise of that extension of authority appropriate to his role and function affects all portions of the group. However, the individual's acceptance of his own due measure of responsibility contributes to the clarification of responsible participation among the members and conjointly sets the real limits of role expectations for the superior's exercise of authority. From another point of view, the failure of any individual member of the group to realize his own area of expected responsibility upsets the balance of authoritative interaction in the group and creates the imbalance of authority that issues in increasing tension and conflict. This is equally applicable whether the failure to realize individual responsibility comes through deficit or through excess. The balance of interaction is upset when the individual fails to fill his authoritative quota or when he exceeds that quota. Both submission and domination at whatever level in the social organization are violations of responsible subjecthood.

## Responsibility

I would like to place certain emphases on the respective parts of the concept. It is not altogether a simple matter to spell out the implications of responsibility in relation to subjecthood. In more traditional approaches there is detectable a tendency to limit the subject's responsibility to carrying out the superior's directives. This is really an avoidance of responsibility as we are proposing it. Responsibility is met in concrete terms when the individual's response affirms his own inner sense of identity and autonomy. Responsibility affirms the reality of the self. Where this inner sense is uncertain, the sense of self-identity is compromised, and the individual is caught up in conflict. Where man is caught up in conflict, he is able neither to act autonomously nor freely. He becomes to that extent a pawn manipulated by external forces or driven by inner needs beyond his control.

The sense of responsibility implies the readiness of the subject to undertake what is directed by the superior, but the readiness is based on something more complex than that the superior has imposed this directive. It is based more complexly on the implicit willingness of the subject to endorse, ratify, accept what is directed, and to initiate an action to which he has autonomously and unconstrainedly set himself. Responsibility will not tolerate mere passivity or conformity. It calls for personal initiative to that which is directed. The underlying mechanism which erects the basis for this kind of responsible activity is identification. Through immediate identification with the source of the directive, the subject can perceive the directive not as something that is imposed from a foreign source, but as coming from an origin that is not only not alien but is seen as intimately related to, if not as psychologically part of, himself. Superior and subject share in an alliance based on mutual values and shared interests. Through identification with the source of the directive in a more indirect manner, the subject can accept the directive insofar as he recognizes it as reflecting the basic values of the community. Through identification, the individual participates in the common value system of the community. He sees the directive as related to, or as expressing the value system. It should be remembered that the effect of identification in the individual is spelled out in terms of intrapsychic structure. The sense of identification is enhanced insofar as the individual to whom the directive is given is able to feel that he has had an active share in the decision by which the directive was originated. The ultimate benefit of democratization and broadening the basis of decision making (in the sense of shared decision making) is that it lends valuable support to the tendencies to identification on which the authority relation is based.

I have said that responsibility implies activity and personal initiative. Responsible subjecthood, therefore, can independently initiate meaningful action. It need not, and often must not, wait for the superior's directive in order to act. It must be willing to act independently and to initiate courses of action, even with the risk of disapproval or opposition from superiors. The opposite side of the coin, of course, is the necessity of a capacity in the superior to tolerate initiative even in the face of the unavoidable anxieties it generates. The overall safeguard for the anxieties which arise in autonomous and initiating action is again the identifications which weld individual, superior, and group into a shared system of values. The shared dimension of individual and group values guarantees to a point the consistency of individual initiative and group goals.

There is undeniably a risk which is covered by no operative mechanisms, conscious or unconscious. Individual commitment to a project or a course of action may come into conflict with group goals or with explicit directives of superiors. The possibilities are many. It behooves us to keep in mind that the divergency is not always easy to locate. When conflict arises, it somehow seems easier to presume that the initiative of the subject is divergent. The superior, however, may find that his directive is not consistent with the consensus of the group. The rebelling subject may, then, be expressing an implicit position of the group. It is the superior in these circumstances who is divergent. It is the part of responsible subjecthood to maintain that aspect of inner autonomy which enables the subject to recognize the autonomy of other individuals, including the superior, as well as the autonomy which belongs to the group itself. If the subject tries to impose his initiative on the superior or on the group, he violates his measure of authority and is acting irresponsibly rather than responsibly. It is often difficult to appreciate this aspect of responsibility. The path of responsibility lies along a route on which one's own personal autonomy does not interfere with the autonomy of other group members nor of the group itself. Responsibility means that one's own personal initiative does not interfere with the initiative of others or of the group. Yet true responsibility must be capable of autonomy and initiative in the face of group pressures and pressure from superiors.

These remarks prompt a pertinent and important observation in regard to several of the antiauthority movements we have been discussing. I have particularly in mind the student revolt and the black power movement, although these remarks are obviously applicable on other fronts. I have been stressing consistently what I feel to be the positive and constructive aspects of these efforts. But there are also less constructive and less positive aspects. My impression has often been that the participants in these movements have been less responsible than they might. There are obviously reasons for this state of affairs, not the least of which, as I have indicated elsewhere, is the ultimate failure of responsibility in existent authority structures. But from the point of view of the subject role, it seems clear that the excesses that have often marred the course of both these movements, particularly where force and violence have been called into play, have infringed upon the autonomy of other individuals and of the community. It seems clear that student rebels have violated their own measure of inherent authority and the autonomy of other students and faculty members and administrators. They have imposed their own initiatives on other segments of the university community, and in general have acted quite irresponsibly. There is little wonder, then, that such tactics bring about the spectacle of armed police and troops in the groves of academia.

The situation is considerably less clear in the black power movement. Again, the failure of responsibility has been on many sides—government, business, the churches, education, the unions, and other segments of society—as well as in the black movement itself. The excesses are obvious and the irresponsibility at times overwhelming. It is hard for us to know what the course of responsible action might be. It is all the more difficult for those who are caught up in it and torn by the powerful emotions born of want, deprivation, prejudice, and hate. The key question, it seems to me, is whether a minority has the right to violate the rights of a majority and under what conditions. Does the minority have a right to place a demand on the majority which will limit the rights of the majority in virtue of a situation of deprivation and injustice to which the minority is subject? Does the majority, in turn, have an obligation to surrender some of its own prerogatives to balance an injustice which affects the minority? In discussing the black movement, are we discussing a situation in which irresponsible demands are being foisted on the community? Or are we dealing with a situation in which mutually interlocking irresponsibilities in all segments of the community have led responsible Negro action in the direction of disruption and violation of the rights of others?

The argument that I have been advancing makes it clear that the preferred course of action is that which maximizes responsible action not only in the subject but also in the superior. It presumes that the authority relation can be established and that the parties involved can act with reciprocating responsibility. But what is the role of responsible subjecthood when those conditions break down, when responsibility is not met with responsibility but with irresponsibility? Does the subject have a responsibility to accept and support the values of his community when those values reinforce prejudice against him and work injustice against him?

It is easy to take a stand in favor of responsible action as long as one is not forced to decide what the course of responsible action is. My own perception of the matter is that there is a middle way which avoids the irresponsible alternatives of passive compliance or violent overthrow. The black community followed the former course for several hundred years. In the contemporary setting it seems inclined to follow the latter course. Both are irresponsible because they surrender the fundamental authority of the mature black man and the black community. The reasonable course is for that authority to assert itself in meaningful and constructive terms. This means organization and effective leadership within the black community. It is noteworthy that the black community has shown itself capable of such effort, and the effort has brought about significant legal action as well as some initial steps toward economic betterment. The excesses must be avoided. They are destructive on all sides, including that which is in the interest of the black community itself. But the Negro must be listened to; he must be heard; he must assert himself in meaningful ways into the dialogue of contemporary society. He must take upon himself the rights and responsibilities of a significant base of authority within the structure of the community, and he must bring that authority inherent in himself as a mature and responsible human being and in the structure of the black community into active participation and dialogue with other loci of authority in the community at large.

The perspective on subject responsibility must, therefore, be multiple. The subject's responsibility is to himself, to the group and, in religious life, to an order of authority. The latter issue is involved in the question of religious obedience, and I propose to take that subject up separately. Responsible effort is constantly involved in balancing the various aspects of its commitment. The subject does indeed carry a responsibility to accept, support, and participate in the value system of the community. His sense of responsibility also requires adherence to his own inner and personal system of values. These are optimally not in conflict. But conditions are not always optimal. There may be conflict in varying degrees. Nor need the conflict ever be wholly resolved. There is a certain degree of conflict-born tension which serves the forces of value change and evolution as well as the vitality of group processes. It is a measure of the vitality and viability of the group that it is capable of tolerating a certain spectrum of variation in the values of its members. The spectrum of variability is enlarged by the responsible participation of the members whose inner value structure is sufficiently flexible and tolerant to permit interaction with divergent values in the shared action of the group.

The whole issue of subject responsibility in contemporary terms is caught up in the tension between responsibility for oneself and one's actions and subjection to the demands of authority. The perennial tension has a new intensity which derives from the growing awareness in contemporary thought of the significance of the person and the implications of his inherent freedom. More and more the climate is evolving in which structures and institutions of social organization are regarded as historical products of man's free creative initiative and energy. The static modality is giving way to the dynamic and evolutionary mode of conception. Traditional patterns are not absolute God-given entities but human accomplishments with a history and an ongoing development. The contemporary mind does see itself as responsible for its own actions and life. Responsibility is no longer limited to a narrow area of conformity to pre-existent patterns and institutions. Personal responsibility has acquired a broadened perspective. Contemporary man is responsible as well for the very patterns and processes to which and by which he adjusts. Initiative and creative renovation reaching out to touch all dimensions of human experience are the contemporary stuff of responsibility.

It remains, therefore, that mere passivity in the presence of authoritative demands is a refusal of responsibility. The obedience which a subject shows to the claims of legitimate authority must be critical, questioning, and evaluative. Obedience is a dialogue in which superior and subject are engaged in a process of mutual regulation and identification. The subject's response to a given directive calls for a reaction which involves a decision. The subject's choice is to cooperate or not to cooperate; his decision is never a submission in any passive sense. This places a considerably greater burden on the subject, who thereby assumes the responsibility for his personal decision. Through his option to cooperate (to act coordinately) or not to cooperate, he also assumes a measure of responsibility for the good of the community.

It is a part of the subject's responsibility that he make his encounter with the superior a creative one so that something emerges from the meeting which neither could in his own right bring about. There is a line between construction and destruction which is often difficult to draw except in retrospect. The impulse to independence is too easily perverted into mere rebelliousness. But rebelliousness, kindled by hostility and resentment, is destructive. Rebellion may even be a hostile response to the more subtle and devastating destructiveness of authoritarian control. This is an area in which objective judgment is crippled by an abundance of obscurities. The test lies ultimately in the individual's sense of mature responsibility, not only to himself, not only to his obligations as subject to obey, but also to the common benefit of the community.

## Subjecthood

So much for the aspect of responsibility in responsible subjecthood. Let us turn now to the other aspect, that of subjecthood. It is not as easy to speak of subjecthood, since the temper of the times is considerably more concerned with matters pertaining to individuality and responsible action. We are somehow more willing to lend an ear to the claims of individuals on the community. We are at the same time reluctant to concern ourselves with the claims of the community on individuals. But it remains true that the development of responsible subjecthood, both conceptually and actually, requires us to temper subjection with responsibility and responsibility with subjection. The role of subject is highly complex. Ultimately the subject cannot realize a mature responsibility without keeping in perspective his essential subjection to legitimate authority within the group structure.

The first important emphasis, I think, is that subjection is to be thought of less as a state than as a process. The subject is, indeed, subjected. But it is infinitely more important that the subject be seen as subjecting himself. He is subjected by no other. The traditional analyses of authority started from the perspective of subject as subjected, rather than from the perspective of subject as subjecting. The individual is the author of his own subjection. Nor does the process by which subjection comes about terminate at some point where subjection is achieved and finalized. Subjection always retains an active sense. Subjection is a continuing subjecting of oneself to the claims of legitimate authority. Or, to put it another way, subjection is a continuing process of relating oneself to an authoritative source in an order of subordination. This emphasis is important insofar as it underlines the origin of the authority relation in the dynamic engagement and creative participation of individuals. It also enunciates the necessity for individuals to persist in that continuing subjection in order that the structure of authority perdure.

Individuals enter or commit themselves to membership in a community more or less voluntarily. This is particularly applicable to the religious community, in which membership is entirely and elaborately a matter of personal election. The prolongation of membership, however, does not derive from the persistence of an immutable state. It depends on a persisting choice which extends and deepens the original decision. Thus, the subject is responsible for his own subjecthood and for its persistence. Since he is responsible for his own subjecthood, he is also responsible for what is implied in that subjection and in that subjecthood. He is, therefore, responsible by extension to that to which he subjects himself. He becomes in the measure of his participation responsible for the values, structure, and action of the community. He becomes through his subjection an active focus of influence within the community. The values of the community are derivatively his values. The decisions of the community are derivatively his decisions. And the actions of the community are derivatively and ultimately his actions.

A second important, though difficult to accept, emphasis is that subjection implies subordination. Though the process of subjection carries within it the seeds of creative activity and responsibility, the controlling impulse must be tempered. The individual does not control the community. The community controls itself primarily. Individuals control the community only derivatively or secondarily. Individuals control only in and through the group. The objectives, purposes, and goals of the community, therefore, acquire a primacy to which individual objectives must acquiesce. Subjection, therefore, becomes a subjecting of oneself to the primacy of community goals. The superior's command, in this view, acquires its claim to obedience insofar as it presents to the individual the function he is to perform in order to serve the objectives of the community. The individual is subordinate to the community. He is also responsible for the community, for its purposes and for its goals. His subordination, therefore, is not simple. It is in reality a process of mutual regulation, a continuing dialogue of human intentions. Never can the subordination of the subject become mere submission to authority. To submit to what is commanded for no other reason than that it is commanded is to destroy the delicate balance of mutual regulation and abandon all responsibility. The authoritative command is essentially a call to subjection. Regardless of the particular content it communicates, it represents a summons to the subject to renew his subjection to the primacy of community goals.

## Relation to Community

It should be pointed out that the primacy of community goals is neither an absolute nor a static matter. All the goals of the community do not enjoy the same importance or significance. A trivial goal of the community does not have any claim to primacy over a significant goal of one of its members. But significant community objectives do have a claim to primacy over significant individual objectives. So it remains possible for concrete situations to arise in which the superior rightly asks for the obedient response of a subject when the obedient response is a great personal cost to the subject and may even be in direct opposition to his judgment and conviction. Insofar as the multiple mechanisms and processes involved in the authority relation —identification, mutual regulation, dialogue, etc.—are functioning effectively, the room for such value and goal conflicts is minimized. But it is never eliminated and never will be. The stirring of so much conflict and resentment under more traditional approaches lies in the circumstances in which the placing of the authoritative demand occurs. Where individuals are given no share in decision making, are given no play to their sense of responsible subjecthood, are presented in apparently arbitrary fashion with a demand which may have important consequences for their personal lives, when they are made to feel that they are voiceless victims of a process over which they exercise no control—all this is extremely threatening. It is productive of massive anxiety and forces the involved individuals to submission or revolt. Neither alternative is desirable. It seems reasonable that the development of community resources which enable the authority relation to mature and evolve also develops a climate within which such conflicts are minimized, and within which the emergence of the inevitable conflicts can be softened by the individual's underlying awareness that his due measure of participation and responsible involvement has not been violated. It is difficult to rebel against a decision for which one feels in part responsible.

It should be remembered that subjection and responsible subjecthood finds itself in a continuing dialogue with the role of superior which establishes an emerging alliance between them. The alliance has as its peculiar objective the building up of the community. More specifically, the alliance of subjecthood and superiorship is ordered to the realization of a maximal degree of freedom and order. There is a temptation to think of the function of authority as directed to the maintenance of order, and of the function of subjecthood as directed to the preservation of freedom as though these two functions were incompatible and had to be served by separate forces in the community. Such thinking is vertical. It sees the structure of the group only in vertical terms, as organized and functioning in terms of mere power and office. In the true spirit of community, authority and subjecthood are allied in the fostering of freedom in order along with order in freedom. Subjection seeks to support and contribute to order insofar as it involves subordination. It preserves and substantiates freedom in the community insofar as it remains active and creative. The subject, therefore, shares with the superior the fundamental and primary responsibility for the dialogue on which the community is sustained and grows. Superior and subject are both responsible for the ultimate balance of freedom and order in the community. The responsibility is shared and cannot be aggregated to one or the other exclusively.

There is another aspect of subjecthood which is worth emphasizing. Subjection and subjecthood serve a unitive function as well. In subjecting himself to the community the subject joins himself to the community in a particular fashion. He recognizes the community, and in reciprocal response the community recognizes him. This provides an important though often unregarded dimension of the interaction between individual and community. The individual's self-recognition is related to his community's recognition of him. In that interaction, he gains a sense of his own identity and continuity of self as part of a community of agents. Thus, participation in the authority relation plays a role in the forming and stabilizing of patterns of inner self-perception which underlie the sense of personal identity so necessary for maturity of function. Identity, as Erikson has so often pointed out, is dependent on a perception of self along with a perception of self through the response of others. "A community's ways of identifying the individual, then, meet more or less successfully the individual's ways of identifying himself with others."[1] Underlying and completing the individual's subjection there is the more unconscious level of identification by which the individual presents an identity to the community and permits himself to be identified as belonging to the community. The processes are mutually dependent and ultimately serve the interests of both the individual who is identified and the community which identifies him. And in this process the community identifies the individual in two important and interrelated senses—it both recognizes the individual and in so doing gives him an identity.

## Development in Subjecthood

The capacity for communal identification and the participation in mature subjecthood is a human achievement. Man grows in subjecthood. Each person has a history and a development in subjecthood, and his present capacity to participate in that aspect of the authority relation is an expression of the residues of that historical development.

Man begins an exercise in subjecthood in the earliest moments of life. He begins life in circumstances of subjectedness. In his most primitive experience there is no differentiation of self and nonself. There is no recognition of those boundaries of bodily extension which define the borderline where self ends and other begins. The distinction between the infant's body and mother's breast is at first nonexistent. It must grow, at first diffusely and vaguely, then with gradually increasing differentiation and clarification under the influence of frustration of wishes and the need to delay gratifications. The infant begins life in subjecthood, but only gradually develops a subjective sense of subjecthood with his primitive and emergent sense of self and his relation to significant others.

In these first primitive relationships the issues of subjecthood are being worked out. The mother is the first important figure against whom and with whom the child defines himself in subjection. Beginning in that relation, based on and focused on oral needs and a primitive feeding and caring economy, the infant starts the long and intricate process of defining himself in relation to the more powerful and influential figures upon whom he must depend. The manner in which the issues of subjection and subjecthood are worked out in that first relation will have much to do with the child's later capacity to engage in analagous relationships with other important and powerful figures.

If he experiences the relationship of subjecthood in a climate of trust and implicit confidence in the loving constancy of the giving, loving, feeding mother, he learns the important lesson and receives the important impression of subjection without fear of deprivation or loss. Subjection, in its active sense, is a necessity urged by the circumstances of biology, but the quality of that experience is influenced by the quality of the relation between mother and child, by the degree of mutual regulation and responsiveness, by the implicit dimensions of trust. Where such qualities obtain, the child learns that he can subject himself to others, that he can enter a relation of dependence on important and powerful others, without sacrifice of self-esteem and self-integrity, and with a sense of confidence in and identification with the depended on figure.

The comforting and strengthening aspects of that relation undergo progressive definition and differentiation as the child matures and enters into relations with other important figures. The relationship with the father is most important here insofar as the father is viewed as an especially powerful figure in the chld's world and insofar as father is usually the major source of parental discipline. A fundamental aspect of this relation has to do with castration anxieties. The degree of castration anxiety is a function of the quality of the child's relation to the father, but it is also deeply influenced by the quality of his interaction with the mother as he emerges from that intimate subjection. If the maternal relation has been one of loving trust, the child's need to project his primitive destructiveness on the father is diminished and castration fears are less pressing.

Again the child has no recourse other than subjection to the father's authority, but the key question is whether he can learn to subject himself in this authority relation without fear of castration and loss. If the quality of the relation is such that subjection carries with it a burden of such fears, then identificatory processes are impaired and subjection becomes a matter of capitulation to powerful and potentially dangerous powers. The only recourse is placation of these forces by submission, or one can take the opposite course and struggle against them in rebellion and revolt. The father's demeanor in the exercise of his authority is paramount. His authoritarian and repressive stance will increase the measure of castration anxieties and reinforce the hostile and destructive aspects of the child's projection. His excessive permissiveness and lack of strength deprives the child of an important source of stability and external control. The child needs a firm and constant relation to paternal authority in order to internalize the authority which becomes the source of inner control that serves further developmental needs and tasks.

While the relations to the parents are of primary and lasting importance, the child's experience of relating to significant others is diversified as development progresses. His relations to other figures in the family should not be underestimated. He shares with siblings the common problem of relating to parental authority in a relation of subjecthood. He can learn from older brothers and sisters, and he can vicariously reexperience developmental problems in observing the interaction between parents and younger siblings. He can diversify his experience in relating to authority in his subjection to older siblings, who may exercise on occasion some portion of parental responsibility. He may also share in the exercise of such responsibility himself.

An important aspect of development in the experience of subjecthood is the emergence of a sense of selfhood and a correlative sense of responsibility to oneself and for oneself. As we have indicated in many places in this study, this aspect is of the utmost importance for the authority relation. The issues here can be grouped under the rubric of autonomy. The child must emerge from the infantile experiences of subjection to authority with self-esteem and with a sense of himself as active participant in interaction with authority figures. The achievement of a sense of autonomy finds its way between the alternatives of willfulness and will-less compliance. Only in the achievement of real autonomy does the child gain the competence to exercise responsible individuality as well as the capacity to commit himself to free subjection in an authority relation without violation of self or without violation of another. The rudiments of this capacity are laid down in parental authority relations and serve as a foundation on which subsequent experiences and interactions build. A crucial step in the process occurs in the resolution of oedipal engagements, for at this developmental phase the child achieves an internalized authority relation which serves as a source of inner authority and control. The sense of inner autonomy is intimately related to the inner capacity for self-regulation with its attendant release from dependence on the sources of external regulation and control. The processes of internalization and parental identification which build autonomy and the inner sense of personal authority are consolidated and refined by the child's broadening experience and the increasing demands for self-expression and the acceptance of responsibility—at first for himself and his actions and then in many ways for others around him. Such consolidation and extension are some of the primary developmental tasks of the latency period.

Only in the degree to which a sense of inner autonomy and responsibility are realized does the human organism develop a capacity for engagement in the life of community. Only if one is capable of accepting responsibility for oneself can one begin to accept responsibility for others and for a community of others. Thus, participation in the authority relation within the structure of a community is another developmental task which rehearses and extends the previous history and continuity of developmental tasks in the exercise of authority. It builds upon the previously evolved structures of inner authority and capacity for subjection and subjecthood. The individual's participation in subjection to the community rehearses and revives in its deepest unconscious implications the residues of subjection to the giving (or depriving) mother, to the confirming and supporting (or castrating) father, and to the whole of a prior history of the development of inner authority and of relatedness to external authority.

The psychology of subjecthood thus has a complicated history which parallels the furthest reaches of personal development. Moreover, it is constantly evolving and emerging through the course of life. Man can never remove himself from his relation to authority. He can never remove himself from the history of his relatedness to authority. Subjecthood is, in fact, a universal human condition.

There is undoubtedly much more that could be said to elucidate the role of the subject in the authority relation. In a sense, nothing we have said on other pages is really irrelevant to that concern. To be a subject, it turns out, is to define one's identity in the intimate context of community. It is to reach that inner balance of intrapsychic order and freedom which makes it possible for individuals to achieve in communal interaction the external balance of freedom and order toward which authority strives. It is a complex and difficult enterprise.

## Chapter 12

# Authority and Community

One emergent notion which has much to do with the workings of authority in the contemporary scene is that of community. More and more there is a tendency to think in terms of community organization, community structure, and community processes as we approach the problems of authority and its function in the group. More traditional approaches to authority and its problems did not find it necessary to have the community as an operative part of its conceptual scheme. Authority was conceived in terms of a separation of the locus of authority from the community, and the community itself was conceived only in terms of the action and reaction of individual persons of which it was the aggregate.

### Notion of Community

It is apparent that much of the preceding reflection is by way of a prelude to the notion of community. The community is indeed a group, and it functions with all the complexity of group processes. But to speak of community is also to speak of something more than group structures and processes. The notion of community underlies the breadth and depth of shared values which form the communal value system. Groups are of many and varied kinds, but a community is a perduring group whose members are members of the community by choice and commitment. Participation in the community embraces all aspects of the members' life and concern. The notion of community applies primarily to the family. This is the smallest and most intimate of human communities, but life in the family touches on all parameters of human needs and concerns. The notion of community applies also to the religious community, where participation in the community life embraces the fundamental parameters of living. The notion applies on a broader and more complex scale to the Church, which is the community of believers. And it applies as well in analogous ways to a variety of social structures in which significant human values are shared and communicated.

The emergence of the notion of community also points to the dynamic and active participation on the part of its members. Community implies an engagement and an interaction between each member and the group. By reason of this active ferment in the community, we must reckon with the contribution of these processes to the shaping of common values and the generation of authoritative structures within the community. It is this latter aspect which marks the somewhat radical divergence between traditional models of authority and contemporary community-derived or community-related models. All of this requires a rethinking of our notions of authority, obedience, and freedom. The Declaration on Religious Freedom of Vatican II, for example, enunciated a basic principle that the human person has the right to live out his relationship to God in freedom. He is guaranteed in this sense an inviolable zone of freedom which permits him to love and worship God as he sees fit, or not to love and worship if he sees fit. At the same time, the Christian experience is basically one of obedience to the authority of the Church. It is not clear how life in the Christian community is to be lived in freedom. What is the relation between authority and freedom in the Christian community?

## Authority and Freedom

As John Murray has pointed out, the contemporary imbalance of authority and freedom has its historical roots. For Leo XIII, the golden age was the age of Christian unity in which princes and people paid due obedience to the power and authority of the Church. The Reformation destroyed all of this, and in reaction to it the Church reaffirmed and emphasized anew its claims to authority. Who obeys the Church, obeys God. Who disobeys the Church, disobeys

God. The reaction, historically inevitable and quite justifiable, had the consequence of producing hypertrophy of the principle of authority, as well as atrophy of the principle of freedom. In addition, the civil and political structure of society saw the relation of ruler and ruled subjects simply in vertical terms. The ruled were merely subjects who had only one duty—to obey. Authority was derived from God; sovereignty was to be exercised paternalistically in imitation of the divine sovereignty. In turn, the submission of subjects was to be filial. The doctrine was plainly paternalistic and authoritarian—politically and historically embedded and appropriate to its context. It issued in a vision of the Christian community as vertically structured with ruler and ruled related only as those bearing divine authority and those submitting to it in simple obedience. Any notion of the dynamic process within the community as in any way pertinent was simply alien to this conception.

The traditional notion of the relation between freedom and authority was evolved in this conceptual context. The wielders of authority make decisions and produce directives; the subjects submit to these decisions and carry out the directives. Obedience is simply to do what the superior orders. Obedience is more perfect as the will of the subject comes to mirror the will of the superiors. The superior becomes the mediator of divine purpose and the agent of divine providence. To obey the superior is to obey God. Obedience to this will is a sacrifice of self in the model of Christ, who was obedient unto death.

## Emergence of Community

The structure of society is evolving, however, and human consciousness is developing new awareness and new values. There is an emerging consciousness of man's elemental dignity. As that fundamental sense of dignity becomes more conscious, it becomes increasingly an operative principle which demands free and responsible action. There is also an emerging consciousness of the reality of community as a being-with others and being-for others which calls for personal initiative and involvement. The historical shift in emphasis involves a refocusing of truth. The classical concept embodied a truth but not the whole truth. The impetus of contemporary events and the movement of history is forcing us to focus on another fundamental truth, and the refocusing involves an adjustment of essential concepts all along the line. The needs of the times can only be met by a revaluation and reanalysis of the basic notions of authority and community.

The emphasis on human dignity and self-realization may become overly polarized. The direction toward self-fulfillment may run in the vein of excessive individuality. Anything that serves to limit the wish of the individual may be mistaken for a constraint to freedom. Obedience, in this sense, may be taken as a barrier and contradiction to personal fulfillment. The hypertrophy of the principle of freedom leads to the misidentification of freedom with self-will. Self-realization is a function not only of man's capacity for freedom, but of his ability to participate in community as well. The notions of self-fulfillment, freedom, obedience, authority, and community are mutually dependent and mutually corrective.

Putting the individualistic fallacy aside, the contemporary difficulty is rooted in a truth which contemporary experience has brought into sharp relief. Father Murray's statement is admirably succinct:

> What is really being said is that sheer submission to the will of the superior and mere execution of his orders do not satisfy the exigencies of the dignity of the person. They do not call into play the freedom of the person at its deepest point, where freedom appears as love. Still less do they exhaust the responsibilities of the person, which are to participate fully in community and to contribute actively to community. Thus stated, the contemporary difficulty is seen to be entirely valid. It is not to be solved by methods of repression. Nor will it yield to mere reiteration of the principle of authority: that authority is to be obeyed simply because it is authority.[1]

Thus, the emergence of the notion of community is really an attempt to deal with this problem. The effort is directed at the resolution of the dichotomy between traditional authoritarianism and the emergent sense of personal responsibility. Since authority and community are in a sense correlative; since community is in a sense the overriding context of obedience and command; since community is also the matrix within which freedom finds its expression, the essential modification and modulation of the concept and exercise of authority must ultimately be achieved in terms of and in relation to the community and its basic processes. Authority plays itself out within the community as a service to the community. The basis on which the superior commands and the subject obeys is therefore service to the community. It is likewise the motive of service to the community which justifies and substantiates the superior's claim to obedience as well as the subject's duty to obey.

## Authority in Community

Service to the community can be spelled out in a variety of formal terms, not all of which exhaust the functions of authority. Authority unites and establishes the communion which is the central core of community. It is through authority that the community achieves its structure and organization. The finality of authority is, in part, order, and it is in relation to authority that the sense of shared identity and values are communicated through which the community establishes and preserves its sense of solidarity. This is one of the underlying dimensions of authority which is derived from the workings of authority as relation. The function is realized through a continuing dialogue within the relation and by the underlying mechanisms of identification and mutual regulation. The unity is a unity of values, of goals and purposes. The dialogue, at all its levels, builds the community. And the individual, who participates in the dialogue through interest, action, and initiative becomes a creative and responsible force within the community. He builds the community out of his own creative resources so that the community becomes an expression of the creative responsibility of its members. The dialogue not only creates the community, but it must continue in an unending process in order that the community may perdure and evolve. The dialogue also serves to deepen the community's awareness of itself as having a reality and a function in the exercise of authority.

There is a limit, or perhaps better a basic condition, for this function of authority. It works in a context governed by a fundamental respect for human dignity and human freedom. Authority functions under the necessity for respect for this condition. The community achieves its structure on the basis of an inherent flexibility and tolerance for diversity of thought, value, and action. There is a necessary pluralism which diversifies and enriches the life of the community and which derives from the diversity and freedom of the creative sources of community life. There is an unavoidable tension in this. The stability of community structures depends in large measure on the extent to which shared values are internalized by individual members. But individual values are always unique and personalized and, therefore, divergent. Maximal stability is achieved by a delicate balance between a consensus of shared values constituting a common value-system and an optimal degree of variability. The latter contributes to the perdurance of the former by creating an area of permissible variation within which an optimal measure of creative freedom can be maintained.

The community thus stands in need of authority for its existence. The individual's subordination to legitimate authority is also necessary for the survival of community. This subordination to authority is justified insofar as that submission is directed to the common goal —which, as common, is properly his own. If this interlocking of the right to command and the duty to obey is conceived in rigid and authoritarian terms, the subject's function is reduced to mere passivity. The subject's inherent activity and creativity are ignored. The subject, however, remains responsible for his actions, and his influence on the community remains a force for continuing adaptation.

Authority also has a directive function. This is a necessary function since the community is organized for the end of action. The organized action of the community is a correlative of its unification. Direction is an offshoot of unity. Direction also presumes that dialogue is at work in the community. The notion of direction must again be modified in terms of a modified conception of authority and community. Direction was traditionally conceived in a movement from above downwards. The superior authoritatively directed the efforts of the community to one of a variety of available courses of action. Unity of action was a function of unity of judgment—the superior's. Direction in contemporary terms is neither exclusively vertical or single in origin. The origins of the directive genius of the community are to be sought more at large in the community. The superior's directive function is exercised more in terms of his sensitivity and responsiveness to the common will of the community. The institution of new community structures is calculated to facilitate the community's determination of its own common purposes and wishes, the bringing of these to community awareness and their communication

to the superior as head of the community. The superior as the definitive locus of decision in the formal sense must acquire sensitive ears
to go with his traditional tongue. He must learn to listen as well as to
direct.

Authority has another function. The spirit of the times lays a
heavy emphasis on personal rights and responsibility. The person has
responsibilities to self and community, but it must also be remembered that the community also has rights and responsibilities to individuals as well as to itself. Authority also has a corrective function
by which the influence of the group is brought to bear on the individual. The exercise of individual responsibility runs a risk, namely
of overinvestment in personal interests and goals. A discriminating
line has to be drawn between personal goals which are merely individualistic and personal goals which are congruent with community
goals. Individualistic action ought to be possible in any well-functioning community. Optimally the value-structure of a community
enjoys sufficient stability and flexibility to acquiesce in some degree
to idiosyncratic activity. The case can be made that such tolerance
for some degree of individual variability in the system is not only
possible in the sense that individual variation is more or less tolerable, but that it is also necessary for maintaining the stability of the
system. Without some range of permissive variation, individual action and freedom become impossible. The system that tolerates only
a narrow range of variation becomes unduly repressive, restrains
free initiative, and ends by forcing members to mutiny or to abandon
the ship. A given measure of variation in values and behavior contributes positively to the perdurance of shared communal values.

For each community and each social system there is an optimal
degree of inherent variability which maximally stabilizes the community structure and maximally satisfies built-in needs for creative
responsibility and freedom in the community. Authority maintains
the delicate balance between the stability of communal structure and
the variability of individual enterprise. It is a function which aims
directly at an optimal interrelation of order and freedom. The function is, therefore, corrective insofar as it serves to redress the balance
of order in the face of freedom and the balance of freedom in the face
of order. In the service of this function, authority can restrain freedom in the interest of order. It can also and must ease the discipline
of order in the interest of freedom. Properly conceived, both direc-

tions are in the ultimate interest of community. The authoritarian mode has historically tended to sacrifice freedom in the interest of order, undoubtedly with the conviction that the interests of order were most closely identified with the interest of the community. The error glosses over the fact that the interests of freedom and creative responsibility are also closely related to the interests of the community. The latter consideration is a corrective which has emerged on the contemporary scene with increasing insistence. The corrective function, therefore, of authority operates to readjust the historical imbalance which is reflected in the relative hypertrophy and atrophy of the principles of authority and freedom.

## Freedom in Community

Freedom, too, has its functions within the community. Freedom, like authority, each in its own modality, serves the needs of the community. Freedom, first of all, serves the purposes of dialogue. If meaningful dialogue is to obtain at all, it must take place between autonomous persons and in a horizontal dimension. There is no such thing as vertical dialogue. Dialogue becomes possible only to the extent that exchange is possible on the same level. There is no dialogue between teacher and student unless the teacher puts himself in some sense on the student's level. There is no dialogue between superior and subject unless they meet on a level of discourse that both share. The hypertrophy of authority stifles dialogue precisely because it works vertically. The invitation of mature authority to dialogue, however, elicits a response in freedom. The subject cannot enter such a dialogue except in virtue of his freedom. Without it, he has no recourse but submission to a vertical relation. It should be pointed out that the authority relation has elements of the horizontal and the vertical inherent in it. Neither dimension is ever absent from it, nor is either dimension ever obscured by the other. The life of dialogue in which community flourishes requires the participation of free persons in mutual autonomy and regulation. In this aspect of community, submission has no part.

This freedom reveals itself as the capacity for communication of self, as the giving of self in the interest of the community, as the generous impulse to serve the community. We are close to the Ignatian ideal of love, which is to be expressed in deeds rather than in words. The first service of freedom, then, is to participate in the ongoing dialogue of the community. This is the primary way in which the subject is able to realize through freedom his creative responsibility, by which he is at once able to build himself and his community.

Freedom has, in addition, an obediential function. There is an essential insight here which is of critical importance. Obedience must be embedded in freedom in order that it be itself. There is no obedience if it is not rooted in freedom and expressive of freedom. Obedience without freedom is submission. I do not wish to elaborate the inner relation and dependence of obedience and freedom since it is significant enough for consideration on its own. I would like to emphasize, however, that obedience is often spoken of in terms which suggest self-sacrifice on the model of the obedient Christ. The atrophy of the principle of freedom suppresses the inherent element of freedom in such expressions. The sacrifice of self in obedience is an expression of free self-determination and commitment. It is the moment in which the individual may capture that element of creative responsibility in which true subjection is achieved. The obedience of Christ was an expression of ultimate creative responsibility—ultimately responsible for the salvation of the community of men.

What is implicit in all this is the notion that any reformulation of authority and its mechanisms must bear in mind the communal structure within which authority functions. Our awareness in this regard is transitional. Our thinking is only beginning to readapt itself and reconstruct itself in communal terms. The readjustment of this imbalance of authority and freedom as an historical process is taking place through the emergence of community as a regulating force in relation to which both superior and subject must adapt. The role of superior is existentially modified by the presence of community as a self-conscious force. The role of subject is also profoundly altered. It is precisely within the community and in relation to the community that superior and subject can meet in horizontal interaction. This is why the notion and the reality of community is so crucial. It provides a framework in which horizontal relationship and true dialogue can emerge. Even the authority relationship with all its refinements is sufficiently resonant with the overtones of verticality to impede the historical process. One could not expect conceptions which are so historically embedded and psychologically defended to alter much in fact without the emergence of a catalytic force in response to which both are compelled to adapt. Community, it seems, may be just such a force.

*Part V*

# Obedience

The Psychology of Obedience

Pathological Aspects of Obedience

The Problem of Disobedience

Authority and Obedience

## Chapter 13

# The Psychology of Obedience

In this section we turn our attention to the complex problem of the psychological understanding of obedience. Our objective will be to integrate some of the relevant findings and concepts of modern psychology and focus them on the concerns about obedience and authority which form the substance of this volume. That objective is both complicated and difficult. There does not exist a psychology of obedience. That circumstance should simplify the task. But, despite the lack of such a formulated psychological view of obedience, there is extant an abundance of insights, concepts, and empirical data which can readily serve as a basis on which the psychology of obedience can at least tentatively be erected.

It should be immediately evident that our major problem is not to know where to begin, but to know where to end. Religious obedience involves and has an impact on all levels of the human person. The psychology of religious obedience, correlatively, touches on nearly all levels of psychological integration of the human being. There is practically no aspect of human psychological functioning that is not somehow related to the problems of obedience and does not have some influence on the development and exercise of the virtue of obedience and its associated patterns of behavior. Consequently, the initial problem in approaching this subject is to determine how far to cast the net in order to bring into optimal focus the

diverse elements that in fact pertain to obedience—without need-
lessly diffusing or confusing the issues that are most pressing and
relevant.

The determination of where to end has other implications as well.
The approach we are taking in this section is specifically psychological. That approach has its intrinsic limitations. It can address itself only to the inner workings and motivations of the human psyche.
Its findings, conclusions, and implications have only a limited validity
and a limited applicability. It can only draw conclusions validly
within its own perspective and in terms of its own empirical base and
theoretical framework. But the implications of religious obedience
are richer and broader—in the specifically religious and theological
sense. The understanding of intrapsychic processes must be complemented and qualified by other considerations. A psychological approach has certain implications for the overall understanding of
obedience, but its understanding is fragmentary and partial. It must
be integrated with other approaches and with other frames of reference. It is only when the problems of obedience are approached in a
multifaceted manner, through the superposition of a variety of perspectives—psychological, sociological, cultural, and theological—
that an adequate understanding can emerge which would give
promise of providing a basis for judgment and action.

In view of these cautions and the ever-present need to be aware of
limitations more than potentialities, we may approach the problems
of the psychology of obedience with a spirit of humility. The reanalysis of obedience has many implications and it is well that we
approach them in a spirit of tentative exploration and not in the
spirit of doctrinaire assertion. What follows, in fact, is more of an exploration than anything else. Its spirit is heuristic rather than dogmatic. Its findings rest on considerable scientific and clinical experience but, nonetheless, it has its considerable limitations which
can be ignored only at great cost. The variety and infinite complexity
of the human spirit requires that psychological formulations be advanced only to be qualified and that the statement of principles be
cast only in relative terms which carry within them the self-limiting
acknowledgment of wide individual differences and endless exceptions. With these cautions to humble our inquiry, we can proceed.

One of the most significant aspects of the psychology of any subject is the developmental aspect. The importance of the developmental perspective in the understanding of human behavior has come into its own only in recent years. The impetus to this added dimension of psychological understanding came as a result of a number of factors, not the least of which was the stimulus of the psychoanalytic historico-genetic approach. Freud realized and formulated the basic idea that the organization and functioning of the human personality was the result of an organic development which was the expression of biological growth and maturation, but which at each step of the process was influenced and modified by the organism's experience. Freud in fact made some of the first published observations of the behavior of children. Following in his footsteps, at first Anna Freud and Melanie Klein, and subsequently a host of others whose name has become legion, have intensified and broadened the first-hand experience of how babies grow into human persons.

As a result, the understanding of any part of human behavior and activity cannot be regarded as established without some insight into the developmental processes which gave rise to it. The developmental aspect has assumed such importance not only because the pattern of life experiences, particularly the experiences of early life, have an effect which shapes the personality in specific determinable ways; even more significantly, the developmental residues become part of the functioning personality in such a way that their influence on ongoing behavior and experience is still active. It is a basic principle of developmental psychology that each developmental phase, each developmental crisis, each developmental achievement, leaves its own residue in the structure of the developing personality that continues to operate as a vital component of the emerging self.

When we speak of a psychology of obedience, we are immediately faced with a variety of facets that interact in complex ways. Psychologically speaking, obedience is taking place as an expression of intrapsychic processes. Those processes do not take place in a vacuum, however, but in fact are caught up in complex interactions. Obedience is substantially a response that the subject emits to a stimulus that comes from some source in his environment. Obedience is at all points a psychological phenomenon that is derived from a social context. The psychology of obedience, then, cannot take the intrapsychic phenomena as its sole vantage point—there is no point at which the psychology of obedience must not be seen as socially embedded. A given response is not an expression of obedience unless it is a response within the context of an authority structure. Structures of authority arise in human organizations out of specific types of interaction and are modified and influenced in a variety of ways, all of which have an impact on the obediential response of the individual.

We cannot make these complex processes a part of our analysis at this point, but the interesting thing about the developmental approach to obedience is that it implicitly deals with such issues. From the beginning of the infant's experience as it relates to obedience, the child is caught up in a substantially social process. From the beginning of life he is interacting with a social matrix which is actively shaping his responses. It is at this level that the issues of inner intrapsychic development and of social interaction come together in mutual interaction and support. From its first contacts with the mother's breast, the child is interacting socially and at the same time, within that social matrix, undergoes the experiences out of which its own inner development can proceed. In this sense, socialization and inner psychic development are correlative and complementary processes.

I would like to turn now to a consideration of the developmental process itself. I will be basing this analysis on more recent investigations in child psychology and child psychiatry and will try to make broad use of Erik Erikson's frame of reference for the treatment of developmental issues. Our objective will be to try to focus on those elements of the developmental process which seem relevant for an understanding of more mature forms of obedience and, specifically, in this consideration, of more mature forms of religious obedience. The essential note that this analysis will try to sustain is that obedience is a life-long experience that takes its origins in the first moments of life, that grows and is modified with the emerging stages of life and experience, and that reaches its maturity in adult life, and that reaches its fullness and richness only when man reaches the fullest expression in wisdom and integrity of his life's experience.

We must begin, however, where the child begins—at the beginning. We must not make the usual adult mistake of thinking that when the child begins his career his experience of the world around him is like ours. We do not really know what that experience is like; we can only infer it from the way the child behaves. Newborn infants cannot really tell us what it is like—being a newborn in this world of ours.

A considerable amount of effort has gone into studying what is involved as the infant starts the business of living. What seems to emerge from such studies is that the infant organism is relatively disorganized in many of its parameters. Its general reactivity is fairly unstable, the inner physiological regulatory mechanisms are easily influenced so that there is a relatively wider fluctuation of autonomic responsiveness. Temperature regulation and bodily functions are poorly controlled and regulated, and so forth. The infant's perceptual world is not well organized either. He is not able to clearly discriminate objects. He is not able to recognize the boundaries between himself and the outside world. There is in the infant's behavior, then, a quality of disorganization, diffusion, lack of differentiation and specificity. All of that will come with time, the maturation of his physiological mechanisms, and his learning through interaction with the significant persons around him.

At the same time, even from the beginning there is some degree of organization and structure in the infant's experience. His eye movements are not random, but follow very specific patterns of organization. Attention studies, for example, have described a preference for complexity in even newborns of a few hours of age. Eye movements tend to follow more complex aspects of simple geometric forms: corners rather than straight lines. The infant does not start from complete lack of structure by any means. But, from the very beginning, structure is developing and the infant is caught up in processes that encourage and sustain his development. The most important aspect of this developmental matrix is the human beings who surround, care for, feed, nurse, and communicate with the baby. Important interactions are taking place from the first hours of the baby's experience which, if successful, can sustain the processes of normal growth and development and, if unsuccessful, can result in impairments which hinder further development and create maladaptive aspects to the child's future functioning.

Some of the studies of infant development have focused on the first two years of life as the crucial stage of development. Many of the child's experiences in that crucial stage of life lay the foundation for successful or unsuccessful adaptation in later life. I would like to describe briefly some of these phases as well as some of the later ones, and comment on their significance for the growth of the capacity for obedience.

## Trust

The most important interaction in the child's earliest experience is with the mother. From the beginning, mother and child are involved in a continual process of active give-and-take. Each is trying to influence and accommodate to the other in a wide variety of subtle ways. In the successful mother-child unit, there is a process of mutual regulation that Erikson[1] has pointed to as so important for the child's development. There has to be an intermeshing of the mother's mothering and caring activities with the child's needs and capacities. Conversely, there has to be a successful adapting and responsiveness in the child to enable him to receive the mother's mothering and find gratification in it.

In the very beginning of life there is an initial phase of mutual adaptation between mother and child. This is the beginning of their career together. It is the first of several discriminable phases of their progressive interaction. These phases are organized around specific developmental issues which reflect the child's stage of development and which lay the groundwork for future steps. Each of these developmental issues becomes the focus of a real negotiation between mother and child. The success with which they negotiate any one of the earlier issues influences the child's development as it becomes organized around that issue and also influences the relative success of the negotiation of future issues.

The period of initial adaptation between mother and child deals with the primary adaptive task of establishing a suitable meshing of mothering activities with the baby's cues. The infant emits signals of his inner states of distress and need. These signals are important because their correct reading by others and a response to them by others are a matter of life and death to the infant. He is not a self-sufficient organism, but depends in critical ways on the mothering activity of others both for sustaining life and, less drastically, maintaining the homeostatic balance of his natural bodily functions which provides for him a sense of well-being and security. Only if this balance is maintained can he thrive. Thus mother and child are caught up in this mutual negotiation over matters of basic vital processes—feeding, eliminating, sleeping, and waking. The successful negotiation of these matters is normally achieved within the first few months and is reflected in the extent to which the child establishes a stable rhythm of such activities. The child also develops a capacity for discrimination in his responsiveness to handling by the mother. He is more responsive to her and quiets more readily for her than for anyone else. From the mother's part, the success of the negotiation is reflected in her assurance that she knows her baby and understands him in a way that no one else does. This may also be reflected in a considerable decrease in her anxieties about providing these life-sustaining ministrations for the child.

Mutuality must be established in this earliest phase. The mother must be sensitive to and responsive to the cues that the child is able to emit. An essential aspect of her responsiveness to the child is a balance that she must maintain between her empathy with what she feels to be the child's needs and her objectivity in viewing him as an independent unit apart from her own thoughts and feelings. A certain measure of objectivity is essential if the mother is to pick up the unique functional qualities that characterize individual infants from the moment of birth and to which she must adapt her mothering activities. If she cannot do this she fails to respond to the child's cues and runs the risk of responding more to her own inner thoughts and feelings, which she begins to mistake for the child's.

What are the basic life issues that are established in this earliest period of mutual regulation? The most striking aspect of the process is that, for the basic regulation of his inner states and the balancing of vital processes, the infant must depend on another human being, usually the mother. He must learn to depend on another for the control of inner states which cause him discomfort. The degree to which he can count on that other, rely on her, find assurance that she is a constant and reliable object for him to relate to and depend on for these necessary and life-sustaining functions, and more specifically the extent to which he comes to know her as sensitive and responsive to his inner needs are vital aspects of this early interaction. Homeostatic regulation and the maintenance of a sense of well-being in the child are at this level intimately tied to and dependent on the mother's mothering responsiveness. The child's primitive and vaguely undifferentiated sense of wholeness, goodness, and internal security and comfort are a result of how this interaction goes. This can be viewed as the basis for what Erikson has described as "basic trust." The baby's trusting is reflected in his ease in feeding, in the confidence that what is being taken in from another is good and comforting, in the depth of sleep which can be entered with the assurance that the needed and sustaining person will be there when he wakens, and in the ease of elimination. The infant's familiarity with the mother becomes, as Erikson puts it, an inner certainty as well as an outer predictability.[2]

This process leaves a fundamental residue in the emerging personality that will go a long way in shaping his basic orientation toward other persons in his environment. The rudiments of basic trust or of basic mistrust are what is in question, and the question of which direction the child's development will move is decided within the context of this earliest interaction. The capacity to trust is fundamental to any kind of human relatedness and the extent to which that capacity is impaired will determine much of what later passes for psychopathology and the inability to get along with other people. Its severest defect is seen in schizophrenic or autistic states in which all human relationships are permeated with dread and the threat of destructive engulfment. Even at the best, it hardly seems possible to speak of perfect trust—every human being carries with him a residue of mistrust that reflects the partial breakdowns in the mutual regulation that might have obtained in the interaction of mother and child. The process is bound to have its slip-ups as all human processes do. But there is a balance struck in the interaction which gives a basic resolution to the polarities of trust and mistrust and lays the foundation for the individual's future capacity to enter into trusting and mutually rewarding relationships with others.

Erikson adds a significant note:

> But let it be said here that the amount of trust derived from earliest infantile experience does not seem to depend on absolute quantities of food or demonstrations of love, but rather on the quality of the maternal relationship. Mothers create a sense of trust in their children by that kind of administration which in its quality combines sensitive care of the baby's individual needs and a firm sense

of personal trustworthiness within the trusted framework of their culture's life style.[3]

The child's trusting is a response to and an interaction with the mother's own inner sense of trustworthiness. The infant's inborn capacity to take in by mouth must mesh with the mother's capacity and desire to feed him. The breast-feeding situation is more or less a prototype of the mother-child interaction at this early stage. As Erikson puts it, "At this point he [the child] lives through, and loves with, his mouth; and the mother lives through, and loves with, her breasts."[4] While this immediate mouth-breast contact is important, we should remember that it is only representative of a whole series of interactions between mother and child in which the mother is responding to the child's needs and is caring for him. Trust is built out of this matrix composed of countless acts and responses of both mother and child which build in the child a sense of comfort, security, well-being, and a sense of his own inner trustworthiness—that the discomforting sensations and states of inner disorganization are manageable, that states of inner tension can be relieved. There must develop a sense of inner stability which allows the child to build a sense of trust in himself and to find a sense of trustworthiness within himself. As his own inner capacities for even physiological regulation mature, the sense of secure stability that has been provided by the ministrations of the mother becomes increasingly the child's own.

The significance of these rudimentary developments for obedience, as well as for all human interaction, is profound. Trust is at the root of any meaningful and mutually rewarding human relationship. Any human interaction that is of any significance or lasts for any length of time carries within it the seeds of ambivalence, of elements of both hate and love, mixed in conflicting and interlocking ways. The ability of any human being to find satisfaction and reward in the other humans around him—especially the significant others who have an influence over the course of his life and activity—depends on the capacity to trust the other and to have a basic sense of the reliability of his good intentions. This is so fundamental that the alternative is either paranoid suspicion and dread or schizophrenic withdrawal. Obedience is such a context and it calls uniquely on the individual's capacities for trusting relatedness.

I have tried to develop the notion of the authority relationship as based on the principle of mutual regulation and responsiveness in the preceding chapters. But I would like to point out at this juncture that the basis of any meaningful and humanly sustaining relationship between superior and subject must be the element of basic trust. As in the relationship of mother and child on which trust builds psychologically, the relationship of trust between superior and subject must involve mutual regulation in such a way that the trusting and trustworthiness are apparent in both terms of the relation. The subject must have a sense of trust in and confidence in the trustworthiness of the superior. Similarly, the superior must have a sense of trust in and confidence in the trustworthiness of the subject.

A basic notion that makes the developmental consideration of aspects of human personality so pressing and pertinent is that the residues of even the earliest levels of development are not simply left behind. Rather they form a functional residue in the personality which remains active and determining through the rest of the individual's life cycle. Impairments in the basic sense of trust which are laid down in the early stages of the child's experience may have profound effects on his later capacity to relate to others in a trusting manner and may severely prevent any sense of his own inner trust in himself. These impairments may be in operation within the authority relation and may have important implications for the individual's capacity to obey.

The commitment of oneself and one's resources to a course of action prescribed by someone else requires a degree of considerable trust of that someone. We must trust his judgment, his knowledge, his good intentions, etc. There was a time in the operation of obedience when an automatic appeal could be made to the will of God made manifest through the superior to substantiate the claim to trust and trustworthiness. But the naive simplicity of that view of religious obedience is no longer sufficient. The need for trust cannot be so easily gotten rid of. One of the strengths of the traditional view of obedience was that it gave individuals a rationale and a source of trust. No matter how foolish the order seemed to be, one could always take recourse to a deeper purpose and a deeper logic that was somehow guaranteed by divine purposes. If one could not trust the superior, one could at least trust his authority and the grace of his office. That prop of obedience has been taken away, and we are left to work out the basis of trust on other terms.

The result, I think, is that trust must be found within the relationship that obtains between superior and subject. By that I mean that it does not rest simply on the superior or his qualities. It rests on much more complex psychological processes which involve the respective capacities of both participants to trust and on their respective capacities to have a sense of their inner trustworthiness. The basis of trust and its operation, then, has come to rest much more on the mutual relation between superior and subject and derives its confidence from the sense of shared purpose and common value with which they relate and with which they involve themselves in the ongoing purposes and activities of the religious group. If superior and subject share a common conviction of the purposes for which they mutually enter the authority relation—and these involve the goals and values of the religious group, the determinable place of the group in the work of the Church at large, and interiorly the motivations of each for committing themselves to this group and their respective senses of solidarity with the group—their capacity to respond to its demands with a sense of trusting relatedness will be enhanced.

## Autonomy

To return to our developing infant, there are other issues that emerge and must be negotiated as he progresses. The first six months or so are given over largely to the working out of a basic pattern of interaction between mother and child, as we have suggested. The mother's anxieties about providing her infant with life-sustaining care gradually diminishes and she becomes more able to indulge in the increasingly delightful and playful experience of stimulating and responding to the child's gradually emerging smiling behavior. The social interchange remains, however, largely with the mother's initiative to elicit and sustain it. As the child's smiling response develops, a phenomenon usually reaching its height in the second half of the first year, he begins to assume some initiative in social exchange with the mother, and he begins more and more to take on the function of stimulating her to respond to him. A basic question for the infant's development is to what extent his efforts will be successful in gaining a response from the mother, and particularly to what extent he will succeed in bringing about a mutually enjoyable and reciprocal exchange with her.

The child assumes an increasingly active role in this exchange and as he does so another important developmental issue comes into focus. The child gradually extends the range of his initiative and attempts to elicit response from the mother. There is a concerted effort to focus the mother's behavior to meet his needs. He accepts feeding easily from her, whereas before he might have accepted it equally from mother or father. He seeks her lap for comfort and security. The extent to which his attempts are successful serves as the root for the development of his own inner autonomy. He develops a sense of his own inner capacity to control and bring about responses in the significant other. The ability to focalize the mother's responses to meet his own inner needs gives him a sense of inner resourcefulness and control over the discomfort and tension that arise with unfulfilled needs. He becomes increasingly aware of himself as capable of inner regulation and as capable of influencing the predictability of significant others upon whom he has learned to depend. Not only can he find a familiar trust in the caring figure, but he can to some extent succeed in bringing about and eliciting those trustworthy responses as a result of his own initiative.

The prototypical situation in which much of this stage and its conflicts is displayed is that of toilet-training. Much has been written and much mythology has been generated about toilet-training, but we should not lose sight of the fact that it coincides with a developmental phase in which some of the most basic elements of the emerging personality are being worked out at large in the child's experience. The maturation of the child's organism and the gradually increasing control over the operation of sphincters makes the capacity to hold on to or let go of feces a natural ground on which many of these developmental issues are joined. They are joined in multiple other and diverse contexts of interaction between parent and child as well, so that we cannot enshrine the struggles over the potty as having any magical significance.

The child enters at this stage on a period of self-assertion. The phenomenon of negativism in the second year of life is something that every parent knows well. The child learns the word "No" and exercises it in all directions as an expression of his increasing assertion of himself as over against everything else. The child seems almost driven to carry out his own intentions and to extend the area of his manipulation and control. Before, his initiatives had been more or less in the direction of eliciting supportive responses from the mother. Little by little he begins to try out his attempts even in the face of her opposition. A battle of wills evolves. The important issue that must be successfully negotiated at this stage is whether the child can establish self-assertion in his interaction and in what areas. He must gain some sense in this negotiation that his winning out and having his way can be accepted by the mother.

The child begins to define the world more explicitly in terms of "I" and "you" and what belongs to "me." The mutual regulation between child and parent at this stage is crucial. The child still needs the support of outer controls, but if the outer controls are too rigid or too early, they deprive the child of the opportunity to exercise his own control. If the child's attempts to control his own functions are interfered with, he may develop a sense of powerlessness that forces him to resort either to earlier patterns of behavior or to progress prematurely to a pretended and fragile autonomy. He may regress to whining and demanding or begging behavior or to forms of oral gratification like thumbsucking. Or he may become hostile and willful, assuming a pretended autonomy and a wish not to lean on anybody or depend on anybody.

The development of autonomy extends and depends on the earlier development of a sense of basic trust. The child must learn that the sense of basic trust in himself and in the world will not be jeopardized by his emerging wish to have a choice and to exercise his own willingness or willfulness. His potential willfulness and disruptiveness must be met by parental firmness, which can protect him from his own destructive wishes and can guide and support him in his wishes to hold on to and let go of with appropriate discretion. Otherwise he runs the twofold risk of stubborn holding on or letting go without control. In either case real autonomy would be prejudiced by shame or self-doubt. The objective of this stage of development is to establish a sense of self-control without loss of self-esteem. As Erikson puts it:

> This stage, therefore, becomes decisive for the ratio between love and hate, for that between cooperation and willfulness, and for

that between the freedom of self-expression and its suppression. From a sense of self-control without loss of self-esteem comes a lasting sense of autonomy and pride; from a sense of muscular and anal impotence, of loss of self-control, and of parental overcontrol comes a lasting sense of doubt and shame.[5]

If the child is encouraged to stand on his own feet, he must at the same time be protected from experiences which threaten him with either doubt or shame. The child not only tests out his own capacity for self-assertion, but gradually begins to test out the extent to which he can carry out destructive and aggressive wishes, especially when the mother or father are present. The manner in which these assertions are answered and treated by the parents is of the utmost importance for the development of autonomy. If the child's aggression is treated with too much permissiveness, the child will develop a sense of his own dangerousness and the dangerousness of his impulses which neither he nor the powerful others can control. If it is treated in an overly controlling or punitive manner, the child will develop a sense of his own inner wickedness and destructiveness and feel that the inner destructiveness needs to be carefully guarded against. In either event he falls prey to shame and self-doubt.

The issue of autonomy is fundamental in the understanding of the psychology of obedience. The rudiments of autonomy start being laid down, in a sense, from the very beginning of the child's interchange with the mother, particularly in terms of the mother's capacity to maintain some objectivity in her interaction with the child which allows her to be responsive to him as an independent source of specific cues to which she must respond, rather than her responding to him in terms of her own inner impulses and feelings. As that rudimentary sense of self that the child builds in the first year of life becomes more definite, the child must solve the tension between dependence and independence. His dependence on his mother at first, and later on both parents, changes as he progresses in his development and with it he enlarges and solidifies the area of his own independence. The crucial issue in the development of autonomy is what degree of independence can the child establish and in what areas. In the normal course of development, this relative autonomy undergoes a gradual increase and extends to more and more areas of the child's life, in a manner, hopefully, that is age-appropriate.

This is the point at which the mutual regulation between parents and child becomes a vital factor in determining whether the child's development in autonomy proceeds on a normal timetable. The parent can blend firmness with permissiveness in order to help the child find the area of appropriate exercise of his autonomy, and thus save him from the embarassment or uncertainty of overreaching his independence and suffering a correlative loss of self-esteem. The aspect of mutual regulation assumes central importance since the child's gradual emergence toward greater independence cannot be regulated unilaterally, by either parents or child, without a mutual exchange and understanding between them. The child's natural drive toward increasing autonomy and self-expression must receive sufficient latitude to permit it to reach its own level of optimal expression. The child's attempts to extend the areas of his independent functioning must not be met with punitive retribution or loss of love. He must be able to make these explorations into increasing autonomy with the threat of loss of support or loss of that measure of dependence that is necessary to sustain his independence.

In all of this the child is undergoing a development in obedience. The interrelation between obedience and autonomy is closer than the relation between obedience and any other developmental parameter that we shall consider. The character of the child's obedience changes as he grows in autonomy. The area of obedience becomes the vital ground on which issues of autonomy are played out and through which they obtain their most pertinent expression. It must be said immediately that obedience from the very beginning, even in its most rudimentary form, is a matter of mutual regulation and interchange. Even the earliest exchange between mother and child can be formulated in terms of a relationship of authority. Mother and child must work out certain necessary tasks in a relationship in which one is superior and the other dependent and submissive. If the mother treats that relationship unilaterally as an authoritarian situation, in which the child only submits to her directives and must adapt to her scheduling of vital functions, the effects on the child's development will be profound and will undermine some of the most vital aspects of his personality development. While the lines of the hierarchy are not difficult to discriminate in that relationship, we must not lose sight of the centrality of mutual regulation if the essential developmental tasks are to be accomplished. Obedience, then, from its earliest roots has the element of mutuality and mutual regulation as a vital part of its inner structure.

It is perhaps obvious, but still worth emphasizing, that mutual regulation has the relative autonomy of the participants in the interaction as a necessary constituent. There can be no mutuality unless the autonomy of the interacting parties is established and is maintained in the interaction. Even the simplest mutuality between mother and newborn child requires a sense of the child's independence and objectivity in the mother. The mother must respect the potential autonomy of her child or else she will not be able to respond to the subtle cues that he emits to indicate his inner state. The principle of mutual regulation extends through the full range of obedience, and consequently the issue of autonomy is an integral part of the problem of obedience at all levels. Obedience, then, must be seen as a process involving an interchange in mutual regulation between autonomous persons. Obedience, particularly religious obedience as we are developing the notion here, is built on autonomy and derives from it, so that any form of the exercise of authority which violates autonomy is to that extent a violation of and a deviation from authentic obedience.

To say that as the child develops in autonomy he becomes less needful or less capable of obedience is to endorse a very partial and limited notion of both autonomy and obedience. Such a position would see autonomy and obedience as somehow opposed, so that insofar as one achieved personal autonomy, obedience had to suffer. This is a central presumption of more traditional views of obedience which postulated a childlike lack of autonomy in the subject and attributed autonomy only to the superior. Obedience in that formulation had to be a form of submission only, in which the optimal exercise of obedience manifested itself in the complete surrender of personal autonomy. The point of view that we are developing here, however, takes its stand on completely different ground. We suggest that obedience and autonomy are intrinsically related and mutually dependent. One cannot have one without the other, and to the extent that autonomy is lacking in the authority relation which serves as the matrix of obedience, obedience is deprived of its true meaning and impact.

Obedience is *not* seen, therefore, as involving the command of an autonomous superior to a nonautonomous subject whose only modality of response is submission and acceptance. Mature and authentic obedience is rather based on a relationship between autonomous individuals who relate to each other in virtue of their respective roles as superior and subject, and who work out the issues of direction and action by mutual regulation which respects the autonomy and responsibility of their respective positions. Their mutual participation in the relation of authority imposes on each a set of responsibilities which are prescribed under the obligations of obedience. It is the interaction of these respective responsibilities which constitutes the essence of obedience. Each of the participating individuals cannot meet and accept those responsibilities except insofar as he does so freely and autonomously. Consequently, there is a cluster of related and mutually dependent elements which must go together and which are intrinsically proportioned to each other—freedom, responsibility, autonomy, and obedience.

Obedience, then, develops in a manner correlative to autonomy. The child grows in his own inner autonomy and capacity for responsibility, at first over himself and gradually over aspects of his world. His capacity for obedience grows in a parallel fashion. The quality of his obedience alters as his development progresses. At first his obedience is an obedience of utter dependence. Even at that earliest level, the importance of the awareness of his incipient autonomy and uniqueness on the part of significant caretakers is essential to further development. He must also develop an incipient sense of the separateness and independence of those important figures on which he depends for nurture and care. In this aspect of his development lies the basis for his evolving awareness of those around him as separate and his ability to differentiate between himself and the objects in his world. The roots of autonomy and independence are present even in the basic dependence of the symbiotic union of mother and child. As the child develops in relative autonomy and independence, the quality of obedience changes accordingly. He is able to extend the areas of his own control and decision and to become increasingly independent of his parents. One of the most difficult tasks for parents as the child develops is to recognize the area of appropriate autonomy and self-direction for the child and to provide him with a sufficiently protective context within which he can exercise and extend that autonomy without running afoul of the Scylla and Charybdis of autonomous development—either excessively limiting the child's exercise of self-judgment and self-direction by repressive overconcern, or permissively allowing the child to overextend the area of his autonomous functioning and thus running the risk of loss of control and, correlatively, loss of self-esteem and self-confidence.

In the exercise of mature obedience, the same factors are at play, in their proper proportion as determined by the level of maturity of function and capacity for responsible engagement achieved by the participating individuals, both superior and subject. The subject, however, enjoys a much more developed sense of self-direction and control, so that one of the risks in the mutual regulation between superior and subject is minimized; that is, the risk of overextension and loss of self-esteem. The overriding risk, then, in the exercise of mature obedience is the alternate risk of excessive and overcautious limitation. Such limitation is both regressive and repressive. It is repressive because it tends to deprive the individual of the proper exercise of his own autonomy, and it is regressive because it tends to force upon the individual a kind of autonomous functioning that belongs to an earlier stage in his developmental history.

The difficulty in the working out of the mutual regulation of the authority relation and its correlates in obedience is that the developmental strata in the individual's life course are not left behind, but remain as continuing presences in the individual's personality structure. They can be activated and become influential at any point in his experience. The workings of mature obedience, therefore, are overladen with a double jeopardy. There is a precariousness that is inherent in the very working out of obedience on the contemporary level. The essential interaction between superior and subject depends on the success of the process of mutual regulation. That depends on the capacity of each to function in a maturely autonomous manner and in so doing to allow each other to exercise their respective responsibilities. Mature autonomy involves not only the acceptance and acknowledgement of one's own independence and responsibility, but also the capacity to accept and acknowledge the other's proper independence and responsibility. These two are correlatives that cannot be separated. Taken simply on the level of their present involvement and interaction, these qualities of the mutual regulation of superior and subject are susceptible to countless invasions and impediments. But there is jeopardy also from the fact that prior developmental levels are still available as an active basis for determining the individual's involvement in the authority relation and his obediential response. Therefore, all of the conflicts and developmental impairments that might have marred his growth in obedience —and who does not have his share of these?—can become operative in the present context and have their influence on the present response in obedience. We will have more to say about these matters later in terms of the functional aspects of obedience, but the point we are stressing here is that developmental aspects of obedience are not simply interesting history. They provide a present and often actively determining aspect of the current exercise of obedience. In this deeper sense, then, the superior represents, in an unconscious and overdetermined sense, all of those figures in the subject's life who have held the position of controlling authority, so that the response of the subject to the exercise of the superior's authority is a complex amalgamation of all the preceding levels of his experience of obedience.

## Initiative

I would like to return again to the image of the developing child to pick up another developmental parameter that has considerable significance for the life of obedience. The whole issue of initiative is one that is closely related to the workings of obedience. The rudiments of initiative really take their origin in some of the earliest negotiations that the child undertakes in dealing with his environment and particularly with his caretaker. The rudiments of self-assertion are there very early in the process of human development. The early issues are centered around the question of the degree to which the infant can succeed in controlling and focalizing the mother's caring activities. It is therefore closely related to and dependent on the establishment of basic trust and also correlative to an emerging sense of autonomy.

Initiative does not become a central issue in development, however, until the child gets to be about four or five. The emergence of initiative as a central development issue is related to the maturation of a number of aspects of the child's functioning. The child seems to become more integrated physically and psychologically. Locomotion is no longer a skill to be acquired or a task to be mastered. It is a capacity to be unconsciously relied on and assumed. The child can then begin to explore the limits of his walking or running capacity. He begins to propel himself into space and assert his sense of mastery over it. Similarly the child by this time begins to gain a sense of mastery over the use of language, and can begin to exploit it in the semingly endless asking of questions. The child's curiosity becomes endless, and his mind becomes as curiously intrusive as his body becomes in relation to space. Along with this corporal and linguistic development, there is an expansion and a coming into play of the child's imagination. This is the age at which children are most taken up with fantastic stories and fairy tales. The imagination runs riot, and the child's world has an animistic and magical coloration which is at once fantastic and often frightening. In all of this there is a quality which Erikson has described in terms of the intrusive mode.

> The *intrusive mode*, dominating much of the behavior of this stage, characterizes a variety of configurationally "similar" activities and fantasies. These include the intrusion into other bodies by physical attack; the intrusion into other people's ears and minds by aggressive talking; the intrusion into space by vigorous locomotion; the intrusion into the unknown by consuming curiosity.[6]

There are two important aspects of this whole phase of development that deserve special emphasis. They are the aspects that involve the development of the child's instinctual life. With regard to the development in aggression, it becomes immediately apparent that the intrusive character of the child's activity operates on the basis of a considerable mobilization of aggression. The basic issue for the child's growth in initiative is whether the child can undertake such aggressive intrusiveness on all of the many fronts of its expression without incurring the risk of guilt. The contest of wills that took shape in the struggle over autonomy in the younger child is continued and extended in the child's increasing efforts for self-assertion and initiative, even in the face of parental wishes to the opposite. The child's insistent intrusiveness can provoke parental frustration and anger. What the child needs is firm acceptance and clear-cut setting of firm limits. What the child does not need is angry retaliation and punitive restriction. The latter tends to reinforce the mechanisms that underlie guilt in its many forms.

The significant aspect of this phase of development is the sexual. The child's all-consuming curiosity extends at this age to the sexual sphere. He becomes curiously preoccupied with bodies, his own, his mother's, his father's, his siblings', especially those of the opposite sex. The interest becomes centered on the genitals of both sexes. In his own body, particularly in boys, his phallus becomes a focus of sensations, feelings, and interest. While erections may have occurred before this, they now become more specifically associated with sexual feelings and wishes rather than with states of diffuse arousal. There is an increased wish and impulse to engage in sex play and to seek out means of sexual investigation. Children at this age become increasingly aware of sex differences and sex roles. Erikson places an emphasis on the notion of "making" in the twofold sense of goal-oriented and pleasureful competition, and in the slangier sense of being "on the make." For boys this takes on an active and intrusive quality. For girls it takes on a more passive sense of making oneself attractive and endearing. For both sexes there is an emerging sense of sexual initiative that has distinctive characteristics for each sex.

The child's emerging sexual interest sets the stage for his growing awareness of his similarity to the parent of the same sex and his dissimilarity to his parent of the opposite sex. This provides him with a stimulus to the realization that he can be like one parent and that he must find a basic style of relating to the other parent. This gives him on one hand the promise of growing up to be like Daddy or Mommy and provides the stimulus for the crucial identifications that organize and structure his own personality. It also raises significant threats with which the child must deal. The emergence of sexuality brings with it the increase of sexual wishes which are incestuous and forbidden. The increase of his own powers brings along terrifying fantasies and a sense of the capacity to carry out his forbidden wishes. This also sets the stage for the emergence of guilt, particularly where the parents' own sexual conflicts do not permit them to deal with the child's flowering sexuality in reasonable and factual terms.

The entire complex of interlocking phenomena gives rise to the development of conscience. This whole aspect of the child's development is essential for the understanding of obedience. The child acquires a sense of internal control and regulation. The origins of conscience begin to take shape around the parental prohibitions. These prohibitions are at first simply extrinsic, but little by little, the child takes them in and makes them his own. This gradual internalization is prompted and sustained by the child's increasing need to carry on his emerging sense of initiative and to extend himself as the source and master of his activity. The necessity for making parental prohibitions his own is related to his need to guarantee that his increasing initiatives are carried out in such a way as to find acceptance from the important and influential—as well as powerful—figures about him. His initiative, involving as it does the expression of both aggressive and sexual interests and impulses, runs the risk of disapproval, punishment, and the threat of abandonment. Initiative runs the risk of loss of love.

The child's gradual internalization of parental attitudes and prohibitions also makes him more like his parents. Psychologists speak of this essential process of personality formation and development as identification. The identifications that take shape at this stage of the child's development are crucial for the patterning of his adult personality. Parental prohibitions that are excessive, punitive, hostile, or restrictive create a sense of inner danger, inner insecurity, and a sense of inner evil and need for caution and control in the child. He distrusts and fears his own inner impulses. Not only aggressive but also sexual feelings and emotions become frightening, with the result that his capacity to pass on to more mature levels of life in which such impulses must be used and integrated is limited. The more severe the parental restrictions and prohibitions, the more archaic, punitive, and constricting will be the child's own inner attitude toward himself and the control of his impulses.

The child's conscience can be quite cruel, harsh and uncompromising. It expresses itself in feelings of guilt. He can begin to feel guilty not for actions and deeds, but for mere thoughts, wishes, and impulses. The importance of this aspect of development for morality cannot be overestimated. It leads to a form of obedience that is rigid, overly exacting, and more literal than even parental standards might exact. Often parental prohibitions restrict the child from doing things that parents allow themselves. Sexual activity is a primary example. The child inevitably comes to resent this arbitrary (in his view) imposition of standards and promotes a deep hatred for the parent who served as a model of control, but who can get away with the very things that the child cannot tolerate in himself. There is thus an inner store of infantile and primitive rage that must be controlled. There can develop a rigid sense of moral right, of moralistic intolerance, which is continually prompted by the need to resist instinctual pressures and comes to exercise itself more in the prohibition of initiative than in guiding it to constructive ends. Initiative comes to represent in the first instance the threat of internal and instinctual disruption and excess, and in the second instance the threat of disruption and excess in others. There comes about an insistence on control, restraint, organization, and prohibition which extends not only to the direction and organization of one's own life, but where possible to the organization and direction of the lives of others. This sense of self-righteous initiative, then, finds ready justification in repression and restriction to the point of violence—in the name of goodness and right order.

Correlative with the emergence of initiative, the child develops a sense of himself as an autonomous source of his own activity and self-direction. In this aspect of initiative, we can begin to look for the rudiments of responsibility. The sense of responsibility declares the reality of oneself and of one's uniqueness. It bespeaks a sense of one's inner difference from all other human beings. It expresses a capacity for responding to the world on one's own terms and of eliciting responses from the world. Subjective responsibility accords to man a position as the initiator of his own acts. It recognizes the reality of choice and freedom, as well as the capacity of the individual to direct his own purposeful action to specific ends. The capacity that each individual achieves for accepting responsibility both for himself and his actions and for the world in which he lives, depends on the pattern of his own development in initiative. If he has the experience of growth in initiative without an excess of guilt, if he can come to a sense of inner trust in his own capacity to regulate and control his emergent impulses and interests, if he can achieve a sense of mastery and competence in the exercise of his powers without the need for severe restrictions and punitive retaliations, responsibility has a chance to grow and to find its rightful place in the mature personality.

The relevance of these aspects of development for the life of obedience is not difficult to see. The exercise of obedience in all its multiple forms is susceptible to all of the impediments that mark the course of development. The mature relation between an authority figure and a subject calls forth the same elements that obtained in the course of each individual's developmental experience. The response of obedience calls forth all of the constituent elements that were once elaborated in the previous contexts of obediential response. If the development in initiative was in some way impaired, the individual's capacity to respond to the current demands of authority figures will be correspondingly limited.

The essential point that this analysis brings into focus is that obedience in the mature context builds on and evokes the individual's capacity for initiative, freedom, and responsibility. These parameters of the human response are correlative. They emerge together and correlatively from the same developmental matrix. One cannot have one without the others, and the degree to which one achieves any one determines the degree to which one possesses the others. I am focussing this pattern of development specifically as a development in obedience. The development in obedience follows a course of increasing autonomy, increasing initiative, increasing freedom, and increasing responsibility. In that course of development, there are innumerable pitfalls and pressures which operate to fix the process of development at some less than mature level. Correspondingly, in the exercise of mature obedience, there are extant pressures which tend to evoke a response that derives from one or other of the less than mature levels of obedience. The response in obedience, therefore, is liable to regressions to less than mature levels of initiative or responsibility or freedom.

These are ever-present risks and indeed temptations. It is more difficult to sustain a more advanced and mature level of obedience than to regress to less demanding levels. Moreover, there are often institutional pressures at work to draw individuals back to less mature levels of functioning. One can even say, from this point of view, that the more or less institutionalized model of obedience that has been long operative in religious groups—a model in which obedience was equated with an evacuation and denial of initiative, freedom, autonomy, and responsibility—is an expression of and a reflection of a developmental stage that is considerably less than mature. The developmental process, however, teaches us that human beings normally grow beyond the constraints of limited levels of their development, and that the process itself is open-ended and continuous. One is never finished growing and developing.

## Identity

The term identity has become so much a part of the linguistic landscape in recent years that it is almost unnecessary to consider explaining what it means. We are primarily indebted to the efforts of Erik Erikson over the past score of years for the more developed notion of identity that we possess today. Insofar as identity is an expression of the development of the self, it has its roots in a course of development that reaches back to the earliest levels of self-awareness. But as Erikson particularly has developed it, identity has been applied, in the sense of a developmental achievement, to adolescence. Identity in this sense is the result of the integration of the achievements of preceding phases of development and their integration into a more or less autonomous sense of self that has an assured sameness and continuity and that is integrated into the social context in terms of the applicability of roles and skills. Erikson expresses the basic notion of identity in these terms:

> The integration now taking place in the form of ego identity is, as pointed out, more than the sum of the childhood identifications. It is the accrued experience of the ego's ability to integrate all identifications with the vicissitudes of the libido, with the aptitudes developed out of endowment, and with the opportunities offered in social roles. The sense of ego identity, then, is the accrued confidence that the inner sameness and continuity prepared in the past are matched by the sameness and continuity of one's meaning for others, as evidenced in the tangible promise of a "career."[7]

I would like to focus on those aspects of identity that seem particularly related to the understanding of obedience. It must be remembered that by and large the young people, men and women, who come to religious orders are adolescents. They are caught up in the inner struggles of self-definition and identity formation that mark that period of their growth. The crucial emphasis in identity formation lies not only in the necessity for inner integration and definition of self, but also embraces the necessity for identifying oneself as belonging within a certain social and cultural context. Youth is a period of earnest and enthusiastic searching for ideas, ideals, values, purposes, and objectives to which one can commit oneself and with which one can identify oneself. Youth is a period of active affiliation, of commitment to causes, of embracing ideologies. Erikson describes this aspect of the process, by which youth seeks to find and consolidate its sense of identity, in terms of fidelity. Fidelity is the virtue that integrates the purposeful energies of youth with the pre-existent structures and institutions of society. Such structures are the bearers and preservers of tradition. The measure of youthful fidelity that they inspire is an index of their vitality. The strength of social institutions and of the culture that they are embedded in expresses itself in the ideals and values and functional roles that it provides for young people to embrace.

A sense of fidelity and identity is essential to the further growth of any human being beyond the vicissitudes of adolescent turmoil to the more mature and deeper levels of meaning and purpose. The religious organization must provide the context and the substance of faithful commitment and identification in order to assure the young religious that the strengths of the religious tradition are responding to his inner needs for faithful affiliation. The significant task to be accomplished in the formation of young religious is the formation of a sense of personal identity as a religious person. There are a number of parameters to such a development. There is the significant area of inner personal growth in which the residues of earlier developmental phases must be integrated into a consistent and coherent sense of self. One must develop a sense of meaning within oneself and a sense of one's meaningfulness to the community within which one functions and whose life becomes a meaningful part of oneself. There is a need to integrate into a meaningful whole the roles and functions and patterns of behavior that constitute a pattern of life that he can identify as specifically religious. There must be an overall sense of integration within oneself, but also a sense of integration with the goals, values, purposes, and intents of the religious organization. One must have a sense of one's personal function in an over-all structure of meaningful activity which has specifiable religious objectives and is governed by a determinable set of religious values. A sense of authentic religious identity incorporates a sense of meaningful participation in God's work and of having a share in God's plan and purpose.

Obedience, particularly in its specifically religious meaning, is a commitment to such a context. The individual's capacity to grow in religious obedience, then, is not merely a problem of the integration of the significant residues of earlier stages of personal development. The extent to which the individual has mastered and integrated the basic issues of trust, autonomy, initiative, etc., determines the inner resources that are available to him as he seeks to integrate these residues and form for himself a sense of identity with which he can meet the expectations of the adult world and find a meaningful pattern of existence within it. His potentiality for identity and faithful commitment, however, must be met in the fashion of mutual regulation. Society must offer him a meaningful context; it must provide for him the necessary structures and value-orientations within which his emerging sense of identity can find expression and sustenance; it must give him an organized pattern of purposeful direction with which he can identify and which he can make his own in the conviction of fidelity and the assurance of trust.

When we move to the level of identity and its formation, an element of human development that has been more or less implicit, but nonetheless significant, comes into explicit focus. From the earliest phases of human development, the child's emerging personality depends in specific ways on the social matrix in which he is embedded and within which he grows. There is a kind of cultural nutriment that the social matrix provides the growing child that irresistibly shapes and molds his emerging personality. The mediators of that influence in the first instance are the parents; in the earliest stages the mother, and later both parents. The child begins the course of his life as a member of a group, the family. His membership becomes more explicit and more active as he grows and becomes more capable of active participation. As he moves on toward maturity and the pressures for development of identity and the need for fidelity grow, the social matrix broadens. The family becomes less and less influential as the determining matrix and context of meaningful participation. The broader social contexts become more meaningful, whether they be the world of education or work that the young adolescent enters. The religious group becomes the meaningful social matrix for the young religious, and the process of formation of religious identity depends in a crucial sense on the mutual interaction and regulation that accrues between the evolving individual and the matrix of meaning and value that the religious group provides.

I think one can usefully ask whether the problem of obedience as it arises in the contemporary scene is not in some part a reflection of the uncertainty and diffusion of objectives that afflict many religious groups. Religious groups are experiencing a relative disengagement from institutional commitments and a corresponding reorganization of goals, objectives, and purposes. As a result, the purposefulness and meaningfulness of religious activities are neither so clear nor so forceful as they once might have been. This must inevitably raise significant questions in the minds of religious of all ages, but particularly in the minds of younger religious in whom the concerns for personal identity and fidelity are more pressing and immediate. The disorganization and diffusion of purpose at the institutional level must have its impact on the personal level. It can only undermine the individual sense of meaningful personal commitment and thus undercut the motives underlying and supporting individual fidelity to the purposes and objectives of the group. Furthermore, it tends to undercut the individual's sense of identity and the security of his sense of meaningful relatedness within the group and in relation to broader religious purposes.

One cannot disengage the problem of obedience from this complex context. The maintenance of a mature sense of obedience relies on the integration of these many levels of development; it derives from a secure sense of identity and fidelity of commitment; it requires a meaningful integration of the residues of trust, autonomy, and initiative into an adequately functioning sense of identity. These are all important developmental perspectives. But it also relies on the integration of these developmental achievements within a stable and meaningfully organized social and institutional context. We shall have occasion to return to a consideration of this functional aspect of obedience later on, but the point that I wish to emphasize at the moment is that the functional aspects of obedience are intimately related to and are constantly influenced by developmental aspects. The adequate understanding of obedience requires that we be able to see their respective influences and the manner and extent to which they interact.

## Generativity

Up to this point in our consideration of the developmental process, we have been concerned with early development, with the development of the child and the young person. But development is only in a limited sense the process by which one grows to adult maturity. In a broader and more meaningful sense, it is a process that persists throughout life. When a man has achieved a mature sense of identity and self-mastery and of the purposefulness of his life, he has not completed the tasks of development. As he passes through adulthood and follows the inexorable path of growing old, he must face new challenges and new demands for adaptation which require his continued development.

I would like to focus on one aspect of mature development which has special relevance for the life of obedience. Generativity is an aspect of adult development which goes beyond the concern for self-meaning and self-integration. It is that quality of human growth which leads it to move beyond learning to teaching, beyond following to guiding, beyond dependence to caring. It is the concern which reaches beyond a focus on self and its interests and purposes, and brings into the focus of concern the bringing of the next generation to maturity. Generativity expresses itself in intergenerational concern. Erikson writes:

> Generativity, then, is primarily the concern in establishing and guiding the next generation, although there are individuals who, through misfortune or because of special and genuine gifts in other directions, do not apply this drive to their own offspring. And indeed, the concept of generativity is meant to include such more popular synonyms as *productivity* and *creativity,* which, however, cannot replace it.[8]

Thus generativity may be related to, but cannot be identified with, the impulse to produce the next generation by sexual means. On the contrary, many parents do not reach a level of true generativity.

Generativity, then, is an aspect of mature personality development which broadens and deepens one's own sense of belonging and meaningfulness in the concern for erecting those conditions in which the next generation can bring itself to the fullness of identity and maturity. I wish to emphasize that generativity is a developmental phase which involves a growth of personal commitments and resources. In bridging over to generativity, the individual inevitably undergoes a deepening of a sense of his own capacity and meaningfulness. He acknowledges his own place as responsible bearer of a tradition and a trust which must be communicated to the young if they are to be able to achieve the rudiments of trust and responsible autonomy. One must become not merely responsible for oneself and one's own actions and decisions, one must must become responsible for a tradition and a faith. One must further become responsible even more for its secure transfer in trust and meaningful relatedness to the next generation.

I would see generativity as a most significant aspect of the life of obedience. Obedience in the fullness of its meaning is not merely the response to a command of a superior. It is what Rahner has called a "life-form." It is an expression of an inner sense of identity and fidelity. It is not a pattern of activity but a structure of meaning in one's life that becomes a part of one's own inner sense of identity. It represents one's sharing in the life of a community which is directed to specific goals and objectives. It is this pattern of shared conviction and commitment that lends meaning to one's life and activity. Obedience is thus, from one aspect only, the individual's response to and participation in the authority relations that constitute the structure of the group. By it he is defined to the group as participating member and by it he is defined to himself as member, sharing in and committed to the ideals, values, and intents of the group. Obedience is an essential aspect of the individual's sense of religious identity.

Since obedience is such a central aspect of religious identity, generativity becomes an essential ingredient in the growth to maturity of religious obedience. The full flowering of obedience reaches beyond the concern with one's own obeying or one's own sense of religious belonging or sharing. It extends to a concern for meaningful continuity within the religious group. It extends to a concern for the meaningful integration of young religious into the shared religious experience of the group. It extends to a concern for their member-ship, for providing them with the guidance and support to enable them to grow in a sense of religious identity and fidelity. It extends to a commitment of oneself to the guaranteeing of the religious tradi-tions and their vitality and meaningful implementation, so that young religious have available to them institutions and structures perme-ated with a sense of purpose and guided by the inner conviction of fidelity to God's will and God's purposes.

The view of obedience that emerges from this developmental consideration places it more in the context of personal growth than in the context of responding to the commands or directives of a superior. To see it only in those terms is to see it only in the most limited of its perspectives. I have tried to bring into focus the idea of obedience as an aspect of personality that has its place in any human develpoment insofar as man is responsive to and participating in the social structures that sustain and give meaning to his life. Social structures are built around and embody structures and rela-tions of authority, and obedience is a necessary component and aspect of authority relations. Obedience has a special relevance in the religious context, however, since it is an essential aspect of the individual's sense of religious identity.

I have also tried to bring into clearer focus the interplay between obedience and a number of developmental parameters. Obedience emerges as an aspect of human personality that is subject to growth and development. It builds on and incorporates other significant aspects of development. It integrates in its fullness of development the elements of trust, autonomy, initiative, responsibility, and gen-erativity. Its functioning is derivative from and dependent on the degree to which each of these developmental parameters has been successfully achieved and integrated into the functioning personality. The impairment of development or the regressive deterioration of any of these aspects—for whatever reason, whether personal or in-stitutional—will limit and undermine the mature expression of obe-dience and will contribute to the persistent problem of obedience in all of its many forms.

*Chapter 14*

# Pathological Aspects of Obedience

It will sound somewhat extreme or perhaps threatening to some readers to focus on the pathology of obedience. Pathology implies a disorder in the functioning of a process. It carries the implications of disease and sickness. By pathology I mean to refer to those aspects of the functioning of obedience which reflect a developmental impairment in obedience, as well as those factors in human personality and the structure of authority relations that act to inhibit personal growth or impair the functioning of obedience in its mature sense. The impairments that we will address ourselves to in this section are pathological in the sense that they represent deviations from a norm; they are not necessarily pathological in the sense that they represent forms of diagnosable psychopathology or mental illness.

What we are dealing with in the consideration of deviant aspects of obedience are more in the order of traits of character which have been formed in the course of development and which take their expression in a style of thinking, acting, and experiencing. Such traits make up the substance of personality and may be quite normal and adaptive for individuals in the day-to-day living-out of their experience. They may at the same time reflect developmental defects or characteristic attitudes and styles of defense that can influence their patterns of response in obedience and can limit their capacity to achieve a more mature level of functioning in obedience. The same traits, however, can take a more extreme and neurotic shape and express themselves in ways that can no longer pass for normal, but can be diagnosed and described in formally pathological terms. What we are dealing with, however, are not primarily these limiting cases of disturbance, but rather the broad range of personality styles and character traits that make up the functioning personalities of the people who make up the living contexts within which obedience must be exercised and expressed.

## Developmental Deviations

We can approach this aspect from the point of view of the developmental framework that we have been considering in the preceding section. The defects that we are talking about have their roots in the developmental process. If that process runs its course in an optimal fashion, there will be an optimal growth in personality which will allow the individual to reach a relatively mature level of obedience. As we have seen, the earlier phases of development set the stage for and create the conditions within which later stages can be worked out. The issue of trust, for example, which is focused particularly in the earliest stages of the mother-child interaction, is fundamental for all further personality development. If there is a defect in basic trust, the infant will not have the support and inner security that he needs to meet and successfully resolve the issue of autonomy. The original impairment can affect all subsequent levels of development. The same thing is true for each of the respective stages. The more successful the resolution of the developmental crisis at each stage, the more probable is it that succeeding crises will be more or less successfully resolved.

Keeping this dynamic developmental perspective in mind, we can focus on each of the aspects and try to determine what influence its relative impairment might have on obedience. The impairment of each aspect can be either by way of excess or by way of defect. Each aspect has an optimal range in which the issues are resolved in such a way as to maximize growth potential and optimally serve the needs of further development and adaptation. The resolution of each crisis may be impaired by a relative excess or a relative defect of the aspect in question. Each of these deviations from the optimal range carries with it impediments and risks for the development of obedience and has a characteristic expression in the life of obedience.

If we look first at the element of trust, the deviations from basic trust can take the form either of a deficit in trust, which Erikson has called basic mistrust, or of an excess of trust. The influence of mistrust in the workings of obedience can be quite pervasive and profound and insidious. At its most deviant and disruptive worst, the defect of basic trust impairs all human relationships and makes any meaningful contact with other human beings a dreaded threat to one's own existence. The infant's primitive fears of devouring the other person or of being devoured by him if he gets too close underlies some of the most severe personality disturbances. At less pathological levels, however, mistrust introduces a chronic hesitation and uncertainty into relationships of all kinds. The lack of trust introduces an element of suspicion and doubt into the authority relation. Consequently the individual's capacity to respond willingly and spontaneously to the directives of another can be qualified to some degree—from very minor to very severe degrees depending on the measure of trust attained—and introduces a basic flaw into the authority relation that impedes its effectiveness and congeniality.

If the relationship between a superior and a subject is governed by mistrust, to that degree it is impossible for the authority relation to work itself out in any but the terms of power and position. I have analyzed the authority relation at length in order to make it clear that the authority relation derives from and depends on a mutual regulation between superior and subject. In order for that balance in the relation to obtain, there must be an input of trust on both sides. Each of the participants must enter and share in the relation with a sense of trust in the trustworthiness of the other and a sense of his own trustworthiness. Both aspects are essential and they must be operative on both sides of the relation. Mistrust undercuts both. It inhibits the subject's capacity to trust the superior, to have confidence in his judgment—fallible and limited though it must be—to trust in his intentions, to have a sense of optimism and faith about the course of events. The subject cannot open himself to this kind of determination by the will of another without feeling a sense of loss, of impediment, of diminution of self, of loss of control and dread, all of which reflect the basic uncertainty of a state in which the organism had to depend on the other for life-sustaining operations and in which the failure of trust threatened the loss of self and a sense of impending disaster. At the same time, mistrust undercuts the subject's sense of his own trustworthiness, of his own capacity to deal with the demands of his environment, to take the measure of reality and deal with it, to compensate for the failures and inadequacies of the other where needed, to achieve an optimal result in a cooperative context of a directive taken in faith.

Looking at it from the other end of the relationship, if the superior enters the relation with a sense of mistrust it has significant effects on the working of obedience. The superior will have only a limited trust in the maturity, reliability, and responsibility of the subject. His reliance on the subject's judgment and good intention will be undercut and their interaction will be pervaded with insecurity and uncertainty. The superior will tend to feel an uneasy sense of things going wrong unless he assumes responsibility for their carrying out. He will have difficulty in assuming an easy reliance on his subject and will lack a sense of the subject's trustworthiness. In the face of such mistrust, then, both superior and subject have no recourse but to retreat to more secure and more defended positions. The problem is, however, that these positions are governed by the degree of mistrust and represent less mature levels of the development of obedience. Trust, therefore, provides a basic substratum on which obedience builds and without which the structure of obedience is built on sand.

Trust can also err in the direction of excess and that posture also brings with it certain impediments to mature obedience. If the subject is too trusting, his obedience takes on a quality of naiveté. It undercuts his sense of self-reliance and his capacity to take a critical and relatively objective view of the superior's and his own actions. The excess of trust can lead him to a position of unquestioning acceptance and assumptions to the effect that, whatever and however the superior should decide an issue, it is good and right. The more traditional view of obedience idealized this aspect of obedience. The more trust, the better. The model of obedience as hierarchical and based on power which was vested in the superior worked best when trust was maximized in the subject's attitude. His response in obedience would thus tend to be unquestioning, accepting, and uncritical. But such obedience becomes fixated at an early developmental level by an excess of trust so that the individual is inhibited from moving on to more mature and more meaningful levels of obedience. The difficulty with such an excess of trust is that it tends to impede the capacity for autonomy and thus tends to undermine the individual's sense of responsibility and initiative. A more mature form of obedience, as we are envisioning it here, reflects and depends on more mature levels of personality development and represents an integration of elements of trust, autonomy, responsibility, initiative, and freedom. The excess of trust freezes the process of obedience at a relatively immature and regressive level.

Trust can just as well be excessive in the superior as in the subject. Excessive trust in the superior induces a failure in the superior's responsibility too. In the authority relation, the superior's function demands that he accept and exercise his responsibility in decision-making and direction. It is possible for him to vacate that responsibility by excessive trust in his subjects. Each level in the structure of authority has its appropriate functions in terms of decisions and actions. The superior at any level has responsibility for certain functions, and if he leaves them for subordinates out of a sense of excess trust, he violates them by imposing the responsibility on them and thus disrupts and undercuts the proper functioning of authority.

Deviations in autonomy can effectively undermine obedience, perhaps more effectively than any other developmental parameter. The developmental process can lead to a hypertrophy of autonomy, or conversely to an atrophy. The parental failure to meet the child's need for an emerging sense of self-direction with firm guidance can intensify the struggle for autonomy and drive the child to an extreme of willfulness and stubbornness that represents a desperate clinging to his own will in the face of all opposition. The struggle for autonomy takes the form of a desperate holding on to and a refusal to let go except on one's own terms and at one's own time. Such autonomy is threatened and insecure, so that it must assert itself all the more vigorously and all the more absolutely. It is perhaps wrong to speak of a hypertrophy of autonomy. Autonomy achieves its fullness in an optimal range and the deviations from it, whether by excess or by deficit, entail a lessening of real autonomy. It is essential to the notion of autonomy that one not only have a sense of one's own independence and capacity for inner direction and control, but also that one have a respect for and responsiveness to the independence of others. Autonomy involves a sense of independence that does not abstract itself from a healthy dependence on others and does not ignore the dependence of others on oneself. Autonomy maintains a sense of inner direction and control as a potential resource that is available when needed, but that inner resource is secure enough so that it does not need constant and unremitting assertion. The autonomous person can open himself to direction and control from his environment without a sense of loss of self-esteem or without feeling that his compliance represents a subjugation or submission. Where autonomy fails, either in the excess or in the deficit, yielding to external directives becomes a question of power and the individual's response must be governed by the concerns of power—who has it and who does not, who wins and who loses, who is humiliated and who is victorious. These are not the concerns of true autonomy.

Thus the excessive stubbornness and willfulness of hypertrophied autonomy is in another sense a violation and an evacuation of autonomy. It is a fearful autonomy that must have its own way and cannot accept the direction of another without seeing it as an attack, as an infringement on itself, without feeling that accepting such direction is a form of subjugation, without feeling a sense of loss and diminution of self in such acceptance. Such an individual cannot obey without submission. He sees the directive of authority as depriving him of autonomy and not as an opportunity to exercise his autonomy. There is a tendency to absolutize such deprivation too. The individual tends to feel that he is not only giving in and subjugating himself, but that the subjugation is total; he is not only giving in to another's control but he is completely surrendering himself to that other's power. He is left with a feeling of empty and desperate powerlessness.

The authority relation for such people is a threat, precisely because it is seen in terms of power and control. True autonomy does not see the authority relation in these terms at all. For the truly autonomous person, obedience is not an evacuation or lessening of autonomy, it is an opportunity to exercise it. Autonomous obedience is neither a mere acceptance of an authoritative directive nor a submission of one's will to another's. It is a request or stimulus for the individual to engage himself in a common effort, to participate and contribute to the achievement of group goals, to direct his activity to some objective. The individual's response in obedience is a deliberate commitment which derives from his own sense of autonomy and free initiative. The obedient response requires an acceptance of such responsibility, it requires an independent self-determination, it requires the exercise of critical and independent judgment, it requires a sense of responsible self-commitment and involvement. Obedience is violated in this sense by a willful and rebellious refusal, just as much as by an unthinking and unquestioning accomplishment of the task. Both are a violation of the individual's responsibility and autonomy and in both obedience suffers.

The atrophy of autonomy also wreaks havoc with obedience. Such an individual lacks a sense of his own independence and possesses a basic insecurity and uncertainty about his own capacity to control his inner impulses and to direct himself to meaningful and constructive goals. He cannot assert himself without a sense of inner doubt and shame. He cannot look to himself as a source of trustworthy or reliable judgment or direction. In the face of his inner insecurity and lack of autonomy, his capacity for responsibility and initiative are minimized and he seeks security and reliability in the judgment and direction of others. He also sees himself as powerless and others as powerful, but his involvement with authority is not a struggle for power and control—it is a struggle that he has already lost. He need not react against the threat of loss of power by willful stubbornness or rebelliousness, he has no power to be threatened. His only recourse is submission and meek acceptance of the directives and control of others. Such an individual serves as a caricature of the more traditional view of obedience. Self-effacement, self-sacrifice, self-immolation, and total submission to God's and the superior's will were the parameters of the model of obedience.

Such an individual, however, is incapable of mature obedience. Mature obedience derives from the individual's capacity to see himself as an independent source of responsible judgment and action. Unless he has that inner sense of self-reliance and autonomy, he cannot respond to and meet the request made of him by authority. He cannot take up and exercise what I have elsewhere referred to as "responsible subjecthood."[1] He cannot enter into that process of mutual regulation that is the essence of the authority relation and of the participation in it through obedience. Without a sense of himself as an autonomous source of responsible direction and control and without a sense of his own inner resourcefulness, the individual has no recourse but to cling to sources of stability and strength outside of himself. This is not mature obedience by any means; it is rather a caricature of obedience along the lines of an infantile model.

There are deviations of autonomy on the side of the superior as well. Hypertrophy in his sense of autonomy interferes with obedience by overriding the autonomy of the subject. As we have pointed out, such autonomy is a false autonomy that covers an inner sense of insecurity and uncertainty. The tendency, therefore, is for the superior to try to exercise control over all decision making and to leave little room for subordinates to exercise their proper judgment. Such pseudoautonomy is unable to recognize the respective autonomy of other individuals and cannot allow itself to leave room for the exercise of the autonomy of others. Such a superior tends to be rigid, controlling, and repressive. He tends to cast the model of authority in the mode of power and power-conflicts. His position is the reciprocal of the atrophy of autonomy in the subject. Where the subject sees no power in himself and all power in the superior, this kind of superior sees all power in himself and views any exercise of autonomy in the subject as a threat and a challenge to that power. Such a superior will be highly threatened by the hyperautonomous subject—such that the authority relation between them and its correlative obedience will degenerate into a willful and stubborn struggle for control and the exercise of power that cannot help but be marked by repression and rebelliousness. The capacity for mutual regulation and responsive autonomy on both sides would be severely undermined.

The superior can also demonstrate an atrophy of autonomy which leads him away from responsible exercise of his authority to a weak and overly permissive evacuation of authority. The appropriate exercise of authority demands that the superior see himself as an independent and responsible source of influence on others. He must see himself as capable of making meaningful decisions and as capable of directing others to meaningful goals. Insofar as he lacks this sense of inner reliance and resourcefulness, it represents a deficit of autonomy and ·impairs his capacity to act responsibly and effectively in his capacity as superior. He must look to the responsibility and initiative of others to take over the vacuum of authority that his own insecurity creates. Mutual regulation fails and the subject is put in a position of inappropriate decision making. The subject's exercise of self-direction and autonomy is no longer obedience because it takes place in a context of defective authority rather than being derived from a matrix of effective authority. Obedience must take place within the context of the authority relation or else it ceases to be obedience.

Returning to our developmental perspective, we can now turn to the deviations of initiative. Initiative is the extension of the child's impulses to self-expression and aggressive intrusiveness into his environment, an intrusiveness that expresses itself in many modalities and rests on the assurance that the child can be allowed to explore the limits of his capacities and reach out into the unknown without a loss of the assurances of love and support and without a loss of the inner sense of self-reliance, reliability, and competence. Competence in the sense I am using it here has a special meaning that refers to an individual's sense of capability of more or less competent performance and a sense of mastery of necessary skills for the adequate performance of what he seeks to accomplish. Initiative, then, expresses itself as the capacity for self-direction without fear of loss of competence and without guilt.

Mature initiative is again embedded in the structure of an authority relation and is caught up in the interaction of multiple initiatives. One's own initiative is optimally limited by the initiative of others, just as one's autonomy is limited by the autonomy of others. It is true conversely that one's own initiative derives from the initiative of others and depends on it, just as one's own autonomy derives from and depends on the autonomy of others. Excessive initiative can ride roughshod over the initiative of others. It can become a respecter of its own prerogatives and a disrespecter of the prerogatives of others. Excessive initiative can violate obedience by removing itself from the context of authority and expressing itself in a form of hyperindividualism which ignores the goals, objectives, and needs of the religious group. In this form excessive initiative is linked with hyperautonomy.

Optimally initiative functions in the context of the intermeshed initiatives of the group and its members. There is room, however, in the responsible exercise of initiative for the initiative of individuals to be brought to bear on the group. This is an essential aspect of the continuing vitality of the group. The group needs new life and new purpose injected into it in order that it continue to serve a meaningful purpose and that its functions remain meaningful and relevant. The continual process of adaptation in the group and the continual refocusing of its goals and objectives can come about only through the influence of individuals interacting with other members of the group and influencing the group in one or other direction. This requires initiative on the part of the members. The initiative that brings new life and vitality most often comes from the young of any culture —and even more so in the religious group, the vital initiatives come from the younger members of the religious group who are more attuned to the need for change and adaptation. Consequently, the religious group has a stake in the initiative of its younger members insofar as this is inextricably involved in its own survival and relevance. The strength of institutions lies in their capacity to foster and nurture the initiative of the young—serving it at the same time with the support and guidance which allows it to integrate itself constructively with the inner dynamisms of common goals and values. The religious community must find it in itself to offer that guidance with the acknowledgment and acceptance of the possibility that the integration of new initiatives may bring with it the alteration, if not growth, of the structures, values, and goals with which it identifies itself.

It is worth re-emphasizing here once again that obedience is essentially a call to initiative. It is an initiative from a superior to reach out and elicit the initiative of the subject. The subject's initiative becomes congruent with the initiative of a superior or the group he represents to the extent that he identifies with the group and has internalized the group's goals and values as his own. To that extent he becomes part of the group and his initiative becomes part of the group's initiative. Excessive initiative, however, sets itself up in opposition to the group and as divisive from the group. It is important to grasp the distinction between an initiative that opposes the group initiative and an initiative that contributes a new sense of direction to the group initiative. The former separates itself from the group initiative and is either indifferent to the group initiative or works against it. The latter joins itself to the group initiative and in so doing modifies the group initiative. This latter is the form of responsible initiative that serves as a constructive force in the religious group and which is elicited in mature obedience. These remarks are equally applicable to the initiative of all members of the religious group, superiors as well as subjects.

The lack of initiative, therefore, must be seen as equally detrimental to the functioning of obedience. The lack of initiative is a violation of obedience in that it serves as an evasion of the responsibility to which one is called by obedience. One owes the religious group the contribution of one's own initiative. It is an essential resource of the group and a vital source of institutional vitality. If individuals are in default by reason of their withholding of initiative, it also is true that the religious group can be in default by its refusal to acknowledge or encourage the initiative of its members. Initiative must be met with initiative. The individual's initiative must be met with a response in initiative from the group in order for it to be meaningful or for it to effect anything. The failure of initiative, therefore, that so plagued earlier forms and structures of obedience was not so much a failure of the initiative of individuals as it was a failure of the initiative of the group. The failure of initiative on one level required the suppression of initiative on another level. The result was a situation in which individuals tended to withhold their initiative and to leave all initiative in the hands of superiors. Individual initiative atrophied and the response of obedience came to be little more than doing what one was told.

The superior's initiative is closely allied with his leadership function, if not identical. At least leadership is the primary channel of expression of his initiative vis-à-vis the group. Currently the functions of the superior in the religious group are undergoing significant changes. Traditionally he was primarily a decision maker who made the important policy and operational decisions which other members of the religious group carried out under obedience. The superior is less and less in that position. The complexity of matters of decision makes it impossible or foolhardy for the decision-making process to be left in the hands of a single person. The decision-making process is thus gradually becoming more and more diffuse and is involving more and more of the active membership of the religious group. However, as this process continues, the role of the superior is concurrently changing. While he still holds the formal decision-making position, his function is tending more and more toward the exercise of leadership. In times of rapid and radical change, such as the period of transition in religious life we are currently experiencing, the function of leadership becomes crucial for the adaptability and effectiveness of the religious group.[2] Part of the current crisis in religious life can be ascribed to a failure in effective leadership within the religious group. Part of the Problem is that superiors see themselves in terms of an older model of functioning and have not yet generally responded to the demand for leadership in a broader and more personal sense.

Leadership in the context of obedience as we have been describing it is best envisioned in terms of the interaction of respective initiatives. The superior is most effectively exercising his leadership when his initiative operates in such a way as to elicit and stimulate the initiative of his subjects. If the superior errs in the direction of excess, he can easily override the initiative of his subjects. This inevitably tends to repress the initiative of subjects and the operation of authority tends to drift in the direction of a centralization of initiative. The superior thereby deprives his subjects of the area of their own appropriate initiative. If the superior errs by way of defect, he fails to exercise his leadership function and the group runs the risk of a diffusion of initiative away from group concerns and objectives. Individual initiative then becomes divisive and directed toward individual goals rather than group goals. The leadership function of the superior is required to organize and direct the initiative of individuals toward group goals and objectives. It should be noted that such initiative cannot take the form of merely giving orders. It rather requires the enlistment of interests and personal investment, so that the function of leadership in the religious group is a much more complex and difficult matter than the earlier and more traditional views of the superior's role would allow.

When we turn to the developmental issue of identity, we touch upon that aspect of personality integration which is most central and which in a sense underlies the others. Identity and its related mechanism of identification bring into focus many complex issues which are involved in the relationship between the individual and the group. Identity has to do with the integration of patterns of identification and role constellations by which the individual identifies himself as belonging to a certain group and by which the group in turn identifies him as belonging to it. The "belonging" is not merely a matter of card-carrying affiliation, but it involves real membership and a sense of belonging to the group as both an object of commitment and the place of one's self-interest. The degree to which the religious attains a sense of identity as a religious, i.e., as a participating member who belongs to this specific religious group as the group belongs to him, reflects the degree to which he identifies with group values and objectives. Through his identification he makes the group his own and thus internalizes group values and invests group goals with his own personal interest.

The excessive risk in identity is overidentification. The individual can become over identified with group goals, values, and patterns of action. There can result a failure of objectivity. The individual can lose his sense of critical evaluation and judgment, and his capacity to test reality can be impaired. His real sense of autonomy can thereby be eroded. Such an individual will tend in the direction of unquestioning compliance and conformity. His overidentification leads to a rigid adherence to group standards and norms. This kind of identificatory excess lies at the root of fanaticism in its various forms. While identity derives from a sense of fidelity to the group and its values, the excess takes the form of a hypercommitment by which the individual's own individuality becomes dissolved in the attachment to the group. Fidelity tends to become fanaticism and initiative turns to compliance.

Excessive identification with the group can take more subtle and enduring forms. One's own sense of identity can become linked with a certain set of structures and patterns of activity in the group, such that any attempt to change the existing pattern can undermine that identity and place it in jeopardy. This is one of the major psychological problems that have arisen in the context of renewal and the postconciliar transformations that have taken place in the Church. Religious orders have been severely affected by the currents of change, and the structures of religious groups are undergoing a metamorphosis. The strong and somewhat rigid identification with preexistent structures places the inner sense of identity of many religious in jeopardy as the structures on which they depend are modified. The phenomenon is not restricted to older religious, but it presents itself in a most pressing fashion in their regard. There is no surprise in this. The commitment of self and personal investment of the individual tends to increase in proportion to the amount of time he has been a member of the group. His identity is defined in terms of specific roles that he fulfills within the group, and he defines himself as a person in relation to specific structures and patterns of organization within the group. Older religious have defined their own identities much more in terms of the extant structures, and the investment that they have in preserving and maintaining those structures comes to be the investment that they make in the preservation of their own personal identities. The threat that is posed by significant changes is readily understandable in these terms. The problem is less one of liberalism versus conservatism, and more one of the maintenance of inner continuity and the sense of belonging that is implicit in identity.

The fidelity that is implicit in identity at its best allows the individual a sense of faithful commitment, but it does not prevent him from critical evaluation and autonomous determination outside of the group or in opposition to it. One of the aspects of excessive identification that plays a significant role in contemporary difficulties over obedience is that it tends to foster an adherence to more traditional and familiar forms of obedience. Part of the problem is that many religious, who overidentify with prior structures of religious life, identify themselves as religious according to a modality of obedience that dictates passive conformity and self-sacrificing acceptance as the proper demeanor of the religious person. This is bolstered by a well-developed rhetoric of obedience which constantly holds up the model of the crucified Christ who was obedient—even to the death of the cross. The point that I wish to emphasize here is that this model of obedience is closely linked with the manner in which individuals identify themselves as religious, with the effect that any other posture becomes difficult and provokes anxiety. At a deeper level, however, no human being can violate his own inner sense of identity, autonomy, and responsibility without the stirring of anger, resentment, and hostility. Unconscious hostility is the price one pays for overidentification and the submission of obedience. These issue in the channeling of aggression externally in rigidity, punitiveness, discontent, hypermoralism—or they are channeled within to produce depression, poor self-esteem, self-defeating or self-destructive practices, work inhibition, and alienation from the religious group. The form of obedience that flows from overidentification and expresses itself in self-effacement and submission is a cloak for deeper resentments and hostility.

If overidentification is the risk on the side of excess, the defect of identity takes the form of a lack of identification and an unclarity in the definition of roles by which one defines his place and function in the group. The failure to achieve some sense of identification with the religious group and its goals and values undermines the individual's capacity for faithful commitment and diminishes his sense of fidelity. He is left without a real sense of belonging or sharing. Even as nature abhors a vacuum, the human personality abhors a lack or diffuseness of identity. The danger is that the individual who has not achieved a sense of religious identity will crystallize for himself a divergent identity—what Erikson has called a negative identity. The individual may set himself up as the protagonist of religious views and values. He may set himself against anything and everything that is traditional or which is valued by the religious group. The issue in such a posture is not only a difficulty with pre-existant forms and structures, but it is driven by the inner need to find a meaningful identity where that identity has not been available—for one or other reason—in the religious group. This does not mean that every opposition to traditional structures and values has this inner dynamism. One must distinguish carefully between the pressure toward negative identity that flows from a failure of the formation of religious identity and the opposition that derives from a more autonomous sense of identity which expresses itself in the initiative that brings new life and vitality to the group.

The deficit in identity expresses itself in a kind of diffusion of identity—an inability to find one's place or define oneself within the reference systems that compose the structure of one's life. This may involve work, personal relations with other people, or the general orientation to the society and culture that one claims as one's own. The picture is one that is frequently met among contemporary youth who in their wish to escape from the intolerable purposelessness of the sense of identity diffusion resort to cliques, gangs, drugs, delinquency, etc. One of the major defenses that can be directed against this sense of deficiency of identity is overidentification. We have already discussed the effects of such a flight into hyperidentity, but we must appreciate that the flight is driven by the anxiety connected with the underlying sense of lack or diffusion of identity.

The problem of obedience is so complex and as difficult, precisely because mature obedience requires and derives from an underlying and secure sense of identity. All of the deviations and difficulties can be related to an underlying sense of lack of identity—in superiors or subjects or both. The maturity of superiorship and of subjecthood and the capacity for mutual regulation and interchange that is the hallmark of an authentic authority relation rests on the inner sense of identity of the respective participants. The tendency to rigid authoritarianism, dogmatism, and the hard and fast insistence on the prerogatives of obedience are reactions to a lack of the sense of identity. Tendencies to submissive compliance or insolent rebellion share the same underlying sense of lack. The loss of a sense of identity exposes the individual to the residual conflicts and uncertainties of his own childhood. The result for the exercise of obedience is that individuals regress to a less mature and more infantile form of obedience—one that retreats from the mature exercise of autonomy, responsibility, initiative, and freedom—and resort to the extremes of rigid domination and submissive compliance. The result for religious life and the vitality of the religious group is that the inner resources of such an individual become unavailable to the group, either because of psychological impediments or because the individual seeks to resolve the intolerable ambiguity and ambivalence of identity diffusion by seeking another, nonreligious identity. This dynamism I would guess lies at the root of many of the defections from religious life we have been witnessing in recent years.

To complete this consideration of pathological deviations in obedience, let us turn to the issue of generativity. It is easier to speak here of the defect of generativity. Generativity is the natural prolongation and extension of the mature sense of identity and the sense of achieved identification with the religious group and its goals and values that interpenetrates the sense of identity. The risk that it runs is the extension of the risk of overidentification, that the sense of excessive commitment and rigid adherence to the existing structure can bring about a willed imposition of the structure on younger members of the religious group. Adherence to the structure can be imposed on those who are coming to align themselves with it with a rigidity that overrides the essential individuality and initiative of younger members. Authentic generativity concerns itself with the fostering of true obedience, which implies and demands the growth to the fullness of trust, autonomy, initiative, responsibility, and freedom. These are the building blocks and essential bases of mature identity, which is the correlative of true obedience. The excess of generativity, however, dedicates itself to the preservation and prolongation of the structures of the religious group, not to the fostering of mature identity in those who may find their identity within and through the religious group. The rigid adherence to the structure can thus impede the growth to real religious identity, and generativity becomes a caricature of itself. Mature obedience is scarred in the process because what is sought is submission to and acceptance of the structures as they presently exist.

Generativity more frequently can be observed in its defect rather than its excess. Individual religious lose a sense of themselves as the bearers and conveyors of the tradition of the group. The failure to achieve a sense of generativity is most often a reflection of the failure of identity and the correlative of loss of self-esteem and value of oneself as a participating member of the religious group. There is a tendency to feel lost and inessential. One feels that the group goes on whether one is part of it or not, that it has a life of its own independently of one's own sharing in it or contribution to it. This position is essentially self-devaluing and tends to manifest itself along with other components of depression. One feels helpless and inadequate. There develops the "what's the use" or "who cares" syndrome. The essentially depressive condition is relatively common among older religious who feel left out and bypassed by the flow of events and ongoing changes that are taking place in the religious group. Not only is there a context of fairly rapid change which makes them feel like outsiders, but the internal changes that come inevitably with age and the slow deterioration of one's strength and capacity tends to produce a loss of function that severely threatens their self-esteem and pushes them into feeling that they have nothing of value to offer. While such attitudes are easy to understand, it is also apparent that they omit the important considerations that we are urging in terms of the issue of generativity. Older members of the religious group are pre-eminently the bearers of tradition in the group, and they owe to the group and its younger members the guidance and confirmation of trust that is and has been their possession.

The failure of generativity leads inevitably to a form of self-absorption and self-pity that undermines not only the individual's capacity to function, but severely injures the vitality and adaptive potentiality of the group. The capacity of the group to adapt to the inevitable and inexorable changes in which it is caught up depends both on the constant injection of new vitality and new initiative from the influx of younger members and on the continuity with the strengths of the past and the guidance of wisdom and experience that can come only from the older generation. Conditions that minimize or reduce the potential contribution of either source of strength likewise impede the effectiveness and adaptive capacity of the religious group.

## Pathological Types of Obedience

The pathology of obedience can be approached from a variety of standpoints. An approach from one or other perspective will overlap considerably with those of other perspectives, but each perspective brings different factors and dimensions of the problem into clearer and hopefully complementary focus. We have been considering the deviations from a basically developmental schema. Such deviations can align themselves in a variety of constellations with almost infinite variation. I would like to focus at this point on several more or less consistent and relatively general patterns of response to obedience. Under this heading I would like to discuss the authoritarian, the obsessive, the paranoid, and the narcissistic approaches to obedience. Points of conjunction and overlap with our previous considerations will become apparent as we proceed.

The first type we can consider is the authoritarian personality. The authoritarian personality was originally studied in relation to anti-Semitism in Nazi Germany in the 1930's. Interest in anti-Semitism and ethnocentric attitudes was carried on in the postwar years in a massive study carried out at the University of California.[3] A variety of testing data and other studies pointed to a certain consistent pattern of characteristics which designated the "authoritarian personality."[4] Significant aspects of this constellation included a rigid adherence to conventional middle-class values, a submissive and uncritical attitude toward idealized moral authorities, a tendency to be sensitive to and punitive toward anyone who violated conventional values, a tough-minded attitude and an insistence on "objectivity," a tendency toward superstitious belief in the mystical determination of fate and a tendency to think in rigid categories and stereotypes, a general preoccupation with power-control or strength-weakness and a tendency to identify with powerful figures, a general attitude of hostility and punitiveness, a tendency to project unconscious emotional impulses and to believe that dangerous things are happening or could happen, and finally an excessive concern with sexual fantasies.

The California study demonstrated that these characteristics tended to be related to each other and to occur together. This kind of finding does not force us to the conclusion that such covariance indicates an underlying personality type, or for that matter that personalities exist which carry these qualities. The characteristics do have a certain consistency regardless of how frequently they are associated, so that we can reasonably speak of authoritarian characteristics or attitudes. Such attitudes are found at large in the population and may represent aspects of every human personality. The differences are matters of the degree to which such attitudes are manifested by individuals. The authoritarian personality, therefore, is a construct and represents a typology that may be difficult to identify in reality. It is important to keep these qualifications in mind when we are discussing such personality types.

The authoritarian attitude derives from a feeling of inner inadequacy and weakness. The threat of autonomy and independence is too great, and consequently the authoritarian seeks to adhere to something outside of himself by which he can acquire the strength that he lacks. The position is essentially sadomasochistic and expresses itself in strivings for domination or submission. The authoritarian attitude rests on basically masochistic feelings of inferiority, powerlessness, and insignificance. Sadistic feelings are often involved, even in the same person, and express themselves in the tendency to make others dependent on oneself, to have absolute power over others, and to make others suffer. Such tendencies are often repulsive to those who have them and they remain unconscious. They are masked and defended against by reaction formations and rationalizations of excessive concern for the welfare of others. "I rule you and control you because I know what is really best for you." It must be remembered, however, that the sadistic aspect of authoritarian attitudes does not dominate others out of a real sense of care and concern, but he cares for others and is concerned about them only insofar as and because he can dominate them.

The authoritarian need for power, therefore, is not rooted in strength, but in weakness. It admires authority and tends to submit to it, while at the same time wishing to have authority and to have others submit. Moreover, authority and its exercise is conceived and responded to in terms of power. We have already seen Erich Fromm's description of the authoritarian view of power.[5]

The authoritarian character looks at the world in terms of power and sees all relationships and structures in terms of power. He sees himself as having to submit to fate, in the form of destiny, or providence, or natural law, or even more specifically as the will of God. He seeks out of an inner compulsion a higher power in the face of which he has no recourse but to submit. He does not lack courage or strength of belief. But the rootedness of his existence in powerlessness gives his activity a specific quality. Action is taken in the name of the higher power. Courage becomes the strength to endure and accept whatever fate a higher power designates for him. The highest virtue is suffering and the epitome of heroism is submission to fate— not to change it or direct it.

The roots of the problem for the authoritarian personality lie in aggression. Aggression is a fundamental dimension of human existence and experience. It is universally expressed and almost as universally denied. It is a basic human instinct and the problem in human development is not whether an individual will be aggressive or not, but rather how he will learn to modify and direct his aggression. There is no human relationship of any significance that does not elicit and serve as a channel for the expression of aggression. The difficulty for the authoritarian is that he cannot tolerate his own aggressive impulses. He must deal with them by various stratagems and defensive manoeuvres. He lacks a sense of mastery over his own aggressive impulses and feelings. Poorly controlled and regulated aggression retains a primitive and destructive quality which is threatening and terrifies the weak ego. The issue of control is a major one for such personalities; in the first instance, the control of inner impulses, but in the second instance the control of aggression in and from others. A preoccupation with problems of power and control is no surprise in these circumstances.

The inner insecurities about the control of aggression have large implications. The individual seeks reinforcement in his struggle to gain control by allying himself with the sources of power and control in his environment. He bolsters his own inner sense of fragile control by a psychic alliance with the power centers around him. His submission to moral authorities thus tends to become rigid and uncritical; his investment has to be in maintaining their power and position of influence. His anxieties are aroused whenever anything threatens the security of the prevailing power alliance. Any change in the power structure thus becomes a threat to internal security. If he exercises authority, he does so insecurely and is threatened by anything that challenges the absoluteness of his power and the security of his control. His anxiety can be alleviated only by unquestioning submission from his subordinates. Any initiative from a subordinate has to be outside of his control and is thus a threat to his control and a challenge to his power status.

We have observed that such tendencies are widely distributed—even though they are also widely denied for a variety of reasons. Conflicts over aggression are the common human lot and authoritarian types of solution are frequent. The influence of authoritarian tendencies on obedience can be quite significant. The authoritarian attitude approaches the authority relation in terms of power. It thus becomes impossible—or very difficult—for such individuals to enter the authority relation in any other terms than dominance-submission, or to see the relation in any other terms than a vertical, hierarchical structure in which power and control are vested in the superior, and not in the subject. The authority relation cannot be seen in terms of the interaction and mutual regulation of autonomous, free, and responsible individuals. True obedience is unavoidably impaired.

Data dealing with the extent or intensity of authoritarian attitudes are hard to come by, and conclusive data are not available. The research conducted by Stanley Milgram and his associates at Yale has already been discussed.[6] If one thinks for a moment of the atrocities of the persecution of Jews in Nazi Germany and the horror of the concentration camps, or if one thinks for a moment of the more recents events surrounding the My Lai incident, one shudders at the horrors that can be wrought in the name of obedience and legitimate authority. It does not escape the psychological observer that the administration of painful punishment is in itself a sadistic and aggressive act. One wonders what repressed impulses may not have been legitimized by the experimenter's command and thus motivated the subjects' responses.

We can speculate that these surprising results reflect the operation of an authoritarian need which expressed itself in a willingness to ally oneself with an external source of power, the experimeter in this case. The degree and extent of this tendency is what is so surprising. It suggests that the tendency toward more authoritarian attitudes to authority and obedience are more general than might otherwise have been suspected. At this point we can only speculate about the extent to which authoritarian attitudes influence the pattern of the exercise of obedience in religious life. We can at least suggest, however, that the authoritarian need for an external source of strength may find a congenial and responsive context in the ready-made structures of hierarchically organized authority that have so characterized religious groups in the past, and in the ultimate appeal to the need for submission to and acceptance of a divinely dictated fate behind which there stands the infinite assurance of God's omnipotent will. Such a context, so intensely held and advanced in the traditional rhetoric of obedience, provides a ready ground for authoritarian attitudes to flourish and take root. It may also provide an underlying psychological attractiveness that authoritarian needs in religiously inclined individuals may find very appealing. If that speculation is supportable, we could expect the structure of obedience to assume an authoritarian form in religious life.

The obsessive personality presents a somewhat different picture. Like authoritarian traits, obsessive characteristics can manifest themselves in an individual's personality across a wide range of degrees of intensity. Many well-functioning personalities show a certain degree of obsessiveness and compulsiveness which serves them in good stead and enables them to be comparatively productive and hard-working members of society. A certain degree of obsessional defense is to be expected as a normal developmental phenomenon. One would find it suspiciously abnormal not to find some degree of obsessiveness and compulsivity in the latency-age child. A certain moderate degree of adaptive obsessiveness is well within the limits of normality for well-functioning adults as well.

But obsessional and compulsive traits can be shown with increasing degrees of intensity. At more severe levels such traits can combine into what is called the obsessive personality. The obsessive traits come to dominate the person's style and organization of his life and put a definite stamp on the overall pattern of his experience and activity. The degree of pathology and personal impairment in such individuals can vary considerably. At the extremes of severity, obsessive and compulsive elements can take over the functioning of the personality and cause the individual considerable discomfort and impairment of his daily living. This is the pattern of the obsessive-compulsive neurosis. Such individuals are overwhelmed with doubt and guilt. They are often driven to resort to elaborate rituals which they must compulsively carry out in exact detail; otherwise they live in anxious dread of the consequences of omitting any part of this ritual. The rituals thus carry a magical significance which is quite characteristic of obsessional thinking. Common rituals are repetitious hand-washing, often in the service of undoing the guilt over masturbation, or things like not stepping on sidewalk cracks. These ritualized acts have a definite purpose, usually a magical undoing or controlling of underlying sexual or aggressive impulses. The childhood rhyme comes to mind—"Step on a crack and break your mother's back." The essential insight into the obsessions and compulsions that mark the trial of these unfortunate people is that their characteristic patterns of obsessive thinking and compulsive acting represents an elaborate attempt to avoid and at the same time control their underlying instinctual impulses. The emergence of impulses of a sexual or aggressive nature are so threatening to these people that they often spend tremendous amounts of effort and energy to defend themselves against such impulses.

It is important to realize that in addition to the compulsive and ritualized activity which is so striking in these patients, there is an obsessive pattern of thinking which is based on the same underlying dynamics. These patients are subject to spells of obsessive brooding in which they swing back and forth between the same set of pros and cons without ever reaching any decision. The thinking of such a one is permeated with uncertainty. He cannot affirm any belief, thought, proposition, observation, or recollection. He cannot trust his own perceptions or his own memory, even for the most trivial things. One of my obsessive patients could not leave his apartment without going back several times to check whether he had locked the door. He could not put out a cigarette without checking several times to see that it was really out. He then developed the magical thought that if he touched anything after he smoked a cigarette it would burst into flames. The only way he could undo this fiery Midas' touch was by washing his hands. He would then perform this ritual countless times. It turned out that these compulsive acts and their obsessive thoughts were all based on his underlying hostile and destructive wishes.

The doubt, indecision, and uncertainty of obsessional thinking, as well as the magical quality of such thinking, are familiar in religious circles in the form of scruples. Such people are driven by guilt and doubt. They confess and reconfess their "sins," which frequently enough are sins by no possible reckoning. Their guilt, doubt, and uncertainty, however, are driven by their struggle with unconscious impulses. The seemingly unending repetition of their obsessions and ruminations reflects the fact that the instinctual sources of their conflicts have not been resolved, thus necessitating the continuation of their defensive efforts. Occasionally in such troubled people the impulses break through in the form of terrible temptations to commit some evil deed, e.g., to kill someone, usually someone close to them. These disruptions of instinctual material throw the patient into a paroxysm of guilt and anxiety.

Such a patient usually demonstrates obsessive traits in varying degrees. He tends to be excessively conscientious, concerned with minute details and the meticulous observance of rules—even to the most detailed prescription. His investment in detail runs the constant risk of missing the essential. He pours a great deal of time and effort into maintaining orderliness and neatness, often to the detriment of real creative or productive effort. He tends to be perfectionistic, not being satisfied until he has completed a task to its last detail or mastered a given subject matter to a secure degree. His standards are high, but at the same time he is harshly critical, spiteful, and even vindictive of the efforts of others. He is not a man of imagination. He does not value art, literature, music, or poetry. His is the realm of common sense and facts. He prefers mathematics, technology, the exact sciences. He is proud of his intellectual capacity and resorts to it as a means of dealing with reality and his own inner conflicts. Intellectualization and rationalization are characteristic methods of defense.

The obsessive-compulsive traits tend to organize themselves, even at relatively benign levels, into a style of life and experience. The cognitive functioning of such individuals is characterized by rigidity —in thought, attention, and interest. The range of attention tends to be narrowed rather than broadened. There is a preference for focusing on a relatively small area of interest and for exploring it in exquisite detail. There is an interest and a focusing on technical details. Attention is rigidly and intensely directed. All of the individual's activity tends to be organized in terms of purposeful objectives and aims. The purposefulness and directedness of this style is usually ordered to the accomplishment of work. Work becomes the leitmotif of such lives—driven by an inner necessity. Such individuals remain rigidly fixed in their intentions, they remain relatively imperturbable and self-willed. If one attempts to urge or pressure them in any way, they can become quite stubborn and obstinate. Such a pattern of life leaves little room for spontaneous activity or expression, it may leave no room for affective or emotional expressiveness. Such individuals find the giving or the receiving of affection or love very difficult. They tend to avoid and to narrow their subjective experience of emotion—something that psychiatrists call "isolation of affect."

Their lives are driven under the constant pressure of conscience. If they do not continue to work and apply themselves seriously, or if they allow themselves some degree of relaxation and pleasure, or if they loosen their relatively rigid control to give expression to feelings of love or hate, they fall victim to feelings of guilt and remorse. Their lives are governed by an inevitable "should," the feeling of obligation and resignation to duty. Their general reaction is to assume a posture of ambivalent submission to authority or to authoritative principles, often in the form of moral principles. Obsessive morality tends to be a rigid, harsh, and demanding morality, a hypermorality which provides a defense against, even as it forms an expression of, the underlying impulses. In this regard the obsessive personality comes close to the authoritarian personality. Both are deeply conflicted over problems in the management and control of aggression. Both are caught up in concerns over power and control. But whereas the authoritarian tends to submit to authority as a means of allying and identifying himself with a source of external power, the obsessive submits out of the fear of his own inner power and aggression, which he fears and over which he must exercise a rigid control. The authoritarian submits out of a sense of inner weakness; the obsessive submits out of a sense of and a fear of inner destructive and uncontrollable power.

There is obviously considerably more that might be said about obsessive-compulsive symptoms and traits. It is fairly obvious that such traits can be mobilized in the service of quite positive and constructive ends. The life of scholarship thrives on such traits. Dedication to work and assiduous application are virtues that are praiseworthy and strongly reinforced in our culture. If one looks around, he becomes readily aware that such traits are quite common and widespread. They are the stuff on which the wheels of civilization turn. But they nonetheless constitute a discriminable style of life and experience which has certain implications for the life of obedience.

It becomes immediately obvious that the obsessive-compulsive life style fits quite congenially with the traditional model of obedience. The idealized pattern of religious life and religious observance can be described as essentially obsessive-compulsive. There was a strong emphasis on the observance of the religious rule, even down to the minutest detail. There was a strong emphasis on practicality and productive work, to the exclusion of pleasure and enjoyment. Art, literature, and the pleasures of music and poetry were given little place and less consideration. Religious life in general was quite organized and structured. There was little need for self-direction or decision; one had only to follow the order of the day. Moreover, virtue lay in the detailed observance of the daily order, the rules and customs. Such was the standard of the good religious and the measuring stick by which virtue was evaluated. It does not take much insight to see that those characterized by obsessive traits would find such a structured life setting most responsive to inner obsessive needs.

The obsessive style of obedience is one of more or less rigid adherence to the prescriptions of the superior or of the religious rule. The adherence is to the letter of the law rather than to its spirit. An appeal to the spirit of the law is not much to the taste of the obsessive, since it requires too much interpretation and application of principles. The obsessive prefers to have things spelled out in specific detail; the more detail the better. He then tends to follow out the specified detail in a compulsive and often ritualized way. The obsessive is uncomfortable with any opportunity for initiative. He leaves little room for it, or if he allows it he does so only in contexts in which the safeguards are elaborate and secure. Initiative is threatening precisely because it calls for self-direction and self-derived spontaneity. Such spontaneity is avoided by the obsessive, since it involves a disruption of established patterns of regulation and control. It gives some room for the expression of inner impulses and wishes. It is precisely these wishes and impulses which are so threatening.

The obsessive style has little toleration for initiative, but also tends to function in terms of a distorted form of autonomy. The obsessive tends to be rigid, stubborn, and generally willful in his obedience. He will follow the superior's directive quite rigidly as long as the superior follows an established and predictable pattern. But should the superior give directives that require change, he will find his obsessive subject stubbornly resistant. The obsessive does not change easily. He clings to the established way of doing things. If change and flexibility are imposed on him from any source, superior or inferior, his reluctance to change and his insistence on a return to the established way of doing things can become quite willful. One should not mistake such willfulness as simply wanting to have his own way. The last thing that the obsessive would want is his own way, even though his willfulness can have that appearance. What he wants is the familiar, the secure, and the established way. Change is a threat to him because it confronts him with the unknown, and with the unknown comes the possibility of insecurity, of loss of control, of loss of the established pattern of regulation and ritual upon which he depends to manage and deal with his disruptive inner impulses. Change for the obsessive provokes anxiety—often severe anxiety—which forces him to work to oppose change. For this reason, the obsessive often tends to be more conservative in his outlook, and to participate in and identify with more conservative types of organization.

Similar characteristics can be identified when obsessive traits are exercised in the superior's role. Obsessive superiors tend to place a great deal of emphasis on order and organization. They have a distrust for and an intolerance of initiative, not only their own initiative, which is threatening enough, but for the initiative of others, especially their subjects. Initiative is threatening because it disrupts and runs counter to the necessary control that is afforded by order and regulation. The obsessive superior tends to be hyperresponsible. He feels that he is somehow personally responsible for whatever happens as a result of the activity of his community or his subjects. Consequently, the more responsibility he is able to concentrate in his own hands, the more comfortable and the less anxious he feels. This leaves less room for the responsible activity of subjects, of course, and it tends to reinforce a paternalistic framework for obedience. It undermines the initiative, responsibility, and freedom of subjects in the exercise of obedience. The insecurity that forces the obsessive superior to retain responsibility in his own hands derives from his own inner conflicts over responsibility.

One way of understanding this pattern is to remind ourselves that every human being is capable of responsible action, but that every human being also has impulses to irresponsible and impulsive behavior. The obsessive is threatened by such impulses because they are associated with destructive consequences and loss of control. He tends, therefore, to repress them and project them onto others. When this sort of mechanism is at work the superior tends to see himself as the sole source of responsible judgment and action. By the same token, he tends to see his subordinates as less responsible than they really are, insofar as he projects his own irresponsible impulses onto them. While he tends to see subordinates as irresponsible —and concludes in consequence that he needs to take responsibility for them—he also tends to see his own higher superiors as excessively rigid and demanding and as imposing the responsibility on him. The latter perception is transparently again a projection, but this time the projection is of moralistic and superego attitudes. The projection tends to work in both directions; impulsive irresponsibility is projected on inferiors and excessive demands for responsibility are projected on superiors. When obsessive individuals interact in a social system, there is a tendency for individuals at each level of the hierarchy to split the two sides of their respective inner conflicts over responsibility and project them in this fashion. This creates an interlocking system of projections in which superiors are seen as rigid, demanding, and repressive and inferiors at every level are seen as immature, impulsive, and irresponsible. This sets up a system of social defense which serves to reinforce individual intrapsychic defenses and which operates inexorably to shift effective responsibility and responsible action from lower levels in the structure to higher levels. There are countless examples of the working of this process in religious groups, in the Church at large, and for that matter wherever in human organizations obsessive traits and obsessive characters are involved.[7]

I would like to turn now to a consideration of the paranoid style and of paranoid traits. Paranoia can exist in its most striking and extreme form in severely pathological forms—paranoid psychosis or paranoid schizophrenia. But the traits can assume a much milder form and can display themselves in much of relatively normal behavior. The paranoid personality is marked by suspiciousness and a tendency to blame other people for one's misfortunes. Paranoid individuals tend to be quite actively and intently attentive to details, much like the obsessive, but more intensely and for different reasons. Paranoid attention is always searching for something, always on the lookout, tensely directed and purposeful; it has been described as "rigidly intentional." The paranoid is intent on finding what he is looking for. He does not approach reality to find out what is out there, but rather to find what he is already convinced is out there. He searches intensely for the confirmation of his anticipations, but at the same time these same rigid anticipations allow him to feel that he can discredit or disregard anything that contradicts or runs counter to his conviction. Thus, he "finds" what he is looking for—

regardless of what he finds. His intellectual resources and perceptiveness are used, not in the service of attaining realistic judgment, but in the service of guaranteeing his inner convictions and bias.

Approaching reality in this way, the paranoid can arrive at nearly any conclusions he wishes. He can thus at one and the same time be absolutely correct in his perception and absolutely wrong in his conclusion. Parnoid individuals can have in hand all of the necessary information that everyone around them has, but they will arrive at a completely divergent conclusion and interpretation of the state of affairs. Often they will seize upon one aspect or factor in a situation and give it central importance. Others may assign the same element little or no importance. The normal attitude is to evaluate facts and events in relation to some objective standard. The paranoid gives events significance and assigns them value in terms of an inner frame of reference. He tends to see his perception as valid and everyone else's as distorted. It is very difficult for the rigidly paranoid individual to see that events in the real world can be seen in different ways by different people. He lacks sufficient flexibility to allow validity to other points of view. He values his own inner perceptions. All others are wrong or must be devalued in some way. The overlap between paranoid traits and prejudice—a widespread social phenomenon—becomes apparent at this point. What is different is threatening and must be held in suspicion. What is unexpected, surprising, unusual, or just new is provocative for any rigid person, and becomes especially so for the suspicious paranoid individual. Such elements are disruptive and must be reconciled with the paranoid's inner convictions and view of things. The rigid or dogmatic compulsive tends to ignore the new or unusual, but the paranoid cannot afford that. The paranoid can afford to ignore nothing. He must deal with surprise or change by literally anticipating it. The paranoid tends to be excessively alert and attentive. He is constantly scanning the environment to search out anything unanticipated or unexpected. When he finds it, he does not simply become aware of it but tries to scrutinize it completely and examine it in detail to assure himself that it does not violate his inner scheme of things.

The paranoid's hyperalertness and hypersensitivity extend to areas of human experience in which great ambiguity and uncertainty predominate, specifically the area of human interaction and the inner attitudes and motivations of other human beings. Where such uncertainty prevails, the paranoid individual tends to attribute attitudes and motivations to others. He also tends to interpret their actions and behavior in terms of his own inner frame of reference. He may disregard their expressed intentions and motivations—disallowing them as untrustworthy and because they simply do not fit with his preconceived scheme. Evidence of any kind is accepted or rejected not in terms of its objective validity, but in terms of its congruence with his inner scheme and its related biased perceptions. Paranoid thought organization is directed not by objective evidence, but by inner subjective needs.

This tendency on the part of such individuals is described as projection. Projection is not exclusively a paranoid phenomenon but it is characteristically found in paranoid persons. The paranoid attributes thoughts and motives to other people. The thoughts and motives that he attributes are derived from his own inner impulses and unconscious wishes. He may project hostile wishes and intentions, interpreting other people's behavior as reflecting evil intentions toward himself. The projection of such hostility serves as a defense against his own hostile wishes, which he cannot acknowledge. Projection thus serves a blaming function. It enables the person to deny his own responsibility for the pattern of his life and to blame others for his misfortunes. His disappointments and shortcomings are not his fault—they are the result of the efforts of others who want to undermine and frustrate him. Thus the paranoid can avoid his own inner sense of weakness and ineffectualness and his own unconscious feelings of frustrated inadequacy.

Paranoid traits represent a distortion of autonomy which is more severe and more generally pathological than the distortion of autonomy in obsessive-compulsive states. In his discussion of paranoid style, Shapiro has observed:

> Where, for the normal person, autonomy brings a sense of competency, pride, and self-respect, the paranoid person, instead, is either arrogant and pseudo-competent or furtive and ashamed or, perhaps most often, both. . . . There is, however, one other subjective reflection of the paranoid person's unstable autonomy. It is the most familiar of all. While the normal person feels not only competent, but also free to exercise his will, and, in that sense as

well, self-directing, in charge of his own life, and master of himself, the paranoid person is continually occupied and concerned with the threat of being subjected to some external control or some external infringement of his will.[8]

Well-established autonomy can allow itself a certain degree of relaxation. It can tolerate a certain amount of inner relaxation which permits a certain degree of inner spontaneity and abandonment. That amount is essential for any sense of initiative to express itself. A secure sense of autonomy can also allow a certain amount of external relaxation—sufficient to permit one to listen to, and to take into account, someone else's point of view. The autonomous person can even comply with or submit to the will of another without a sense of shame or humiliation. The paranoid person cannot.

The paranoid person cannot tolerate giving-in either to himself or to any external pressure or authority. He must maintain a rigid self-directedness which reflects a hypertrophy of autonomy—in the sense we have already discussed: that the excess of autonomy is really a failure of autonomy. The paranoid must cling to his inner convictions, which include not merely a perception of reality but a conviction about his place and function within it. Directives of an external authority are a threat to that precisely because they derive from someone else's perception of reality—a perception that the rigidly paranoid person cannot accept. The paranoid adopts an apprehensive, anxious, defensive, and basically antagonistic posture toward external authority. He regards such authority as threatening and hostile, as a result of his projective defenses, and he becomes continually preoccupied with the defense of his threatened autonomy from assault. In this regard, the authoritarian attitude and the paranoid attitude approximate each other. They differ in that the authoritarian sees external authority in terms of power to which he must submit and with which he must ally himself for protection, whereas the paranoid sees external authority as not just powerful, but as filled with hostile intent toward himself. He must, therefore, defend himself against it.

The difficulties of the paranoid personality with obedience, therefore, would be considerable. The paranoid could not enter into the mutual interaction and regulation of a mature authority relation. He is too caught up in his own defensive needs to allow himself to identify with the group and its needs and values. Where paranoid types can allow themselves some degree of affiliation, the participation in the group serves subjective needs for support and defense. The individual may thus cling to the group as a source of strength and stability which serves to lend reinforcement to his own inner sense of weakness and inadequacy. In this context there may be a tendency toward hyperidentification with the group. The individual over-identifies with the group, excessively values and idealizes its members and its goals and objectives. There is a corresponding devaluation and hostile rejection of other groups and their values and objectives. The paranoid mechanisms become mobilized in the service of rejecting and attacking the outgroup. The operations of these mechanisms can be seen quite clearly in the process of prejudice. We have already observed that prejudice and paranoia have much in common, particularly the need to reject, exclude, devalue, and demean the objects of prejudice which is based on inner subjective needs and convictions. This serves to remind us that paranoid traits, although we tend to think of them as relatively pathological, may in fact be broadly distributed in otherwise relatively normal individuals.

The operation of paranoid traits, therefore, makes the life of obedience extremely threatening and difficult. For genuine obedience to function at even minimal levels there is required a basic degree of trust and a sense of mutually reinforced autonomy. The paranoid's sense of precarious autonomy makes his capacity for entering into such a mutually responsible relationship negligible. His constant sense of danger and his everpresent need for guardedness and suspicion undermines any capacity for trust. The state of continuing vigilance makes any sort of relationship with other people a difficult area for the paranoid to deal with. Such individuals tend to become increasingly isolated as they go through life, and increasingly independent and self-reliant. To ask such individuals to participate in a group process and to share in relationships through obedience is to ask them to surrender their carefully preserved defenses. It is to ask them to give up the internally elaborated scheme which dominates their lives and by which they preserve their fragile autonomy and to place themselves in a position where they can no longer rely solely on themselves, but must rely at least in part on others.

I would like to turn, finally, to a consideration of the narcissistic character and its implications for obedience. The whole area of narcissistic personality structure is much under discussion these days and provides an interesting area of study. What has become increasingly apparent as we have come to learn more and more about these disorders of personality is that many apparently successful and healthy personalities show real pathological defects when studied more closely and carefully. These defects are often related to difficulties in the development of narcissism. The basic concept of narcissism was formulated by Freud. He based the notion on the myth of Narcissus, the handsome Greek youth who fell in love with his own reflection mirrored on the surface of a pond.

Freud's basic idea was that the infant starts out in a primitive state of narcissism. Early in his development he cannot distinguish between self and nonself so that his loving is directed to himself, primarily to his own body as a source of pleasure and satisfaction. Part of the story of development is how the child moves from a condition of self-love toward an emerging capacity to love others around him. An intermediate phase of this development in the capacity to love finds the child loving external objects insofar as they reflect himself or insofar as they serve his interest or provide him gratification. Many personalities get fixated or hung up somewhere in this phase of development and never really grow to the more mature level of the capacity to love others for themselves rather than for oneself. Thus the interest of such individuals, their investment, their gratification, their love, such as it is, remains centered and focused on themselves. The focus of value in their lives remains on themselves rather than on others. These individuals compose the group of narcissistic personality types.

Narcissistic personalities can and often do commit themselves to organizations, groups, and causes. They are found frequently enough in religious life. But the commitment carries with it an amalgam of self-interest and self-enhancement. Religious life for such individuals becomes a vehicle of promoting self-esteem and self-regard. Rather than a means of self-sacrifice and service to others, it becomes a means of supporting self-esteem and self-interest. Narcissistic persons base most of their interest and activity on self-reference, particularly in their interactions with other people.

Their lives are dominated by the need to be loved and admired. There is often an implicit contradiction between their somewhat inflated concept of themselves and their importance and their inordinate need for recognition and tribute from others.

Narcissistic individuals feel little empathy for the feelings of others. Their enjoyment in life is based primarily on plaudits from others and on their own grandiose fantasies. When the tributes diminish and there are no new sources to feed the inner hunger for approval and regard, they become restless and bored. There is a strong tendency to envy and jealousy. They tend to see tributes and rewards that go to others as being taken away from themselves. Narcissistic personalities often idealize and place high value on others from whom they expect tribute and admiration. Conversely, they tend to devalue and treat with contempt those who do not pay them their due. They tend to exploit and manipulate others in their own interest and advantage—as though they felt entitled to use others in the service of their own enhancement and advancement. They often, therefore, present a very charming and engaging facade.

Deeper exploration of such personalities often reveals that their efforts to enhance themselves and to build up their sense of self-esteem and value is a defensive manoeuvre which is directed against underlying feelings of worthlessness and inferiority. Often enough the grandiosity, self-centeredness, and self-reference cover an underlying paranoid core. The feelings of inferiority and insecurity may alternate from time to time with grandiose and omnipotent fantasies. Underneath these feelings and fantasies there is an infantile sense of entitlement, the conviction that the world owes the individual recognition and reward and admiration and love. When the world does not give him what he is entitled to, the narcissistic person can become quite enraged. His offended sense of entitled justice and the consequent anger may lead to projections, as a means of justifying his rage, and to a more or less paranoid position. The world is not giving him what he feels entitled to because of some conspiracy against him, usually based on the world's envy and jealousy of him. The paranoid construction and the accompanying projections serve to preserve the sense of self-esteem and the narcissistic core that is badly threatened.

Although such elements may be found in some degree in most

narcissistic personalities, many such individuals are capable of functioning at a rather high level of performance. Their social capacities
are usually well developed, they have relatively good control of their
impulses, and they show a capacity for active and consistent work.
Their resources can usually be effectively mobilized in any area of
interest which permits them to realize some of their ambitions and
needs for admiration and rewards. The more intelligent such individuals can become quite creative; they are not infrequently found
in responsible positions of leadership. They are frequently found to
be outstanding performers in some artistic field. The theatre is a
major place for such individuals. It provides them with an ideal context for display of their talents and offers them a ready source of admiration, applause, and notoriety. A narcissistic personality structure does not exclude real creative talent or even genius. Goethe's
narcissism was overwhelming. But the more frequent story is that
narcissistic individuals are too eager for easy rewards, with the result
that their work becomes marked by a certain brilliant superficiality.
Their work is more often marked by promise than solid accomplishment. They are often the promising young talents that never seem to
reach their potential and in whom the promise remains unfulfilled.

Psychiatric attention has been increasingly drawn to the problem
of the apparently well-functioning and adequate personality which
may cover underlying defects in development. Narcissism remains a
central problem in many such cases. Recently, the characteristic
profile in which disordered narcissism plays a major role has been
described as the "Nobel Prize complex."[9] The patterns of personality
development that pass for "normal" is a matter not only of internal
developmental factors but also of the limits and diversity of patterns
that are generated within and acceptable to a given culture. Our own
culture places a high premium on performance and successful adaptation. The narcissistic personality can find an adaptive fit between
his own inner needs for reward and recognition and the externally
imposed and structured demands of the culture for performance, as
well as the culture's willingness to give rewards for various kinds of
performance.

The Nobel Prize complex is exemplified by students, teachers,
professional men, research scientists, performers, etc., who entertain
ambitious life goals—to be President, to gain great wealth and in-

fluence, to become a great leader or thinker, one who can influence men's minds and men's actions. But even more importantly, their ambition is to receive acclaims for their deeds and accomplishments. They wish not only to attain but to be acclaimed for their attainments. The majority are intellectually or artistically gifted and tend to evoke considerable admiration from others. Objective achievement, however, often becomes overshadowed or even inhibited by their preoccupation with acclaim. The dictates of their ambition is in terms of all-or-nothing.

The majority of such individuals are first-born; many are only children. They cherish a twofold fantasy: the omnipotent fantasy of being powerful and influential, and the passive fantasy of being special and being chosen out by reason of exceptional gifts. Because of their developmental imbalance, such individuals who have been singled out since childhood as exceptionally bright tend to be more competitive, seeking recognition rather than love. Those individuals who have been singled out as attractive or artistically gifted tend to seek love and affection rather than recognition. Disappointments or failures loom large in the lives of such individuals. They become hypersensitive to even minor disappointments, and are particularly upset by the failure to receive what they envision as appropriate recognition. These narcissistic expectations and feelings of entitlement are bound to remain unsatisfied in the ultimate confrontation with reality. The problem for so many of these persons is that their early life experience—at home, in the family, in school, and often in the early phases of work and career—reinforces their expectations of success and a belief in their capacity to excel. This becomes consolidated as a way of life and is built into the structure of their personalities.

When such narcissistic fantasies and expectations go unfulfilled, they are plunged into feelings of failure and worthlessness. Disappointment can force them to a quite opposite pole from the excessive feelings of self-enhancement and omnipotence. They become depressed and despondent, often developing a variety of psychosomatic symptoms and complaints. The inflated self-image becomes rapidly deflated, like an overblown balloon from which all the air has escaped.

I have focused on the narcissistic personality disorders and the particular example of the Nobel Prize complex, because it seems to me that this type of personality is seen frequently enough in religious groups. The religious organization is held in social esteem by the Church. Its members are dedicated to lives of special service and special position within the Church. The religious state is seen as somehow more dignified and more sacred than the lay state. The priesthood is likewise accorded respect and recognition as a special state of dedication and consecration to sacred things. The very term "sacred" implies separation from the things of this world and special religious recognition. Religious sacrifice by their vows certain elemental human rights which serve other men for the maintenance and elevation of their self-esteem and self-respect. But by this sacrifice the religious person attains special status and special acclaim which are not accorded to mere laymen. Thus, paradoxically, the religious life has a certain narcissistic appeal. One would, therefore, expect to find a certain proportion of narcissistic personalities among religious groups. The proportion would tend to vary from group to group, in direct relation to the prestige, respect, and recognition accorded a particular religious group. If one compounds this aspect with the increasing trends toward professional training and professionalism in contemporary religious groups, the narcissistic appeal would seem to be even greater.

We can then ask ourselves what the impact of excessive narcissism might be for the life of obedience. The narcissistic personality does not fit easily into any preconceived schema. Such individuals, in their characteristic mode of responding, will tend to show a high degree of autonomy, initiative, responsibility, and may even show all the apparent trappings of the stable and well-functioning identity. But the quality of their response and the underlying motive of their work remains a basic narcissistic one. They are capable of extraordinary initiative and are often willing to take on considerable responsibility, but they do so in the service of narcissistic ends of self-enhancement and self-acclaim. In so doing, they may perform at a higher level and show remarkable capacities for leadership or for creative and productive work. What they do and what they accomplish, however, is always attached with a constant rider, the narcissistic expectation of acclaim and recognition. When that recognition is not forthcoming, they feel resentful, cheated, depressed.

The tendency under obedience, then, is rather toward an excess of the qualities of initiative, autonomy, and responsibility. It is difficult for them to fit their initiative with the initiatives of a superior or of the rest of the religious group. They also tend to take on excessive responsibility. They draw responsibility to themselves and tend to undermine the responsibility and the capacity for responsibility of others. The reason, of course, is that recognition and acclaim usually go to those who accept and hold greater responsibility. Correlative with this hyperresponsibility, such individuals tend to be hyperautonomous in the sense we have already discussed.

The difficulties of the narcissistic personality may come at the level of identity. They may or may not show a sufficiently developed sense of fidelity to permit them to effectively establish a sense of identity, not only as a free and autonomous self, but at the same time as a functioning and participating member of the religious group. They may, however, receive certain narcissistic rewards from affiliation with the group. They may run the consequent risk of overidentification and overcommitment. The identification then flows not out of a sense of commitment to the group and its goals as a major focus of purposeful activity, but rather out of the expectation and anticipation of recognition and acclaim as a result of one's contribution to group goals. This difficulty is most telling in the matter of generativity. True generativity requires the capacity to transcend self and the needs of the self to direct one's efforts to the enhancement of the group and the bringing to full development the potential of the new members of the next generation. The narcissistic character may find difficulty with such a step and may never reach the level of true generativity. Even here, though, if the individual receives sufficient reward and gains sufficient acclaim for his efforts, he may gain the trappings and the appearances of generative activity. The inner reality, however, is beyond him.

In general, the narcissistic personality is so focused on and intent on his own inner needs and ambitions that his capacity for meaningful interaction and relationship with other human beings is impaired. He cannot comfortably enter into any relationship as a subordinate or even as an equal. His difficulties with the authority relation are no less characteristic. He cannot enter into a meaningful process of mutual regulation and mutual regard that is essential to the working of obedience. The superior's directive can come as a request to subordinate his goals and ambitions to the goals and objectives of the group. If that confrontation can be turned somehow to narcissistic ends, the individual may be able to integrate the directive of obedience well enough. If not, there is bound to be tension and conflict, internally if not externally. So often in discussions of obedience, we find ourselves referring to the confrontation of the will of the superior and the will of the subject. What we mean very often is a confrontation of the hyperautonomous and hyperresponsible will of the superior against the hyperautonomous and narcissistic will of the subject. The confrontation then becomes the vehicle of willfulness on both sides.

There is obviously a great deal more that could be said about the pathological deviations of obedience. I have tried to present here a basically developmental schema in terms of which deviations from true obedience might be conceptualized and discussed. I have also tried to bring into focus some more or less typical personality styles and traits that seemed to me to have special relevance for the consideration of religious obedience. The particular patterns of personality organization discussed above seemed relevant both because of the nature of the basic conflicts involved in each and because of the relatively common incidence with which they seem to present themselves in religious groups. The major emphasis, however, that these remarks carry is that obedience is not simply a matter of commands and responses carried out in some sort of psychological vacuum. Rather obedience must be seen as caught up in a life-long developmental process which has broader implications and roots than the immediate situation and the present directive of a superior. It must be seen as an expression of and a derivative of the individual's inner personality structure—a structure which is the progressing and developing end point of a process that begins at birth and does not reach its conclusion until the end of life.

## Chapter 15

# The Problem of Disobedience

There is no problem which is more pressing or urgent in the life of social structures at the current time than the problem of disobedience and dissent. Social structures generally are feeling the increasing tension created by the forces of dissent and the disruption of social organization. The drama of dissent is played out daily on our campuses, in street demonstrations and riots, in nearly every facet of public life and politics. It was made transparently evident in the reaction to *Humanae Vitae,* the encyclical on birth control. The mere fact that dissent from the teachings of the encyclical was so widely interpreted as disloyalty reflects the extent to which the whole question was shrouded in issues of authority and obedience.

One can approach the problem of disobedience from several perspectives. The perspectives may be dictated by a variety of ideologies. One can look at social processes from the point of view of order. This view would envision society as a system of action which was somehow unified in general terms by a shared culture with a general consensus about values (at least within certain limits), and by systems of communication and political organization. Society is, then, a natural system which is ordered to the maintenance of social control. The maintenance of such controls would have to be seen as a necessary good, since the correlative view of man in such a perspective would take the form of a composite of egotistic and altruistic drives and needs, or as an entity standing in need of socialization. There is also a religious dimension to this view of social process insofar as the social body may be seen as composed of morally superior and morally inferior men—a derivative of the Calvinistic conviction regarding predestination and the division of the just and the unjust. In any case, the human components of the social system are seen as requiring constant restraint and control for the collective good of the social system.

The primary good, to which the society directs its efforts and which it views as a major value, is the maintenance of social balance, stability, authoritative control, and the preservation of social order. Acceptance of existing values and the preservation of existing social structures and patterns is seen as positive and healthy. The ideology which is identified with the existing social structure serves a normative function. Any deviation is seen as pathological and deviations are explained in terms of anomie or alienation. The residues of normative function and control are taken to be the institutions and structures of the establishment and those who administer the establishment. Correction of deviance and social pathology is achieved through the extension of social controls and the more efficient institutionalization of values. Emphasis is placed on rehabilitation by adjustment of deviant individuals to the needs of the social system. The need for maintenance of the system and for working within the system is stressed. Correction of evils comes through administrative solution and extension of the system, rather than by change in the system—the philosophy that if some is good, more is better.

One can also view the problem of disobedience from the opposite perspective of conflict. Whereas the order-perspective envisioned order and the preservation of order as the maximal good of the society, the conflict-perspective minimizes the benefits of order and maximizes the benefits of conflict. It sees the social organism as composed of groups with opposite and conflicting goals and perspectives. Society is not seen as a transcendent system of structures and values to which man must adjust, but rather as the expression and extension of man himself, of his wishes, needs, purposes, and actions. Society is, then, what it suits man's purposes to have it. If it does not fit his needs and purposes at any moment in time, man can alter it to suit himself. There is, therefore, an emphasis on and a positive attitude toward change. Man himself is seen as the active creator both of himself, as a freely autonomous and functional participant in social processes, and of society. He participates in the creation of the social system by reason of his practical and autonomous social action. Social processes are seen as involving action, change, and qualitiative growth through change. Moreover, such change and growth is envisioned as a major value in the social process.

Thus there is an emphasis on freedom and autonomous action, rather than on order and social control. The striving toward unrealized standards and satisfaction of the aspirations of subgroups within the society are regarded as positive and healthy. These standards are governed by and directed toward a utopian ideal of how the society should be organized and function. Deviant behavior, far from being seen as destructive or pathological, is seen rather as serving a positive and adaptive function in enabling the society to progress toward the necessary transformation of existing structures and relationships. Deviation is explained in terms of existing obstructions to the achievement of individual and group goals. Since the realization of such goals is held as a maximal value, impediments to such realization are viewed as illegitimate extensions of social control and as exploitations of minority groups. Mechanisms for correction of social pathology are the disruption of social organization and control, and radical transformation of existing patterns of social interaction. The often explicit goal is revolutionary overthrow of the present system and change in its structure. Subordinate and minority groups, striving for greater position and power in the society, are taken as the normative sources of social direction and control. Social evils are corrected by revolutionary disruption and destruction of existing social structures and institutions. The underlying philosophy of change presumes that destruction of an existing evil automatically institutes change for the better, that any change will be a change for the better.

Both of these persuasions, the order-perspective and the conflict-perspective, represent ideological commitments. Among the determinants of whether one stresses the need for order and whether one stresses the need for change, the psychological factors loom large. They stem from the individual's life history and experience, particularly his experience of and relationship with authority figures.

We have traced some of the developmental issues related to one's attitudes toward authority in the preceding chapters. However, one's view of the problem of disobedience and what one might have to say about it must inevitably be critically influenced by what he feels about the issues of order and change. Our effort in the present chapter is to avoid the Scylla and Charybdis of an overemphasis on either the demands of order or of those of freedom and change. The central problem for authority, as we have observed, is to find a way to maximize within the social structure both these elements. The order-perspective would emphasize order to the detriment of freedom, while the conflict-perspective would emphasize freedom to the detriment of order. It is our hope that there may be an ideological middle ground in terms of which both freedom and order may find their proper place and function.

The difficulties and ambiguities of disobedience and dissent are well dramatized in the protests that swirl around us in contemporary society. Ours has become an age of protest and dissent. Besides campus unrest, the areas of particular protest in our present social situation seem to be the question of our involvement in the Viet Nam action and the question of racial justice and prejudice against minority groups. The polarity between those who seek solution to these problems by extension of social control—the law and order proponents—and those who seek solution by means of change and overthrow of existing structures seems to have been clearly and radically established. One wonders whether the breach can ever be closed and healed.

The tensions involved in these confrontations reveal the paradoxes of disobedience quite clearly. We must keep a perspective on such current issues. We have to remind ourselves that protest and dissent are not new phenomena on the human scene. On the contrary, protest has always been a normal process within the social system for initiating change. If we look back at the course of human history, we can select certain men and certain groups which we call pioneers or originators. We imply, of course, that such people did something important for the welfare of mankind or civilization that had to be accomplished by dissent. Any pioneer, whatever his field of human endeavor, must break away from the body of his contemporaries and place himself at odds with them. If he pioneers in a geographic sense, he must break away and go into the wilderness. If he pioneers in an intellectual sense, he must break away from the body of accepted opinion and strike out in new directions. What makes him ultimately a pioneer rather than simply a deviant is that he succeeds in persuading others to accept and follow his views. To accomplish this he must in some manner express his dissent. If it were not so, there could have been no Galileo, no Einstein; there could be no politics, no social reform, no American revolution, no French revolution, no Russian revolution.

The process of dissent is divisive. When the American colonies revolted, the men who carried on that struggle were labelled as rebels, traitors to the crown, and criminals. To those who favored separation from control of the crown, however, these same men for the same reasons were regarded as patriots, men of courage and conviction, heroes. The difference between these views was a matter of political persuasion and social perspective. In any case, the revolution was made by dissenters, political dissenters, but even before that, we must remind ourselves, the men who founded and built the colonies were themselves religious dissenters. We should not wonder at the idea of religious dissent; Christianity, after all, was founded on dissent. We might wonder what the history of Western civilization might have been if Christ had not been a dissenter.

Historical documentation is easy and substantial. The point that I wish to emphasize is that dissent is one of the characteristic processes by which human societies change and make progress. This has been particularly true of democratic forms of government, although protest and dissent are not strangers to other forms of political organization. But the central feature of the democratic process is not simply that the course of government is determined by the will of the majority. We must add immediately that it is also essential to the process that the minority have the right and the capacity to influence opinion so that a new majority can take shape. Unless the minority can bring its influence to bear on the population and persuade them to adopt the minority view, the democratic process stagnates and the capacity for progress and change is lost. It is the strength and source of vitality in the democratic system that dissident minorities are not silenced. They are in fact encouraged to speak out and to try to influence the majority. The strength of the democratic process is that it carries within itself the potentialities for revitalization and progress through social change in a manner that no autocratic or totalitarian form of government can. Other forms of government tend toward rigidity and thus increase the likelihood that significant social change can come about only through revolution. The genius of the democratic process, however, is that it depends on and functions in terms of the mechanisms for social change.

It is not surprising, then, that protest and dissent should take place in our society. Moreover, we could reasonably expect a higher level and intensity of dissent where the communication of new ideas and information has become so immediate and general. As a rule, whenever the free flow and availability of information is increased, the probability of divergent opinions in any group increases. Modern communications and mass media have created a situation of almost immediate and universal availability of information in our society. There is also a widespread dissatisfaction with the more traditional formulations for dealing with problems and an increasing distrust of the sources of organization and control in our society. The views and practices of the authorities and the establishment have come in for increasing criticism and question. This applies to the police, politicians, business leaders, church leaders—practically all of the representatives and functionaries of established social institutions. Also there is a mounting sense of frustration as demands and expectations remain unfulfilled. The sense of frustration permeates the protests of Negroes for equal rights and opportunities, the protests of students in the universities, the protests against foreign military involvement and the war.

The spirit and guiding impulse for protest is not limited to the American scene. It is international in scope and seems to have no regard for political boundaries. It has no ideology, no set of political convictions, no unified direction or impulse. It condemns established ideologies, whether capitalistic or communistic. It stands forth in the interest of change and progress. It is carried on almost exclusively at the hands of youth. The business of protest and dissent is the business of youth. It is the youth of any society who are inevitably least committed to its traditions and established institutions. It is they who are looking for commitment and investment. More and more, however, in our times, they are less and less prepared to accept without question or critical evaluation the circumstances of life and social structure that their elders hand on to them. They are more willing to question, more ready to see evils as evils, and more convinced that evils can be corrected and problems solved by purposeful action. And they are not hesitant to protest, with all the intensity and energy of youth which has found a meaningful direction for its restless drive and sense of urgency.

There is a great deal of propaganda circulated about the "generation gap." There is a generation gap that cuts through all contemporary institutions, from the family to national government. Calling it a "generation gap," however, is a misnomer. It is really a polarization between those who view change as threatening and those who view it as necessary. Undoubtedly those who hold to the former position are more likely to be older and those who hold the latter to be younger, but the dichotomy is not of itself generational. If one must condemn one extreme, one must condemn the other. The air is filled with the noises of hatred and hysteria from both sides. The most devastating charge leveled from both sides and at both sides is the charge of hypocrisy. Parents accuse their children of the basest and crassest of motives, and children can no longer believe that the norms and standards that their parents profess are the guidelines for their real lives. Most young people today are convinced that their elders—their parents and teachers—live lives of self-deception, that they profess and teach a set of values and standards and principles that they are not even aware of violating and ignoring in their own lives. The generation gap has become an hypocrisy gap—and more.

It is relatively easy to succumb to the rhetoric of polarization. It is easy to mythologize (see Chapter 7) and cast either position in terms of its extremes. It is much easier to think in terms of stereotypes of one position or the other. It is easy to cast dissenters as immature, impractical, romantic, and unrealistic. It is easy to condemn their actions as disruptive and destructive. Indeed, all too often they are. Their ideologies are often destructive and negative—inspired by an antidemocratic and revolutionary ideal—and their actions are often destructive and costly. Their objective seems too often aimed at tearing down and disrupting social structures and processes. And it remains true that the course they choose is too often the course of violent overthrow without either the concern or the capacity for purposeful reconstruction. It also remains true that the violence of their protest and its destructiveness is born out of near pathological rage that is displaced from infantile levels to the social and political sphere.

But if we were to satisfy ourselves that this was the substance of the protest of students and the young in our society, we would be missing the most important part of it. The protest of students is not a protest about war, or educational policy or foreign policy, or the ROTC, or whatever—even though these issues become the vehicles upon which the forces of protest are brought to bear. Protest in our times goes much deeper. The generation gap is no longer what it has previously been. It is no longer a difference in the interests and investments between the old and the young. It is not simply a matter of the old standing in favor of the status quo and the youth standing in favor of change. It is not merely and simply a matter of liberalism versus conservatism. The labels fall short of the real issues. The conflict is all of these things, but they express only a part of the problem, and the superficial part at that. The real substance of protest is not simply the realities of structure and organization of the social systems in which they live. The conflict is not merely a matter of criticism of social patterns and action; it reaches below that level to a much more meaningful and far-reaching concern. The substance of protest and the level of basic conflict is ethical. What is under attack is the system of values which guides and directs society at all levels of its organization.

The protest and dissent that have swept over our society at all levels are substantially a search for ethical alternatives. I would like to put the ethical dimension of dissent into a developmental context. We have already addressed ourselves in detail to the developmental issues involved in obedience. I would like to extend that persepctive to embrace the ethical dimension of obedience as well. Ethical capacity is subject to the laws of development, just as all of man's human capacities must undergo development. Erik Erikson has described childhood as the period of moral learning, adolescence as the period of ideological experimentation, and adulthood as the period of ethical consolidation. Preceding stages of development, as we have seen, are not simply replaced by subsequent stages; rather they are absorbed into a hierarchically structured system of increasing differentiation. What is learned by the child by internalizing the prohibitions of his significant elders continues into the moral conflicts of his adolescence, but is brought under the new primacy of ideological convictions and commitments. Erikson defines ideology as "a system of commanding ideas held together more (but not exclusively) by totalistic logic and utopian conviction than by cognitive understanding or pragmatic experience."[1] He goes on to say:

> This ideological orientation as well as the moral one is, in turn, absorbed but never quite replaced by that ethical orientation which really marks the difference between adulthood and adolescence— 'ethical,' meaning a *universal sense of values assented to* with insight and foresight, in anticipation of immediate responsibilities, not the least of which is the transmission of these values to the next generation.[2]

The long and gradual course of moral development builds the substructures of adult ethical maturity and makes it possible for the value structure of the individaul to gain some measure of synchronization with social, economic, and political realities. It also, at the same time, opens the way for a certain instability which may result in partial returns to earlier developmental positions. In young people it is not uncommon to find a certain fixation at an ideological level or even a retreat to earlier conflicts over moral interdicts and prohibitions. In the situation of conflict, frustration, and agitation which characterizes so much of contemporary dissent, youth may find itself alternately reenacting a variety of regressive moral positions. They may act out a premoral position which denies the need or relevance of any ethical norms. They may adopt an amoral position which flaunts and rejects accepted or established norms. They may assume an antimoral position which militantly denies and rejects authoritatively established and defended norms. Or they may take it on themselves to fervently and righteously denounce authority and its ways and means in a spirit of highly moralistic condemnation and denunciation, a position which is at once antiauthoritarian yet highly moralistic.

The process of the generation, support, and ongoing revitalization of values is complex and involves a dialectical exchange among all the resources of the community which participate in the structure of authority. I am using "authority" now specifically in the sense which has been developed in the preceding sections of this study. Authority in this sense derives from the legitimate structure of authority, the legitimately appointed or elected officials, and from the community as a group by way of consensus of its members, and from individuals who by reason of their maturity and responsibility become authentic sources of authoritative direction. The principles have always been recognizable in the structure of the Church, even though they have not enjoyed an even distribution of emphasis or acknowledgment in the course of the Church's history. The principle of hierarchical organization and the legitimacy of authority has always played a prominent role. Authority in the Church has always been vested in the hierarchy and has been centralized in the pope. The image of authority flowing from the head of the Church to lower levels of the hierarchy has always had a prominent place. Alongside the vertical view of authority there has also been a more horizontal view which has recognized the authority of the community. The *consensus fidelium* and the consensus of conciliar decision has been a persistent element in the normative processes of the Church. The authority of the community has enjoyed a certain refurbishing in connection with the emphasis on collegiality and the emerging role of the layman in post-Vatican II theology.

The role of existential authority—the authoritative role of individuals in the dialectic of the sources of authority—has never been given a significant part, even though we can catch glimpses of it from time to time. It played a significant role in the earliest years of the Church. It is reflected in the wisdom of Gamaliel. "If this enterprise, this movement of theirs, is of human origin it will break up of its own accord; but if it does in fact come from God you will not only be unable to destroy them, but you might find yourselves fighting against God" (Acts 5:38-39). It is the prophetic element in the Church that draws its inspiration neither from the legitimate hierarchy nor the consent of the community. The recognition of such an element was implicit in the canonization of individual conscience in the Declaration on Religious Freedom.

The organization of the Church in the post-Tridentine era was governed by the mentality of the Counter-Reformation. There was a strong emphasis on centrality and adherence to the norms of faith and morals as declared by the central authority in the Church. Christian consensus and the unity of the Church was assiduously protected by the examination of suspect teaching and the ready use of the accusation of heresy. Rigid vigilance was exercised in the control of the interpretation of Scripture, formulas of faith, norms of worship, and ecclesiastical discipline. Vatican II reversed this picture. The emphasis on unity and submission to authority gave way to a much more open and liberal set of mind which invited Catholics to think more for themselves even if that meant questioning or criticizing traditionally accepted views. The council fathers set the tone for the Council and for the postconciliar development when they refused to accept the Roman schemata in the first session. They exercised their independence and autonomy in dissent and demanded that the schemata be debated and questioned. By their vigorous dissent and the force of their persuasion they brought about a new consensus which was reflected in the final decrees of the Council.

The Church has moved in the last few years from a suspicious, defensive, guarded position, in which it was turned in upon itself in a posture of frightened insecurity, to a position in which it has begun to enter into a dialectic with the modern world, no longer feeling the need to protect itself from hostile and destructive elements outside itself or within itself, but having a sense of confidence in its strength and divine purpose. I am reminded of the contrast that Robert Waelder suggested between totalitarian governments and autocratic governments. Both are authoritarian in structure, but the totalitarian regime presumes disloyalty among its members, the autocratic system presumes loyalty. Consequently the totalitarian system puts the burden of proof of loyalty upon its subjects; the autocratic leaves the burden of proof of disloyalty on the government. The totalitarian system functions in such a way that its members must constantly exercise themselves to show that they are loyal to the regime and thus keep themselves free from the ever-present presumption of disloyalty. Totalitarian systems, then, must run in an atmosphere of constant suspicion and fear.

What the Church has learned through the experience of Vatican II is that what is required for its continued vitality is not control and the assurance of rigid adherence to established orthodoxy, but rather fidelity. Even further, more than mere fidelity to an established structure or ideology, what the Church needs from its members is faith. The Church has come to know that neither faith nor fidelity are achieved by controls or moral pressure. They must flow ultimately out of a mature sense of autonomy and identity. True fidelity and faith require autonomy and freedom. The internal adherence and commitment to principles and beliefs is a matter of self-direction and self-determination. They can have no vitality or inner psychological reality without freedom.

The point that this development within the Church makes, I think, is that the problem of dissent is compounded by the question of loyalty. It can be taken as basic that dissent is an essential process by which social systems institute and effect change within themselves. But not all dissent is helpful or constructive. It can and often is counterproductive or destructive. A basic issue, then, for this aspect of the problem of disobedience is the relationship between dissent and loyalty. We would suggest that loyal dissent is productive and at least potentially constructive, but that disloyal dissent is more often counterproductive. Dissent that is compounded by disloyalty becomes divisive and destructive; it is the substance of revolutionary intent.

Loyalty is in a sense an external face of the inner quality of fidelity. Fidelity implies an inner capacity, an inner strength, which makes it possible for an individual to pledge and sustain loyalties—to other persons in the abiding relationships that can give meaning to his life, and to social structures, institutions, and values which provide the valued context for and the meaningful support for his own sense of identity. Loyalty, far from representing a submission to forces and structures in one's environment, must mean essentially an affirmation of oneself and one's identity. It implies that developmental tasks have progressed to such an extent and at such a pace that the integration of one's sense of self with the social and cultural realities which give rise to and sustain the sense of meaning of that self has achieved a balance and mutual regulation and reinforcement. The consolidation of identity is in part a matter of the integration of meaningful identifications—with other persons, groups, organizations, social structures, and ultimately values. We have discussed these matters at length in preceding chapters, but they are pertinent to our immediate focus on loyalty.

If loyalty is an affirmation of oneself, it is at the same time an affirmation of that to which one has committed oneself. The commitment is a commitment to sustain, vitalize, take responsibility for, and where necessary or appropriate to take initiative to change in order that the value of the object of loyalty remain or grow. Loyalty implies the willingness and responsibility for developing and improving the group or organization both because it is a significant expression of and support for one's own identity, and also because its preservation and development serves to extend and foster those values inherent in its structure. The commitment to the organization or group and its preservation insures the preservation of values and their availability for those who are to come after. Thus the issues of loyalty and fidelity bridge over into the issues of generativity. One extends a care and concern for future generations by loyalty to those institutions which preserve and promulgate those values with which the individual is identified and which form an essential aspect of his own identity. The strengths of one generation are preserved and made available for the following generation.

It is a basic law of social processes, particularly in a democratic community, that there can be no change, no progress, without opposition, divergent opinions, debate, tension, and conflict. The strength of social structures and institutions lies in their capacity to tolerate such inner conflict and the turmoil associated with it and to bring them to a productive and creative outcome. The impediments to such a creative outcome are many. The basic question concerns those strengths and capacities which make growth possible, whether it be growth in social institutions or growth in individual human beings. Even biological growth is a continuing process of relinquishing older structures and replacing them with new structures, which must in their turn be replaced and reshaped. The growth of organs in the body involves both a change in the size of constitutent cells as well as a change in the number of cells. The growth of bones, for example, is a constant process of replacing older structures and a continual remodeling of new bony structure under the pressure of external influences stemming from muscle pulls, gravity, etc. Growth at any level of organization, whether it be biological, psychological, or social, involves change and replacement of the old by the new.

As a psychiatrist I am forced to deal day in and day out with issues of growth. My professional work with patients is a continuous effort to bring about growth, psychological growth. It involves me in a continuing effort to support those elements within each patient that allow and support the capacity for growth and to try to remove those aspects of the patient's inner life that inhibit and prevent growth. Any growth, any change from the old to the new, must involve a surrender and a giving up of the old and a turning to the new. There is almost inevitably conflict in this. The individual is torn between the attachment to the old and the desire for the new. One must learn to give up the old, to suffer its loss, and to commit himself to the uncertainties and risks of what is new.

Growth and the change associated with it also involve dangers. The same elements that allow for progression and improvement also allow for regression. We have come to recognize that all growth involves both progression and retrogression. If one seeks the benefits of progression and development, one also must take the risks of regression. Progression and regression are so closely intertwined, at least psychologically, in that real progress, and the resolution of conflict require that there be a capacity for regression to the relatively infantile sources of inner strength. In the course of therapy, it is almost axiomatic that patients must be able to regress before they are able to progress. The regression serves not merely the function of uncovering unconscious infantile conflicts, but it allows the individual to recapture or resolve the basic capacities for trust, autonomy, and initiative which are essential for future and healthy psychological growth and which were defective in his original development. The psychotherapeutic process, therefore, is in a real sense a reliving, a re-experiencing and reworking of the basic life issues that must emerge into new strengths in order for growth and mature adjustment to be realized.

Dissent, therefore, which is the social analogue of internal conflict and the stimulus and motive of social growth, is not without its risks. What is of major concern, however, in the consideration of dissent is that dissent does not become disloyalty. Disloyalty is the major risk in dissent. We should make it clear, then, that to regard dissent and loyalty as opposite or contradictory would be a gross misconception. They are not only not contradictory, but their coexistence and mutual interaction is essential to the process of social growth.

I will carry the argument even further. Not only is dissent not to be identified with disloyalty, not only are the coexistence and inter-action of dissent and loyalty desirable and necessary, but in my view dissent is a necessary and essential part of true loyalty. Loyalty in-volves not merely a commitment of oneself to an organization or institution as it exists at this moment. It is a commitment to a set of values which that organization or institution embodies and pre-serves. It is also a commitment to foster, nourish, improve, and de-velop that organization so that it better serves its functions in the social order and more effectively embodies and expresses the values for and by which it exists. Such a commitment is a commitment to continuing growth, change, development, progress. Such a commit-ment involves a willingness and a readiness to dissent. Without it loyalty becomes partial and ineffective. With it loyalty becomes a source of institutional strength and vitality, insuring that the institu-tion and its values and strengths remain vital and relevant and effective.

If dissent is essential to the very concept of loyalty, we must ask ourselves how it is that dissent can so often become disloyalty. The answer that I would propose to this problem would look on both sides of the conflict. The factors that transpose dissent into disloyalty arise both from the side of those dissenting and from the side of those dissented against. From the side of the dissenter, the retreat from established convictions leaves him in a vulnerable position. He is in a position of conflict, caught between the abandonment of inner commitment and convictions that have served to stabilize his own inner identity and sense of adaptation and a reaching out to an un-certainty. The dialectic of loss, abandonment of commitments, and recommitment can open the way to regressive solutions of the con-flict. When the basic issues of dissent have to do with basic values—as we have suggested is the case in much of the dissent of con-temporary youth—the regression can take the form of ethical regres-sion to amoral, antimoral or hypermoral positions. The dissenter runs the risk, therefore, of a recommitment to a relatively regressive solution. He also runs the risk of moving to an excess in his recom-mitment as a result of his own inner need to resolve the conflict and tension involved in his abandonment of old commitments and values. He may rush to embrace alternate solutions and commit himself to them with an excess born out of his inner need for commitment to some ideology that will resolve his ambiguity and the threat to his identity.

From the side of those dissented against, pressures arise which tend to transform dissent into disloyalty. There is a tendency among those who adhere to an ideology to view any divergence or questioning of it as rebellious and disloyal. There is often a misidentification of dissent as disloyalty. If there is an excessive identification with an institution or ideology among nondissenters, there can be an insistence on adherence to the ideology that tends to be absolute. Any dissent automatically becomes disloyalty and the adherents of the ideology feel compelled to rush to its defense. This mentality has governed the history of the post-Tridentine Church until our own day. It lay behind the zeal for the condemnation and destruction of heretics and the inquisitorial enthusiasm of the late Middle Ages. It also lies behind the occasional efforts of Roman authorities to suppress debate and maintain doctrinal control. I have written elsewhere:

> The danger in the dialectic of loyalty and dissent is ideology. Ideology creates disloyalty out of dissent. Ideology creates compliance and blind obedience out of loyalty. The closure on accepted truth and the intolerance of ambiguity that marks ideological commitment derive from an inner insecurity and lack of strength. The tension of the dialectic is intolerable and the associated anxiety can find relief by suppression of one or other polarity. The suppression of dissent leads to an authoritarian rigidity; the suppression of loyalty leads to a destructive rebelliousness. Either defense is deviant and destroys the dialectic, which alone gives promise of renewed confidence and hope, thus eliminating the conditions of inner freedom and outer communication that allow continued growth toward ethical maturity both in individual Christians and in the body of the Church.[3]

The problem in much of the contemporary working out of dissent is that there is a tendency on the side of those who dissent to radicalize their dissent to the detriment of loyalty. Dissent tends to gravitate into disloyalty. There is also a tendency on the part of those who oppose dissent to try to suppress it, thereby radicalizing it even more and placing themselves in the position of authoritarian suppression. The participants in this deadly conflict must learn that there is a place for loyalty in dissent and dissent in loyalty. The young must somehow come to realize that there is room for loyalty in their need to dissent. Their elders, those who hold authority and exercise it, must somehow come to realize that dissent does not necessarily imply disloyalty, but that it may indeed be a form of and an expression of genuine loyalty.

All of these elements and currents swirl through the problem of disobedience. By disobedience we have traditionally meant a combination of dissent or deviance with disloyalty. The presumption is no longer operative. Obedience is the subject's participation in the authority relation. He must respond with freedom, responsibility, and initiative, or else his response is not obedience but a caricature of obedience. Obedience is therefore an engagement of his autonomous judgment and initiative. The laws of social and institutional development demand dissent; without it they wither and die.

Obedience, therefore, must be directed to the fostering of ethical maturity. Only out of a sense of commitment to universal values can an individual find the mature strength in his own identity and fidelity to allow him a convincing loyalty to given institutions and groups. Only in this can he achieve a sense of care for values that supersede his own needs and interests. One can only be truly obedient when his response to authority is directed not only to the authority but beyond it to a set of values to which both subject and authority in the mutual regulation of the authority relation are committed. If either the superior or the subject falls short of ethical identity in the working out of authority, they run the risk of a regressive interaction which reduces the authority relation itself to a relationship of power and deprives it of those ethical values without which it becomes meaningless.

*Chapter 16*

# Authority and Obedience

It is inevitable of course, that we turn our attention to the highly specific problem of religious obedience. The emerging and changing perspectives on authority and its exercise in the contemporary setting have a very profound influence on attitudes toward religious obedience. Those attitudes have been in transition for some time, and they are still very much in the process of transmutation. As the notion of authority and its concrete exercise undergo gradual change, the complementary notion of obedience must be given a correlative new understanding. We have been much preoccupied on the preceding pages with matters of authority and obedience. The momentum will now carry us on to an examination of the correlation between them.

The overriding context for a reconsideration of obedience is that of the authority relation, as already developed, and the more general context of community life and processes. Obedience is not a simple matter of command and response between a superior and a subject. It has an implicit complexity and profundity which touch all aspects of the religious commitment. It involves as Father John Courtney Murray describes it, "the third great encounter . . . the encounter with his [man's] own spirit."[1] We must shape an understanding of obedience, then, which matches the concept of authority. That understanding must touch the profoundest depths of human experience and responsiveness, and it must embrace the broadest reach of social involvement and complexity. Our understanding must also embrace the inherent paradox of human freedom, if only that we may recognize to what extent freedom is essential to any meaningful obedience.

## Mature Obedience

As Father Karl Rahner[2] has pointed out, religious obedience is quite different from filial obedience. The obedience of a child to its parents is different in kind from the obedience of a subject to a superior. The former is inherently transient and directs itself to its own transcendence; the latter, on the contrary, is permanent in form and intention. The obedience of childhood produces those inner qualities which ultimately make that very obedience irrelevant. The child begins life in utter dependence on parents, and his obedience is correlative to that dependence. As his dependence diminishes, the degree and quality of his obedience is transformed.

Every child begins life in a context of authority through which he is schooled in obedience. The schooling of early years reflects the child's immaturity and incapacity for mature and responsible action. It is not at all surprising that the dominant model of obedience should be that of infantile obedience—particularly in a context in which the model of authority was paternalistic and authoritarian. There is a gravitational pull which drags us back toward the infantile model which we have all mastered. It is not without a disciplined effort that we achieve a more mature level of adjustment in obedience. But the model of obedience in which the superior's command is obeyed only because he commands it is infantile because it reflects the basic presumption of infantile obedience, that judgment and decision are reserved to the superior for want of such capacities in the subject. Such a concept of obedience, which clings to a more or less infantile supposition, must be regarded as regressive. As the child matures, his obedience matures. The obedience of religious is the obedience of mature and responsible adults. Insofar as religious obedience clings to an infantile paradigm, it is thereby regressive.

The capacity for mature obedience is correlative with intrapsychic development. Obedience represents a free, responsible, and autonomous response to authority. Such obedience cannot display the subject's dependence on authority or authority figures in any univocal sense. Infantile obedience is, indeed, correlative with and derivative from dependence. Mature obedience, however, is derivative from and correlative with autonomy. Infantile dependency is, therefore, an impediment to mature and effective obedience.

## Intrapsychic Aspects

From an intrapsychic perspective, mature obedience is a matter of the capacity of the ego to respond to the extrinsic demand of authority without the loss of a sense of responsibility, autonomy, and freedom. Infantile obedience involves none of these dimensions of the inner life, since the emerging ego has not sufficiently evolved to permit release from the extrinsic reliance on parents, which gives no play to responsibility, or from the inner dependencies and instinctual forces which preclude real autonomy and freedom. The inner sense of freedom requires that the individual have a developed sense of mastery and inner control; that he be unimpaired by the constraints of anxiety, conflict, or guilt; that he have a sense of his own personal autonomy and competence to judge and to act responsibly. The sense of freedom or oppression is determined by the degree or kind of restrictions which are imposed. Life is filled with multiple restrictions and limitations imposed by our environment, by social life and culture and law, etc. Yet we preserve a sense of freedom because we do not recognize such restrictions as relevant to our freedom. Such restrictions are in the interest of some advantage or benefit that we find useful. The restriction is in the interest of an ideal, and when that ideal is so internalized that it becomes part of our own inner values, we accept the restriction as one that leaves our sense of freedom intact. If, however, the restriction is not consistent with our inner values, not acceptable to our superego, we experience it as oppressive and as a violation of our freedom.

Mature obedience, then, rests upon an integration of inner psychic structures. That integration is disrupted by the activation of poorly controlled, instinctually derived energies. It is disrupted by the prolongation of conflict and dependence, which limit the inner sense of autonomy and diminish the sense of inner mastery. It is disrupted by the neurotic rigidities of a superego which cannot tolerate responsibility without guilt or self-reliance without shame or doubt. These inner psychic impediments are also restrictions on the sense of freedom. The sense of freedom is attained only through the inner integration of mature personal identity and psychic functioning. Without the inner structure, the complex interrelation of freedom, autonomy and responsibility cannot be maintained regardless of the extrinsic relation to authority. But mature obedience finds its expression in relation to authority. It is specifically a response to a claim from the authority structure, but it is a response which preserves and ultimately confirms the sense of freedom, of responsibility, and of autonomy which characterizes the mature identity and the well-integrated personality.

## Role of Identification

The integration of these inner parameters must be achieved in the authority relation. We can recall here the essential role of identification in the construction and preservation of that relation. Identification issues in an alteration of inner psychic structure so that identification with authority, resident in the group or in the superior, implies an internalization of a shared system of values. To the extent that such identification is realized, the claim of authority to obedience does not present itself as something purely extrinsic. It is not merely a demand placed on the individual from some alien source. It is perceived as originating and deriving from the shared values which are seen as congruent with one's own inner values and intentions.

Thus, through identification there is an internal modification of psychic structure which makes it possible for the claims of authority to be received as congruent with individual values. It is possible for the individual to preserve a sense of responsibility and autonomy in regard to these claims since he perceives them, not as infringements on his freedom, but as ordered to his own objectives and consistent with his own intentions. It is perhaps more difficult to understand objectively how a man can be both obedient and free, or more specifically, how he can be free insofar as he is obedient. But the function of identification, I think, sheds some light on the relation of obedience and at least the inner sense of freedom. Ultimately, the inner sense and the reality of freedom are related.

## Religious Obedience

There is, of course, a very pedestrian side to obedience. The individual religious is asked to submit to any number of customs, practices, and directives which have little more intent than a very practical one of making a smoothly functioning community life possible. A certain degree or order is required for a common life to exist, and it is the function of authority to direct this organization of community life. Organization of the community is also required in order that the energies of the community be effectively directed toward common goals. Obedience at this level serves very pragmatic purposes.

But religious obedience is also much more than a matter of organizing community behavior. It is a matter of personal commitment which involves the individual in a profound and meaningful manner. It is a commitment of self which permits authority to exercise a claim on an individual subject, and by which the subject obligates himself to recognize and respect the claim and to respond to it. Religious obedience, therefore, is based on a right of authority to command and a correlative duty of the subject to obey. We must continually remind ourselves that neither the right to command nor the duty to obey can function in violation of the fundamental element upon which obedience itself rests. Insofar as obedience is a matter of response to authority on the part of mature and responsible individuals joined in a community governed by Christian ideals, authority cannot command nor obedience respond unless in terms of the free responsibility and autonomy of individuals, both subjects and superiors. We must keep in mind as well that obedience must also preserve the freedom and autonomy of every member of the community. Consequently, authority cannot be exercised in such a manner as to permit freedom and autonomy to one individual at the cost of freedom and autonomy to others. Order balances the relative autonomy of individuals. So authority can find itself involved in the restriction of freedom in the interest of order. But we must recognize that the restriction works to preserve the distribution of freedom, and thereby it ultimately maximizes freedom and autonomy in the community.

## Initiative

It is apparent in all this that there are many things that authority directs, but many others that it does not direct. There is room, therefore, for initiative in the exercise of obedience. There is room for initiative, not only in tasks and actions not appointed by authority, but also in tasks and actions which are appointed by authority. There is often an implicit assumption that initiative and the origination of action have a place in religious communities, but only on condition that the course of action take a direction congruent with a pattern previously endorsed by authoritative decision of superiors, or that the initiative itself be given authoritative approval. This creates a situation in which only that initiative which is at least tacitly approved by the superior is legitimate. There is an inertial effect in such an assumption which tends to discourage independent effort. It suppresses real initiative and leaves all initiation of responsible action in the hands of superiors. To succumb to such an effect is to abandon initiative and responsibility. Obedience, in a word, does *not* require that everything that a subject undertakes be given a stamp of approval by legitimate authority. The preservation of legitimate initiative, however, is a cooperative venture. It requires a willingness to initiate and explore on the part of subjects, and it requires a willingness and capacity on the part of superiors to tolerate and even encourage the impulses to initiate and originate on the part of subjects. The ultimate benefit is primarily to the community, but both superiors and subjects share in the profits.

Unfortunately, there is too often a temptation to repress initiative. Superiors who are insecure in the management of their own responsibility or are overburdened by it find it hard to accept initiative. They are caught in the conflictual bind which makes them feel that they are responsible for everything that is going on about them and that other agents cannot be relied on as sources of responsible action. There is no temptation so subtle and so easily justified as interference in another's freedom. This is the greatest single difficulty in the exercise of authority. The superior who extends his own concerns over responsibility to the point of inappropriate restraint of initiative violates the freedom of his subjects.

There is also room for real initiative in tasks appointed by the superior. This aspect of obedience is much neglected. The superior's command is a stimulus which elicits the obediential response. The response should never be mere submission. The command, properly understood, does not demand submission. If it does, it is regressive and does not appeal to obedience at all, but to neurotic fears and conflicts. The command is really an invitation to cooperative responsibility. It is a concrete expression of the superior's legitimate expectation that the subject participate responsibly in the work of the community. Consequently, when the subject responds merely passively to the superior's command and when he shows an obedience of mere execution, that is a caricature of obedience. It is not authentic obedience. Blind obedience is not obedience at all. It is a distortion.

Blind obedience in any literal sense is unsound philosophically, theologically, and psychologically. It ignores human dignity and maturity, and it obliterates moral judgment. Man must accept responsibility for his own actions. Responsibility cannot be handed over to someone else, even under the guise of religious obedience. We are saddled here with a traditional rhetoric which is a vestige of a former age. The rhetoric of blind obedience—the staff in a man's hand, the dry stick, etc.—is frankly archaic, and it is no longer illuminating in the modern context. Because it places mistaken emphasis on the nature of obedience, it is misleading and ultimately harmful. We need a new rhetoric which expresses the obedience proper to the contemporary setting and its evolving needs.

It is important, therefore, to emphasize that obedience and responsible initiative are not opposed. They are correlative. Mature obedience demands initiative. If the superior's command is an invitation to cooperative enterprise, the subject's unique contribution requires a certain critical objectivity, independence of judgment, and willingness to assume responsibility for the course of the common enterprise. This requires a basic capacity to think and act as an independent agent which is implicit in initiative. The individual must be capable of independent thought and action divergent from the pattern established by authoritative forces without feeling guilt and without succumbing to destructive or irresponsible impulses. Initiative finds its way between the extremes of instinctual disruptiveness and guilt-laden conformism, between irresponsibility and hyper-responsibility. A subject is capable of such initiative to the extent that he can respond to the claims of authority and can contribute of his own creative resourcefulness to the benefit of the community.

## Initiative in Community

Thus, the community is a seedbed of initiatives which express the creative responsibility of its members. The members provide the initiative and give it origin—not authority. Authority unifies, directs, organizes, integrates, and implements the interplay of initiatives. Inner group processes interplay with the influence of authority to complete the modifying mechanisms by which individual initiatives in the community are orchestrated. Such diversity of initiatives is not only necessary for the continuing vitality and adaptability of the community; but it is also the stuff out of which a more mature and responsible participation in community life is made. The community needs the initiative of its members to survive. Authority need not stimulate such initiatives, but it must not suppress them. That basic disposition, maintained without conflict or unconscious threat on the part of the superior, is sufficient. An added element, however, requires something more from authority. The orchestration of initiatives is not mere passive permissiveness. Superior and subject are involved in a cooperative enterprise through initiative. That cooperation requires mutual regulation in the interest of order and freedom. Authority must actively restrain initiative at some points in order to preserve community interests. It should be apparent, however, that the restraints are not purely a matter of opposition between superior, representing authority, and subject, representing individual interests. Their cooperation and mutual regulation involves and extends to such restraints whenever necessary.

It does not really need emphasis, but it is apparent that these processes, even when operating at their best, will not obliterate all differences and divergences. What is most difficult to appreciate is that a certain amount of divergence is a source of strength for the community. The value system of the community is neither so compelling nor so rigid that it cannot be complemented. The shared values of the community are less a set of inflexible ideals than a more or less tolerant spectrum of permissible norms. Initiative plays within this range. The range of variation contributes to the stability of the system as a whole. Variations form a channel for release of necessary strain in the system. If such variation is suppressed, there is an inevitable increase in the level of strain in the system with correlative increases in the level of anxiety and conflict. Dissatisfaction and anxiety in a community may have no apparent relation to the concrete situation in which they arise, but may reflect the underlying tension in the repressive character of the structure as a whole. It is inevitable, therefore, that initiatives and divergences which authority cannot regulate will exist. By implication, initiatives will arise spontaneously, independently of and without approval of legitimate authority. The superior's service to the community is spelled out in terms of his ability to encourage and nourish the creative resources of his community. Ultimately, he must rely on the initiative of his subjects, and his resources depend on the degree to which he can enlist the creative energies of his subjects for common purposes.

## Obedience and God's Will

The nature of obedience is such, then, that it cannot consist in mere submission to another's will. It is ultimately a submission to the will of God, who alone commands irrevocably and unequivocally what is right. The will of God is manifested in a variety of ways and is real in many sources. As Father Karl Rahner has pointed out, authority is only one of the sources of divine inspiration and stimulation. There is no special guarantee that God has advised a superior or the structure of authority of his own activity in the workings of salvation history. The superior's command does not automatically and unquestionably represent God's will. Moreover, the giving of the command does not free the subject from his fundamental responsibility to identify and pursue God's will. The question persists—does the superior's command represent the divine intention? Or better— how can we determine whether the superior's command is representative of divine purposes?

This is a complex matter, and I do not think that simple solutions to it are satisfying. Obedience is a free commitment to a way of life, a life of free subjection to the authority of religious superiors. Subordination to the authority of religious superiors is not imposed by the Church without the free and deliberate consent implicit in the vow. Free consent, moreover, does not have its play only in the original vow by which the subject binds himself to this finite life-form. The free consent of obedience is continually in play. Subjection to religious authority calls for a recurrent deliberation and free election by which the life-form of obedience is prolonged and extended. Obedience is a commitment to a way of life which seeks God's will in all things. It seeks God's will primarily and exclusively. By obedience man gives his life a God-directedness which is accepted and responded to in this context. This frame of reference gives obedience to a specific command its inner significance. The subject is required by his commitment to a life of religious obedience to make that evaluative consideration. He takes the responsibility of directing his response to authority to God's will and its fulfillment. He cannot pass that judgment off to superiors. They are in no way responsible for the way in which he fulfills his vow.

Thus, the proper object of religious obedience is a perduring way of life directed to fulfillment of God's will. It is quite possible, therefore, that this object remain intact even if a particular command of the superior must be ignored or disobeyed. The religious does not vow himself to simply execute the superior's nonimmoral commands. The vow is his commitment of himself to accept and respond to such commands when the commands are just and when they are directed to the life-form dedicated to God as specified in the constitution of a given community. The guarantee of this is inscribed in the Church's validation of the religious community and organization. Obedience is specified in reference to the formal constitution, and the superior can command only within this framework.

To strike a somewhat different emphasis, it is substantially true that the religious commits himself to a life-form of obedience in a specific order. The order further specifies the life-form of obedience. There are certain works, certain preferred apostolates, certain institutions within which the order seeks its objectives. In relation to these objectives, the subject formulates his life of God-seeking. The group structures and institutions are subject to change as a function of group processes. But they enjoy a certain stability which gives meaning to the context of obedience. The individual is responsible for maintaining this stability. It is a part of his commitment. If he sees that his community's structures are archaic or moribund, he is responsible for revitalizing or replacing them. His responsibility is to further God's purposes, and he must always seek a better way to accomplish this according to his energies and insight. But he does not serve God's purposes by destructive efforts alone. The destruction of institutions rarely advances God's kingdom unless it is complemented by the construction of new resources. It is too often easy to destroy, but it is frequently difficult to build. The superior commands to advance God's purposes according to the specifics of time and place, and the subject is generally committed to respond accordingly. The presumption, however, cannot be absolute. Obedience translates faith in God's abiding presence into act. If that faith which inspires obedience is to have any meaning, it must issue in a mode of existence in which spontaneouus willingness to carry out the concrete actions, decisions, and programs directed by legitimate authority predominates.

## Renunciation

There is in obedience an element of renunciation. This is a vital element which has been an integral part of religious obedience from the beginning. The traditional formulations have emphasized the element of renunciation and self-effacement. This was consistent with the operative models of authority derived from concepts of divine sovereignty and formulated in terms of vertical relations. The model of renunciation was Christ, who was obedient unto death. This context gave decisive direction to the whole course of religious life. Obedience was measured by the amount of renunciation or self-immolation it occasioned. One might almost come to believe that the obedience which destroyed the individual was best. Such a concept is not consistent with the notion of obedience we are developing here.

Renunciation, however, remains a central element in the notion of religious obedience. The vow of obedience does not commit one to a course of self-interest and self-gratification. It does commit one to a life-form which places the interests of God and his purposes above the interests of self. The average religious dedicates himself to seeking God's will in a given community and in relation to a given set of values, institutions, and concrete undertakings. The commitment to the community and its concerns gives the community a certain priority and preference. The individual by accepting this commitment also takes upon himself a responsibility for the community, for its interests and concerns, for its advancement and evolution, for its developing capability for attaining its goals. Insofar as the religious accepts this responsibility, he also accepts the responsibility for assimilating his own personal goals, ambitions, and initiatives to those of the community. It may be, and most often it is the case that both can be served. It may also be that the goals of community and self are divergent. Thus renunciation of personal goals becomes a possibility in many varieties of degree and kind.

This kind of divergence, however, is exceptional. What is more often in question and more to the point is a kind of inner modification which embraces the entirety of religious life. To undertake the life of religious obedience is to undertake the life of community; it is to participate in the relation of authority with all of the implications of that involvement. It calls into play the fundamental mechanisms of identification and value formation which bring about a modification of inner psychic structure. It modifies the value system which constitutes such a significant part of one's own personality, and it brings that value system into some degree of congruence with the shared values of a community. This is the fundamental renunciation which forms the substantive part of the vow of obedience. If it is a basic renunciation, it is at the same time an enlarging of personal horizons It is a broadening and intensification of personal responsibility and initiative and a deepening of a sense of directedness and meaningfulness of one's life. He who loses, in losing, gains.

## Risks

Obedience cannot survive without a delicate balance between a number of vital elements. There is no doubt that the pendulum has swung and is swinging in the direction of freedom, responsibility, initiative, etc. While this re-emphasis is badly needed, there is a risk in it—the risk of excess. Undoubtedly, many real forces are contributing to this changing emphasis, and there is real need for moderating voices. The risks are real. Father Pedro Arrupe, General of the Society of Jesus, in speaking of a "new obedience" has detailed some of them.

> In place of authority a personal collectivism or capitularism will insert itself. Dialogue will lose its constructive power and turn into endless and decisionless conversation. Delegation of authority will be turned into a scattering of energy and directive power, and this would be the root of internal division and common confusion. A recognition of the value of personality would be mere human respect and not respect for the man, and a denial of the offering of the whole man in the holocaust of obedience.[3]

There are ever-present risks that are undesirable. But insofar as such disappointments come about, they reflect a deterioration in the responsible and creative participation in community affairs for which obedience calls. In the very risks as well, one must balance the needs of order against the needs of freedom. What may seem to be a deleterious excess from the perspective of order, may not be so from the perspective of freedom.

## Change and Evolution

There is a crisis of obedience today which cannot be resolved by a reaffirmation of old formulae. The crisis has arisen out of the confrontation of vital social and cultural forces which strongly emphasized individual responsibility, initiative, freedom, and personal development with a historically derived conceptualization of authority-obedience built on an essential insistence on order, absolute authority, submissive obedience, and resignation to the will of superiors. To rehearse ancient ideas about obedience is merely to contribute to the crisis. Many minds are at work in the Church today seeking to find new ways of thinking about and responding to authority. They are searching for new ways and forms in which a new balance between the needs of freedom and those of order can be struck. The old order is being eroded, but a new order is rising in its place.

Some feel that religious obedience is so wedded to the structure of the old order that it cannot survive the coming of the new. Man cannot, they say, be free and obedient. But such a view is destructive. It is correct in asserting that the exercise of authority and obedience in its traditional form may not survive. But it ignores the capacity and strength of religious institutions to adapt and modify themselves in the face of historical exigencies. Changes are in progress. They are not changes of revolution but of evolution. The balance of responsible effort does not seek to overthrow and destroy the schema of values upon which older authoritarian views of obedience were founded. It does not seek to substitute an entirely new schema of values. It seeks to illumine and bring into sharper focus those basic elements in an integral view of obedience which have become atrophic and nonfunctional. The needs of the time call for a development of those elements. However, it is impossible to make this reformulation without profound repercussions for the concrete exercise of authority and the response of obedience. What is re-

quired, therefore, is a theoretical reformulation which must be supplemented by a translation into practical terms of concrete action by
men of understanding and prudence.

That enterprise will be most difficult and precarious. Its failure
will outweigh its successes for a considerable time. The time of
transition will be one of great anxiety for many as well as a time
of conflict. The ultimate determinant will be the extent to which
those involved in the effort of revitalizing and reshaping the actuality
of obedience are convinced of and dedicated to the principles of the
inherent dignity and freedom of religious men. Within those principles there is a germinative core which provides the dynamic source
of change, adaptation, and ultimately spiritual maturity. That core
is the creative potentiality for growth and the dynamic energy which
can charge the mechanisms of communal life and structure with new
vitality. That energy becomes available for the creative purposes of
the community insofar as the structure of the community itself is
sufficiently evolved and sufficiently mature to give it play and to
channel it meaningfully once it is activated.

The exercise of obedience, then, in its mature and evolved sense
involves more than mere personal maturity. It calls for more than
an evolution and development in the structures of authority. It does
call for these as essential ingredients of any meaningful reorganization, but it calls for something further. There must evolve certain
community structures which will provide the background matrix
within which the exercise of authority and responsible subjecthood
are facilitated. If the crisis of authority and obedience reflects the
impetus of change, we must remember that significant group processes are in operation which serve the community's needs for adaptation and development. As religious communities shift the emphasis
from a vertical-authoritarian constellation of values to a more hori-
zontal-liberal constellation, there will follow a metamorphosis of
community structures. The structures of the community evolve or
are evolved in a teleological sense in order to concretize and perpetuate an underlying system of values. The system of values inherent in a more traditional authoritarianism evolved community
structures which institutionalized and realized, as it were, those
values in community life and organization. Under the impetus of a
reorganization and refocusing of the value system, the community

will in time evolve new structures which again concretize and existentialize the underlying value structure. In the time of transition there is bound to arise a definite but self-limiting tension between older structures and presently emergent values.

## Free Obedience

The ultimate question to which the problem of obedience must address itself is the paradox of freedom-in-obedience. How can religious man in ultimate consistency with his inherent and inalienable human dignity and personal integrity maintain and develop his rightful measure of personal freedom and at the same time pledge himself by solemn vow to a life of obedience? The question can be specified even further. How can religious man be this free in his obedience, i.e., specifically insofar as and in proportion to the degree to which he is obedient? The answer to these questions is by no means simple or direct. The answers will not be attained in the abstract forum of philosophic reflection. They will be reached through concrete existential dialectic involving all the elements in the authority situation. In these pages the discussion of authority in its various dimensions has only pointed to some of the relevant factors. The solution to the problem of freedom-in-obedience is, then, a solution of fact, more than a solution of theory. The solution of theory may wait on the solution of fact. Indeed, the solution of fact may evolve without any theoretical solution.

In any case we have attempted to advance a concept of religious obedience which is erected on the foundation stones of freedom, responsibility, initiative, and autonomy. Obedience so conceived is consistent with the concept of authority which has emerged in these pages. Whether such a concept can find its way into the exigencies of the actual dialectic now in progress remains to be seen. There is reason to believe that it must. At least it can be argued that obedience ought and can serve the best interests of these fundamental human values.

In opening this discussion of obedience, we referred to the third encounter which Father John Courtney Murray has delimited as the encounter with man's own spirit. The encounters are those wherein man becomes a man—with earth, with woman and with his own spirit. Through the vows the religious man sets himself aside from these various encounters. Through poverty the religious is redeemed from the struggle with earth. Security is achieved without struggle; the responsibility for creating the conditions of life is suspended and is assumed by the community. Through chastity the encounter with woman is declined. Entrance into the elemental world of the female is denied, and the possibility of achieving that maturity of sexual identity in which man becomes more of a man through woman and woman more of a woman through man is narrowed.

Father Murray goes on to say:

> Finally, by the vow of obedience one declines the most bruising encounter of all—that of a man with himself, with his own spirit and its power of choice, with his own powers and the problem of their full exercise, towards the achievement of a determined purpose.[4]

The image of the obedient man is dismal, indeed. He is without self-direction. His choices are made for him, and he feels no need to assume responsibility for them. There are no agonies of decision; one need only follow and obey. Aspiration and ambition wither. Deprived of real alternatives and the necessity of choice, the obedient man lives without the necessity of self-assertion and purposefulness. The image is redolent with the ideals of traditional obedience. It rings with the overtones of humble submission, resignation to the superior's and God's will, self-abnegation and renunciation.

The image thus presented is a caricature at least. There have been such obedient men and their obedience has been praised. But those who accomplished God's work somehow managed to violate that image with the strength and confidence of their own inner resources. There was room for initiative and responsibility. But it was an initiative that they seized as though that effort was something to be gotten away with. The harsh lines of the image were softened by many influences. The image itself, however, is disturbing. It is disturbing because it throws into relief a set of values which appals the contemporary mind. It disturbs the religious mind because it emphasizes the imbalance in the thinking about obedience. The truly obedient man recognizes it as caricature and, therefore, as distortion.

Religious obedience does not decline encounters with self. It summons the religious man to an encounter with self at all levels of his moral life. Through obedience he becomes responsible not only for himself but for his community and for God's purposes. It summons him not only to the inner chamber of his own counsels, but to a life of dialogue directed to the achievement of common purposes. It asks of him the exploitation of his resources and imagination and initiative not in the interest of merely personal objectives, but in the direction of divine purposes.

On these terms, then, religious obedience substitutes one bruising encounter with another. It substitutes for the encounter of man with himself and his own spirit a more basic and a more bruising encounter—the encounter of man with God and God's purposes. In the encounter with God, man becomes or can become more fully human than in any encounter with self. That encounter activates his being to its very depths. It requires his judgment, resolution, and decision at every turn. It requires the summoning up and integration of his most basic and instinctual energizing and elemental forces. His life becomes a life-form directed to the most demanding and sublimest of purposes. This, then, is the obedience of which we speak. This, then, is the mature obedience of the sons of God—free, responsible, creative, purposeful, and demanding.

# *Notes*

## Introduction

1. John L. McKenzie, *Authority in the Church* (New York: Sheed and Ward, 1966).

## *Chapter 1*
## The Concept of Authority

1. Decree on the Bishops' Pastoral Office in the Church, 1. References to documents of the Council are taken from *The Documents of Vatican II,* edited by Walter M. Abbot, S. J. (New York: Guild Press, 1966).

2. Pastoral Constitution on the Church in the Modern World, 74.

3. Yves Simon, *Philosophy of Democratic Government* (Chicago: University of Chicago Press, 1951).

4. J. R. P. French, Jr. and B. Raven, "The Bases of Social Power," in D. Cartwright (ed.), *Studies in Social Power* (Ann Arbor, Michigan: Institute for Social Research, 1959), pp. 183-219.

5. *Ibid.*

6. Max Weber, *The Theory of Social and Economic Organizations,* edited by T. Parsons (Glencoe, Illionis: Free Press, 1947).

7. *Ibid.*

8. P. M. Harrison, "Weber's Categories of Authority and Volun-

tary Associations," *American Sociological Review* 25 (1960) 232-237.

9. R. Bierstadt, "An Analysis of Social Power," *Ibid*. 15 (1950) 730-738.

10. T. Eg., D. Cartwright, R. A. Dahl, and K. F. Janda in the papers cited in this chapter.

11. R. M. Emerson, "Power-dependence Relations," *American Sociological Review* 27 (1962) 31-44.

12. C. I. Barnard, *The Functions of the Executive* (Cambridge, Mass., 1938).

13. W. W. Meissner, S. J., *Group Dynamics in the Religious Life* (Notre Dame: University of Notre Dame Press, 1965).

## Chapter 2
## Leadership and Authority

1. J. R. P. French and B. Raven, "The Bases of Social Power," in D. Cartwright (ed.), *Studies in Social Power* (Ann Arbor, Michigan: Institute for Social Research, 1959).

2. *Cf*. R. T. Morris and M. Seeman, "The Problem of Leadership: An Interdisciplinary Approach," *American Journal of Sociology* 56 (1950) 149-155; and C. L. Shartla, "Studies in Naval Leadership," in H. Guetzhlow (ed.), *Groups, Leadership and Men* (Pittsburgh: Carnegie Press, 1951), pp. 119-133.

3. C. A. Gibb, "The Principles and Traits of Leadership," in P. Hare, E. F. Borgotta, and R. T. Bales (eds.), *Small Groups: Studies in Social Interaction* (New York: Knopf, 1955), pp. 87-95.

4. *Ibid.*, p. 94.

5. *Ibid.*

6. K. F. Janda, "Towards the Explication of the Concept of Leadership in Terms of the Concept of Power," *Human Relations* 13 (1950), 345-363.

7. *Ibid.*, p. 355.

8. B. M. Bass, *Leadership, Psychology, and Organizational Behavior* (New York: Harper, 1960), p. 94.

9. W. W. Meissner, S. J., *Group Dynamics in the Religious Life* (Notre Dame: University of Notre Dame, 1965).

10. Sigmund Freud, *Group Psychology and the Analysis of the*

*Ego,* Standard Edition of the Complete Psychological Works of Sigmund Freud, Vol. 18 (London, Hogarth Press, 1955), pp. 65-143.

11. F. Redl, "Group Emotion and Leadership," *Psychiatry* 5 (1942) 573-596.

12. Meissner, *op. cit.,* Ch. 2.

13. R. C. Day and R. L. Hamlin, "Some Effects of Close and Punitive Styles of Supervision," *American Journal of Sociology* 69 (1964) 499-510.

14. French and Raven, *op. cit.,* pp. 150-167.

15. M. Mulder, "Power and Satisfaction in Task Oriented Groups," *Acta Psychol.* 16 (1959) 178-225; and "The Power Variable in Communication Experiments," *Human Relations* 13 (1960) 241-257.

16. M. Mulder, R. Van Dijk, T. Stelwagan, J. Verhagen, S. Sentendijk, and J. Zwezerinen, "Illegitimacy of Power and Positiveness of Attitude Towards the Power Person," *Human Relations* 19 (1966) 21-37.

*Chapter 3*
Authority and Identification

1. Sigmund Freud, *On Narcissism* (1914), Standard Edition, Vol. 14 (London: Hogarth Press, 1957) pp. 73-102.

2. *Ibid., Instincts and Their Vicissitudes* (1915), Standard Edition, Vol. 14, pp. 117-140.

3. *Ibid.,* p. 132.

4. Freud, *Mourning and Melancholia* (1917), Standard Edition, Vol. 14, pp. 243-258.

5. Ibid., *Group Psychology and the Analysis of the Ego* (1922), Standard Edition, Vol. 19 (1955), pp. 69-143.

6. *Ibid.,* p. 134.

7. Freud, *The Ego and the Id* (1923), Standard Edition, Vol. 19 (1961), pp. 12-66.

8. *Ibid.,* p. 34.

9. N. Sanford, "The Dynamics of Identification," *Psychological Review* 62 (1955), 106-118.

10. J. Kagan, "The Concept of Identification," *Psychological Review* 65 (1958), 296-305.

11. T. Parsons and E. A. Shils, *Toward A General Theory of Action* (New York: Harper and Row, 1962), p. 129.

12. Anna Freud, *The Ego and the Mechanisms of Defense* (London: Hogarth Press, 1937), p. 129.

13. Freud, *Group Psychology and the Analysis of the Ego,* Standard Edition, Vol. 18 (1955), p. 108.

14. H. Nunberg, "The Synthetic Function of the Ego," in *Practice and Theory of Psychoanalysis* (New York: International Universities Press, 1960).

15. E. H. Erikson, *Identity and the Life Cycle* (New York: International Universities Press, 1959), p. 113.

*Chapter 4*
Authority and Values

1. T. Parsons and E. A. Shils, "Systems of Value-Orientation," in T. Parsons and E. A. Shils (eds.), *Toward A General Theory of Action* (New York: Harper and Row, 1962), pp. 159-189.

2. S. A. Stouffer, "An Analysis of Conflicting Social Norms," *American Sociological Review* 14 (1949), 707-717.

3. C. Kluckhohn et al., "Values and Value-Orientations in the Theory of Action," in Parsons and Shils, *op. cit.,* p. 395.

4. A. M. Johnson, "Juvenile Delinquency," in S. Arieti, (ed.), *American Handbook of Psychiatry,* Vol. 1 (New York: Basic Books, 1959), pp. 840-856.

5. *Ibid.,* pp. 844-845.

*Chapter 5*
Authority as Role-Relation

1. M. Deutsch and R. M. Krauss, *Theories in Social Psychology* (New York: Basic Books, 1965).

2. R. K. Merton, "The Role-Set: Problems in Sociological Theory," *British Journal of Sociology* (1957), 106-120.

3. *Ibid.,* p. 110.

4. E. H. Erikson, *Identity and the Life Cycle* (New York: International Universities Press, 1959), p. 102.

5. *Ibid.,* p. 114.

6. R. Benedict, "Continuities and Discontinuities in Cultural Conditioning," *Psychiatry* 1 (1938), 161-167.

*Chapter 6*
Authority and Mutuality

1. E. H. Erikson, *Childhood and Society* (New York: Norton, 1958).
2. *Ibid.,* p. 57.
3. W. W. Meissner, S. J., *Group Dynamics in the Religious Life* (Notre Dame: University of Notre Dame Press, 1965), pp. 15-50.
4. R. H. Turner, "Role-Taking, Role Standpoint and Reference Group Behavior," *American Journal of Sociology* 61 (1956), 316-328.


*Chapter 7*
Myth and Authority

1. B. Malinowski, "Myth in Primitive Psychology," *Magic Science and Religion and Other Essays* (Garden City, N.Y.: Doubleday, 1954).
2. *Ibid.,* pp. 100-101.
3. *Ibid.,* p. 146.
4. E. Cassirer, *The Philosophy of Symbolic Forms,* Vol. 3, Mythical Thought (New Haven: Yale University Press, 1955), p. 36.
5. *Ibid.,* p. 45.
6. *Ibid.,* pp. 69-70.
7. H. Nunberg, "The Synthetic Functions of the Ego," in *Practice and Theory of Psychoanalysis* (New York: Nervous and Mental Disease Monographs, 1948), pp. 120-136.
8. J. Arlon, "Ego Psychology and the Study of Mythology," *Journal of the American Psychoanalytic Association* (1961), 371-393.
9. N. Stern, "Ego Psychology, Myth and Rite," *The Psychoanalytical Study of Society,* Vol. 3 (New York: International Universities Press, 1964), pp. 71-93.
10. F. Fearing, "Human Communications," in W. A. Dexter and D. M. White, eds., *People, Society and Mass Communications* (New York: Free Press of Glencoe, 1964).
11. A. J. M. Sykes, "Myth and Attitude Change," *Human Relations* 18 (1965), 323-337.

## Chapter 8
## The Authoritarian Personality

1. E. R. Jaensch, *Der Gegentyous* (Leipzig: Barth, 1938).

2. T. W. Adorno, E. Frenkel-Brunswick, D. J. Levinson, and R. N. Sanford, *The Authoritarian Personality* (New York: Harper, 1950).

3. Erich Fromm, *Escape from Freedom* (New York: Holt, Rinehart and Winston, 1941).

4. *Ibid.,* p. 184.

5. *Ibid.,* pp. 190-191.

6. J. H. Schaar, *Escape from Authority* (New York: Basic Books, 1961), pp. 284-324.

7. S. Milgram, "Some Conditions of Obedience and Disobedience to Authority," *Human Relations* 18 (1965), 57-76.

8. *Ibid.,* p. 75.

9. D. Stewart and T. Hoet, "A Social-Psychological Theory of the Authoritarian Personality," *American Journal of Sociology* 65 (1959), 274-279.

10. J. Weima, "Authoritarianism, Religious Conservatism, and Sociocentric Attitudes in Roman Catholic Groups," *Human Relations* 18 (1965), 231-240.


## Chapter 9
## Systems of Social Defense

1. Sigmund Freud, *Three Essays on the Theory of Sexuality* (1905), Standard Edition, Vol. 7 (London: Hogarth Press, 1953), pp. 130-243.

2. Sigmund Freud, *Inhibitions, Symptoms and Anxiety* (1926), Standard Edition, Vol. 20 (London: Hogarth Press, 1959), pp. 87-172.

3. I. E. P. Menzies, "A Case-Study in the Functioning of Social Systems as a Defense Against Anxiety: A Report on a Study of the Nursing Service of a General Hospital," *Human Relations* 13 (1960), 95-121.

4. W. W. Meissner, S. J., *Group Dynamics in the Religious Life* (Notre Dame: University of Notre Dame Press, 1965).

Chapter 10
The Role of Superior

1. W. W. Meissner, S. J., *Group Dynamics in the Religious Life* (Notre Dame: University of Notre Dame Press, 1965), especially p. 127-150.
2. R. Benedict, "Continuities and Discontinuities in Cultural Conditioning," *Psychiatry* 1 (1938), 161-167.
3. E. H. Erikson, *Insight and Responsibility* (New York: Norton, 1964), p. 126.


Chapter 11
The Role of Subject

1. E. H. Erikson, Identity: *Youth and Crisis* (New York: Norton, 1968), p. 160.


Chapter 12
Authority and Community

1. J. C. Murray, "Freedom, Authority, Community," *America* 5 (December 3, 1966), p. 734.


Chapter 13
The Psychology of Obedience

1. E. H. Erikson, *Childhood and Society,* 2nd ed. (New York: Norton, 1963).
2. *Ibid.*
3. *Ibid.,* p. 249.
4. E. H. Erikson, *Identity and the Life Cycle,* Psychological Issues, No. 1 (New York: International Universities Press, 1959), p. 56-57.
5. *Ibid.,* p. 68.
6. *Ibid.,* p. 76.
7. Erikson, *Childhood and Society,* pp. 261-262.
8. *Ibid.,* p. 267.

## Chapter 14
## Pathological Aspects of Obedience

1. W. W. Meissner, S. J., "Loyalty and Dissent: A Psychiatrist Report," *America* 122 (June 27, 1970), 681-682.

2. *Idem., Group Dynamics in the Religious Life* (Notre Dame University of Notre Dame Press, 1965).

3. T. W. Adorno, E. Frenkel-Brunswick, D. J. Levinson, and N. Sanford, *The Authorian Personality* (New York: Harper, 1950).

4. See p. 153.

5. See Ch. 8.

6. See Ch. 8.

7. Meissner, *Group Dynamics*.

8. D. Shapiro, *Neurotic Styles* (New York: Basic Books, 1965).

9. H. H. Tartakoff, "The Normal Personality in Our Culture and the Nobel Prize Complex," in R. M. Loewenstein, L. M. Newman, M. Sehur, and A. J. Solnit, eds., *Psychoanalysis: A General Psychology* (New York: International Universities Press, 1966), pp. 22-252.

## Chapter 15
## The Problem of Disobedience

1. E. H. Erikson, "Reflections on the Dissent of Contemporary Youth," *International Journal of Psychoanalysis* 51 (1970), 11-2.

2. *Ibid.*

3. W. W. Meissner, S. J., "Loyalty and Dissent," *America* 1 (June 23, 1970), 682.

## Chapter 16
## Authority and Obedience

1. J. C. Murray, S. J., "The Danger of the Vows," *Woodstock Letters* 96 (1967), 428-434.

2. Karl Rahner, S. J., "A Basic Ignatian Concept," *Woodstock Letters* 86 (1957), 291-310.

3. Pedro Arrupe, S. J., "A Talk on Obedience," *Woodstock Letters* 96 (1967), 433.

4. Murray, *op. cit.,* p. 427.